MW00786285

Contested Tongues

to Monica
with love,
Loada

CULTURE&SOCIETY
AFTER SOCIALISM
A SERIES EDITED BY
BRUCE GRANT&NANCY RIES

Contested Tongues

Language Politics and Cultural Correction in Ukraine

LAADA BILANIUK

Cornell University Press *Ithaca and London*

The map on page xvi is adapted from the map created by Adrian Hewryk and Robert DeLossa for Martha Bohachevsky-Chomiak, *Political Communities and Gendered Ideologies in Contemporary Ukraine* (Cambridge, Mass.: Harvard Ukrainian Research Institute, 1994), 8. Copyright © 1994 by the President and Fellows of Harvard College. Reprinted by permission.

The cartoon by the artist Vasyl' Lazun'ko, on page 10, originally appeared in *Vsesmikh*, no. 84 (January 1999). Reprinted with permission.

Copyright © 2005 by Cornell University

All rights reserved. Except for brief quotations in a review, this book, or parts thereof, must not be reproduced in any form without permission in writing from the publisher. For information, address Cornell University Press, Sage House, 512 East State Street, Ithaca, New York 14850.

First published 2005 by Cornell University Press
First printing, Cornell Paperbacks, 2005

Printed in the United States of America

Library of Congress Cataloging-in-Publication Data
Bilaniuk, Laada.
    Contested tongues : language politics and cultural correction in Ukraine / Laada Bilaniuk.
      p. cm. — (Culture and society after socialism)
    Includes bibliographical references and index.
    ISBN-13: 978-0-8014-4349-7 (cloth : alk. paper)
    ISBN-10: 0-8014-4349-0 (cloth : alk. paper)
    ISBN-13: 978-0-8014-7279-4 (pbk. : alk. paper)
    ISBN-10: 0-8014-7279-2 (pbk. : alk. paper)
    1. Ukraine—Languages—Political aspects. 2. Ukraine—Languages—Social aspects. 3. Language and culture—Ukraine. 4. Sociolinguistics—Ukraine. 5. Languages in contact—Ukraine. 6. Multilingualism—Ukraine. 7. Ukrainian language—Social aspects. 8. Russian language—Social aspects—Ukraine. I. Title. II. Series.
P119.32.U38B55 2005
306.44'09477—dc22

                                            2005016117

Cornell University Press strives to use environmentally responsible suppliers and materials to the fullest extent possible in the publishing of its books. Such materials include vegetable-based, low-VOC inks and acid-free papers that are recycled, totally chlorine-free, or partly composed of nonwood fibers. For further information, visit our website at www.cornellpress.cornell.edu.

Cloth printing   10 9 8 7 6 5 4 3 2 1

Paperback printing 10 9 8 7 6 5 4 3 2 1

Contents

Illustrations

Acknowledgments

This book was made possible by the many people who shared their insights with me on language politics in Ukraine. Since the country became independent in 1991, I have conducted several research trips, living in Ukraine for more than two years in all. Many school directors, administrators, teachers, professors, students, and serendipitous acquaintances helped arrange and participated in my research. I was often moved by the generosity of people who welcomed me into their homes, schools, and workplaces, sharing their thoughts and hospitality. To them I express my deepest gratitude.

Although it is impossible to list everyone, I would like to thank certain people whose friendship and assistance enriched my stay in Ukraine. These include Iryna Parasiuk and her family, Tanya Poliakova and her family, Volodymyr and Oleksii Tokarevskyi, Larysa Sliusarenko and her mother, Ol'ha Ivanivna (an excellent storyteller whom I will always remember fondly), Ol'ha Kocherga and her family, the Povoroznyk family, Mykola Riabchuk, Natalia Bilotserkivets' and Anastasia Riabchuk, the Bilaniuk families in Kolomya and Piadyky, Leonid and Hanna Zalizniak, Max Smetana, Misha Smetana, Veronica Khokhlova, Sergei Diabel, Roma Dvornin, Anton Dvornin, Valentyna Hroza, Alexei Sogomonov, Aliosha (Zaichyk), Anya Glybina, Yulia Antoniv, the Burlaky of Lviv, Lesia (Kovalchuk) Shajenko, Taisa Mykolaivna Kovalchuk, Natalia Chernysh, Volodymyr and Irena Sviontek, the Gayda family, the Muzychuk family, Andrii Zakharov, Svetlana Knyshevska, Lena Denysiuk, Sasha Onyshchuk, Tanya Green, Mara Moldwin, Zhenia Moldwin, and Naomi Feigenbaum.

In Ukraine my research was facilitated by scholars and administrators at the National Academy of Sciences of Ukraine, who helped arrange visas, scholarly affiliations, and letters of introduction. In particular, I thank the scholars at the Presidium of the Academy of Sciences of Ukraine, the Potebnia Institute of Linguistics then headed by V. M. Rusanivs'kyi, the Institute of Ukrainian Language then headed by O. O. Taranenko, and the Ryl's'kyi Institute of Folklore, Art History, and Ethnology, headed by Hanna A. Skrypnyk. I benefited especially from the collegial support and advice of Bohdan M. Azhniuk, Viktor M. Britsyn, Larysa Masenko, and Hanna Zalizniak. Thanks also to Vitalii Radchuk for sharing numerous useful articles. The IREX-Kyiv office staff helped in innumerable ways; in particular, I would like to thank Yaroslav Myshanych and his family, Oksana Maydan, and Myroslava Andrushchenko.

A Shklar Fellowship at the Harvard Ukrainian Research Institute (HURI) provided me with crucial time for research and writing, access to Ukrainian library resources, and a vibrant collegial environment. I thank Eugene and Daymel Shklar for making this invaluable scholarly experience possible. I am grateful to the many people at HURI who shared their personal insights and scholarly expertise, especially Aleksandra Hnatiuk, Tamara Hundorova, Volodymyr Kravchenko, Volodymyr Kulyk, Oleksandr Halenko, and Stephen Shulman, who were my fellow Shklar Fellows; Robert DeLossa, Volodymyr Dibrova, Michael Flier, Lubomyr Hayda, Svitlana Hurkina, Ksenya Kiebuzinski, General Kostiantyn Morozov, Serhii Plokhy, Yuri Shevchuk, and Ukrainian foreign minister Boris Tarasyuk.

This research was supported by two Fulbright-Hays Research Abroad Grants (1994–95, 2002), a National Science Foundation Doctoral Dissertation Improvement Grant (1995, No. SBR-9419338), and three grants from the International Research and Exchanges Board (with funds provided by the National Endowment for the Humanities, the U.S. Information Agency, and the U.S. Department of State): an On-Site Language Training Grant (1991–92), a Research Residency (1994–95), and an Individual Advanced Research Opportunity (2002). Analysis and writing at the University of Michigan were supported by fellowships from the National Science Foundation, the Social Science Research Council, the Mellon Foundation, and the University of Michigan Rackham Foundation. The University of Washington provided travel funding and further support through the Junior Faculty Development Program. The views expressed in this work are my own and not those of any of the agencies and institutions that so generously supported my research.

My interests in linguistic anthropology were kindled at Yale by Harold Conklin, Niko Besnier, J. Joseph Errington, and Ray McDermott. At the University of Michigan, Bruce Mannheim, Lesley Milroy, Laura Ahearn, Michael Kennedy, Conrad Kottak, and Assya Humesky provided invaluable guidance. At the University of Washington, I am grateful to Alicia Beckford Wassink, Celia Lowe, and Miriam Kahn, who provided useful feedback on my writing.

At Cornell University Press, I am deeply grateful for the supportive and constructive efforts of series editors Nancy Ries and Bruce Grant, and for the careful editorial work of John Ackerman, Rita Bernhard, Sheri Englund, and Karen Hwa. Ben Fitzhugh, Volodymyr Kulyk, and an anonymous reviewer provided useful commentaries on drafts of the book. My thanks to Yurii Verbovskyy for his moving photographs of the Orange Revolution, and to Dave Prout for indexing. This book incorporates material that appeared in "Speaking of Surzhyk: Ideologies and Mixed Languages" in *Harvard Ukrainian Studies* (1997, 21[1/2]) and in "A Typology of Surzhyk: Mixed Ukrainian-Russian Language" in *International Journal of Bilingualism* (2004, 8[4]), included here with permission.

My parents, Oleksa-Myron and Larissa Bilaniuk, inspired me and bred my love for studying languages and cultures. My parents, my sister, Larissa Sand, and my grandmother, Myroslava Zubal, all sustained me with their moral support. This project would not have been possible without the support of my husband and colleague, Ben Fitzhugh, who tirelessly helped me at every stage, from field-work to writing. My daughter, Laska, also assisted me in my most recent field-work. She and recent arrival Larissa relentlessly provide joy and humor. I thank them all for their support in this endeavor, for their understanding, and for making it all worthwhile.

Note on Transliteration

References to printed sources are transliterated using the Library of Congress (LC) system, omitting ligatures. The term *surzhyk* (denoting mixed Ukrainian-Russian language), which is used extensively throughout this book, is also in LC transliteration. Place names are transliterated from Ukrainian according to standards established by the Ukrainian Legal Terminology Commission (omitting the optional soft signs), for example, Kyiv, Lviv, and Odesa (instead of Kiev, Lvov, and Odessa, which are transliterations from the Russian forms, generally more familiar to English speakers). The names of persons or groups who publicly use a romanized version of their names are rendered in the orthography used by these persons or groups. All other transliterations of terms and names, transcriptions of spoken pronunciation, and linguistic examples are rendered using the Linguistic System (Kubijovyc 1984, xi–xii). In a few cases, additional specialized symbols of the International Phonetic Alphabet are employed to indicate finer phonetic distinctions. Italicized words denote phonetic transcription unless otherwise indicated. When I need to make the distinction, slashes (/) surround phonemic representations and square brackets ([ ]) surround phonetic representations.

Transliterations, as well as translations from Ukrainian and Russian into English, are my own, unless otherwise indicated.

Transliteration and transcription of Ukrainian and Russian

Cyrillic	Library of Congress	Linguistic Transliteration and [Phonetic Transcription]
Consonants		
б	b	b
в	v	v
г (Ukr.)	h	h
г (Rus)	g	g
ґ (only Ukr.)	g	g
д	d	d
ж	zh	ž
з	z	z
й	i	j

(continued)

Transliteration and transcription of Ukrainian and Russian (continued)

Cyrillic	Library of Congress	Linguistic Transliteration and [Phonetic Transcription]
к	k	k
л	l	l
м	m	m
н	n	n
п	p	p
р	r	r
с	s	s
т	t	t
ф	f	f
х	kh	x
ц	ts	c
ч	ch	č
ш	sh	š
щ	shch	šč
ь (palatalization)	'	'
Vowels		
а	a	a
е (Ukr.)	e	e
е (Rus.)	ie	je['e]
э (only Rus.)	e	e
є (only Ukr.)	ie	je['e]
ë (only Rus.)	ë	jo
и (Ukr.)	y	y[ɪ]
и (Rus.)	i	i
ы (only Rus.)	y	y[ɨ]
і (only Ukr.)	i	i
ї (only Ukr.)	ï	ji
о	o	o
у	u	u
ю	iu	ju ['u]
я	ia	ja ['a]
schwa (centralized vowel	-	[ə]

Contested Tongues

Map of Ukraine

Introduction

Kyiv, December 1991

Gray winter light streamed into the otherwise unlit dingy hospital room crowded with beds. Women of various ages sat or lay on the beds, brought together from all over Ukraine with the hope of curing their ailments or at least having a rest from work. My friend, Anya, suffering from an ear infection, had invited me to visit, as she and her roommates would appreciate the distraction.[1] I saw this as a good opportunity to meet people from various backgrounds and hear their ideas about language, since I had come to Ukraine to study the nature of Ukrainian-Russian bilingualism. At the time American visitors in Kyiv were still rare, so my visit was unusual, although my interest in talking about language issues was seen as normal. Ukrainian had been declared the state language two years earlier, and this brought language into the center of public debate.

The first woman I spoke with brought forth no surprises; as I had expected, she described her language use in various contexts in terms of established linguistic categories, specifying that she spoke either Ukrainian or Russian or in some cases both. But the next woman I talked to, Halyna, started out by telling me that she spoke a "joint" language—neither Ukrainian nor Russian but a mixture. Indeed, the language she spoke was difficult to label—it blended elements of Ukrainian and Russian in grammar, lexicon, and pronunciation. I had heard of "mixed" and "impure" language before, reviled and referred to derogatorily by the label *surzhyk*. But Halyna avoided this term when describing her own speech. As I asked her about her language use in different situations, her answer was always the same—mixed language. Then she told me that she preferred television shows and newspapers in Russian, because they were more intelligible to her than the Ukrainian ones. Her language must be closer to Russian after all, I thought. A moment later she stated that her ("mixed") language was really "just plain Ukrainian, that's all," and she criticized the television stations for using a Ukrainian lan-

---

1. All personal names mentioned are pseudonyms.

guage that had "an accent." She said that if there were shows in Ukrainian as she knows it, she would watch them. To complicate matters, when I asked how she answered people who addressed her in Ukrainian, she replied "in Ukrainian," and stated that she answered those who addressed her in Russian "in Russian." In my observations of how she spoke with me and with others in the room, she did not alter her "mixed" language, regardless of how she was addressed. What was going on here? Many of my assumptions about language did not seem to hold. Nor did my own sense of "Ukrainian" and "Russian" match what Halyna thought.

While at the outset Halyna described her language as "mixed," and asserted her ability to communicate with both Ukrainian and Russian speakers, she also claimed legitimacy for her language and herself as truly "Ukrainian." It was through her confidence in the value of her language that Halyna claimed social legitimacy and established a sense of her social worth. What was at stake was not the empirical reality of what was spoken but how it was perceived, what people believed about it, and what they could convince others to believe about it. Halyna's case, I later learned, was but one expression of an ideological struggle at the core of Ukrainian nation building. Everyone's language is, to some degree, mixed, but powerful agents such as government officials, educators, and activists perpetuate the belief in a "pure" language as a standard against which everyone is to be judged. The ideology elevating a "pure" language establishes a hierarchy in which linguistic values index social values, and awareness of the mixed nature of language is suppressed. While this ideology can mobilize and empower people, it can also be a basis for discrimination.

I have found that this ideological aspect of language is crucial even when people do not see their language as "mixed" and strive to adhere to literary standards.[2] When people name a language, and describe it as mixed or pure, language becomes the site of struggle over identity, social values, and, in terms routinely implied by those I spoke with, a certain "cultural correctness." Heightened concern with correction was a product of anxieties evoked by the disintegration of Soviet hierarchies of value, but its roots lay firmly in Soviet practices that had defined the achievement of culturedness according to conservative standards. These Soviet practices were also generated in response to anxieties resulting from the disruption of standards of value, in the wake of the 1917 Revolution, as peasants and workers ascended to positions of greater social authority (Dunham 1990;

---

2. In Ukraine the term "literary language" (*literaturna mova* in Ukrainian) is used to refer to both written and spoken standards. Perhaps since Ukrainian orthography is basically phonetic (with each letter representing a sound that does not change in different contexts), these two dimensions—the written and the oral—are usually conflated, seen as manifestations of a single ideal language. Regional differences in the production of some phonemes, such as degree of palatalization of /š/ or degree of roundedness of /o/, remain bases for discriminating spoken languages that are not determined by orthography.

Lewin 1985, 266–267, 297; Hoffmann 1994, 2003; Smith 1998). Parallels can be found in conditions of social change and state building elsewhere, such as in the policies of linguistic unification and purification that accompanied the French Revolution, and the tensions over linguistic standards in Britain that resulted from class struggles during late-nineteenth- and early-twentieth-century industrialization (Milroy 1999, 185–188; Thompson 1991, 6). While efforts to police linguistic correctness and purity often take center stage during revolutionary periods, often they are also part of ongoing efforts at social regulation in relatively more stable times (Cameron 1995; Jernudd and Shapiro 1989; Thomas 1991; Wexler 1974).

In the first decade of post-Soviet independence in Ukraine, beliefs about what is and is not correct were as varied as individual life histories, but underlying the tensions between beliefs was a collective desire for the legitimacy of an order whose construction was too recent to be comfortably transparent. That Ukrainian and Russian are structurally close only heightened the symbolic significance of differences between them, and this was reinforced in the marginalization of mixtures of the two. The degree of mutual intelligibility of the standard Ukrainian and Russian languages is very limited without some background knowledge owing to different phonological rules, some different grammatical structures, and a large portion of basic vocabulary without common roots (see appendix). The linguistic commonalties do allow for some basic communication, as would be the case among most of the Slavic languages. An analysis by Radchuk (2000b, 11), on the basis of an etymological dictionary, concludes that, out of 10,779 Russian words, just under 30 percent are common to the Slavic languages in general and only 0.8 percent are common exclusively to the three East Slavic languages—Russian, Belarusian, and Ukrainian.[3] Russophone visitors to Ukraine may, however, mistake local versions of Russian or Ukrainian-Russian mixtures for Ukrainian, leading to the impression of mutual intelligibility. The misidentification of mixtures and Ukrainian-accented Russian for standard Ukrainian has also been propagated on Russian television, most recently in humorous skits such as those of the popular comic figure Verka Serduchka (played by actor Andrii Danylko) who speaks a range of Ukrainian-Russian mixtures. Also, people who have lived in Ukraine, even though they may speak only one language, tend to be at least passively bilingual, as they will have had extensive exposure to the other language through the media and public language use.

Despite the multiplicity of language varieties and mixtures, the assumption persists that there must be a correct standard, making "a language" something

---

3. Radchuk's analyses are based on data from M. Fasmer's four-volume etymological dictionary of the Russian language, using data compiled by Trubachov (1957). Radchuk analyzes a total of 10,779 words whose roots are given, excluding 818 ethnonyms and personal names. See chapter 5 for further discussion.

that can be given a name. Even named language (English or Ukrainian, for example) is always seething with tensions and contradictions. As a new regime is habitualized and naturalized, tensions recede from overt contestation, but they are always present, implicit in language use.

Kyiv, March 1976 to 2002

I first experienced the tensions between ideologies of Ukrainianness and Russianness when my family moved to Ukraine for seven months on a scientific exchange, in January 1976. I was born and raised in the United States, but Ukrainian was my first language. My parents were both born in western Ukraine and, during World War II, had fled west with their parents from the oncoming Soviet army. They spent several years in displaced persons (DP) camps in Germany after the war before coming to the United States. After time spent in the DP camps, my father attended a university in Belgium for several years before rejoining his family in Detroit, where he later met and married my mother. I grew up in an exclusively Ukrainian-speaking extended family household, and learned English once I started attending American public school.

The 1976 exchange that brought my family to the Ukrainian Soviet Socialist Republic (SSR) was organized between the U.S. National Academy of Sciences and the Academy of Sciences of the USSR. While my father took part in physics research and my mother lectured on medicine, I attended first grade in one of only three Ukrainian-language-instruction schools then existing in the city of Kyiv. Russian language dominated city life then, but in the suburb where we lived, almost all the children I played with spoke Ukrainian. I was too young to consider the possible significance of this, but my parents called attention to the problems of Russification, to the erasure of Ukrainianness by Soviet culture, and thus to the need to strive to correct these cultural and linguistic anomalies. I participated in mild symbolic political resistance: on March 9, the birthday of the mythicized nineteenth-century Ukrainian poet Taras Shevchenko, my sister and I wore the white aprons and hair bows that were designated for special holidays, while the other children wore the everyday black. As foreigners we could afford to make such gestures of cultural commentary, whereas, for Soviet citizens, the everyday uniform counterbalanced the potentially dangerous fact that Shevchenko's birthday was being publicly recognized at all, since many of his works highlight Russian-Ukrainian conflicts and decry Ukraine's oppression by Russia. In earlier years people had been arrested for organizing celebrations of Shevchenko's birthday, while at other times he was officially celebrated as a champion of those oppressed by tsarist imperialism. The acceptability of Shevchenko was reinterpreted in shifting Soviet official policies in response to, and in competition with, the ways in which people unofficially mobilized the symbolic significance of this literary figure.

The author during her seven months as a Soviet school pupil in 1976, reciting a verse below a portrait of the Ukrainian poet Taras Shevchenko.

Back in the United States my sense of struggle for cultural correctness persisted, particularly through language. With time I learned to be an "unmarked" American in public, while within my family we tried to protect our Ukrainian language from infiltration by English words. I now realize that, for better or worse, I, too, participated in cultural correction, since I had learned that mixing, especially in language, was degradation of identity, all the more problematic because it was so prevalent among Ukrainian Americans. Our diasporic experience in the United States in some ways paralleled that of Ukrainians in Ukraine with regard to Russian: in both countries Ukrainians faced overt and implicit pressures to adopt the language of power, whether English or Russian, and this often resulted in linguistic mixtures and rejection of the socially limited Ukrainian language, especially by the youth. Russian may be more similar to Ukrainian than English, but that did not diminish the social differences between Ukrainian and Russian forms. The significance of mixing languages was more poignant in Ukraine, however, because it signaled a deterioration of ethnic/national integrity according to the globally dominant national model, which idealizes an essential unity of a language, a people, and a homeland (Woolard 1998a, 17). The disappearance of Ukrainian would help foster the "flowing together" of languages, with the ultimate dominance of Russian, which was part of the planned construction of Sovietness. In the USSR aspirations for linguistic correctness in Ukrainian could be dangerous, since they could be seen as a threat to the centralization of power.

Once I returned to conduct research in a newly independent Ukraine in 1991, concern for correcting Ukrainian had become part of the construction of nationhood. Although I had come to question the implications of cultural correction, I still felt inclined to correct my language, to alter features of my Ukrainian language that were typical of the diaspora. I conducted fieldwork in Ukraine (which, along with archival and media research, is the basis for this book) from October 1991 to August 1992, November 1994 to November 1995, May 2000, and May through August 2002.[4] After more than two years of fieldwork I lost many (but not all) of my markedly diasporic linguistic features. As one Ukrainian linguist put it, I had "pulled my language up to the standard." This left me with the curious situation of being aware that I was speaking my first native language differently than I had learned and spoken it for the first twenty years of my life. I had learned Russian later in life, in college, and while I developed my proficiency during my fieldwork, choices between different variants of Russian were not as closely tied to my sense of identity.

During my fieldwork in Ukraine I found myself frequently weighing the pros and cons of choosing to speak one language or the other in my daily interactions. At times I even consciously chose to use what some people called impure or incorrect forms to conform to the usage of others in a given context. I based my

---

4. My main sites of research were Kyiv, Lviv, and Dnipropetrovsk and nearby villages. I also visited Zaporizhia, Crimea, and areas in the oblasts of Poltava, Volyn, and Ivano-Frankivsk. My field research consisted of observing and participating in everyday life, along with more than one hundred tape-recorded structured interviews (arranged through friends, in a hospital, research institute, and apartment building, as well as with people encountered while traveling). I also learned much from many unstructured discussions with individuals I met. I taped television programs and regularly sampled the print media. In 1994–95 I also conducted a psycholinguistic language attitude test and survey with a total of two thousand respondents from urban and rural schools, universities, and teacher training institutes (findings from these tests are presented in Bilaniuk 1997a, 1998a, 1998b, 2003). Making arrangements for the testing led to further observations and interactions that were a rich source of data.

choices on what felt acceptable, which I judged by other people's speech and people's reactions to my own speech. Such interpersonal dynamics, compiled of everyone's linguistic choices, add up to a crucial dimension of what can be seen from afar as large-scale social and political changes.

Across the years there has been a dramatic shift in public linguistic practices in Ukraine, in Kyiv, in particular, where I spent time during all my visits. During my first research trip, from October 1991 to August 1992, in Kyiv it was rare to hear and awkward to speak anything but Russian in public. During my next stay, from November 1994 to October 1995, Russian was still dominant in Kyiv, but Ukrainian had a small but noticeable presence in public. During this period in Kyiv I tended to choose Russian so as not to stand out, since Ukrainian speech in the public urban environment was still remarkable. Later, in May 2000 and May through August 2002, hearing Ukrainian on the streets of Kyiv was no longer unusual, although still less frequent than Russian, with about a third of people speaking Ukrainian, according to one survey.[5] I often witnessed conversations carried on in both languages, with each interlocutor adhering to his or her preferred language. While my original inclination was to conform to the language of my interlocutor, in 2002 I tried engaging in such nonreciprocal bilingual conversations, speaking Ukrainian with Russophone respondents. In contrast to earlier years, such dual-language conversation felt comfortable, and it came to feel inappropriate to accommodate to Russian when Ukrainian was my stronger language.

My personal experiences of linguistic dynamics highlight the importance of the everyday individual acts of choosing and judging languages that create a linguistic environment. This environment is also shaped by top-down language policies, which people may accept or reject depending on the regulatory consequences, their sense of appropriateness, their desire to express political inclinations, and their sense of confidence in their language skills. The correction of language thus proceeds on many levels.

Correction, Co-option, and the Impossibility of Neutrality

Individual choices in the use of language play a role in the social construction of Ukrainian ethnolinguistic identity. On another level, this book itself could influence the construction of that identity. As I weighed the implications of language

---

5. In 2002 I worked with Hanna Zalizniak of the Kyiv City "Hromads'ka Dumka" Center for Sociological Research to organize a survey of 450 people representative of the city of Kyiv, which included a question asking respondents to identify the percentage of people on the streets of Kyiv speaking Ukrainian. This added statistical data to my own impressions of increased public usage of Ukrainian. On average, respondents answered that 36 percent of people in Kyiv spoke Ukrainian in public.

choice in everyday interaction, I also had to consider the impact of my research topic and methods. By focusing on the ideological constructedness of "Ukrainian," and the blurring and mixing of the ethnolinguistic categories of "Ukrainian" and "Russian," I could provide fodder for those who would delegitimize Ukrainian language, culture, and statehood. Does it help to point out that English, French, Russian—and any other ethnolinguistic or national unit—is just as ideologically constructed, the boundaries similarly blurred in practice?[6] An acceptance of a view of these languages as ideological constructions entails a departure from what is, for most people, a deeply ingrained "common sense" ideology of the essential naturalness of these language categories, bolstered by extensive institutionalization of the myths of their nature as discrete entities. It is much easier for the majority to question the legitimacy of institutionally less established ethnolinguistic categories, like Ukrainian—unless they were brought up and educated in Ukrainian, in which case they are indeed likely to have deeply internalized the naturalness of this category. The analysis I undertake here, including a focus on the mixing and hybridity of forms, risks playing into already prevalent discourses that work to delegitimize less powerful and less institutionalized categories of language and identity. In the case of Ukraine, these date back to tsarist policies forbidding public uses of Ukrainian and denying its existence as a language, continued recently by Russians arguing that Ukraine, Belarus, and Russia are really the same country and should be united (Kaplan 1994; Solzhenitsyn 1990, 1991). This erasure of Ukraine was further supported in the West by the frequent Cold War–era practice of equating the whole USSR with Russia.[7] In the early 1990s many publications appeared in Ukraine that specifically refuted these denials, arguing for the naturalness and legitimacy of the newly independent nation (e.g., Hoian 1991; Ivanyshyn and Radevych-Vynnytskyi; Karavans'kyi 1994; Karpenko 1990; Pan'ko 1991; Serbens'ka 1994).

I encountered the impossibility of being scientifically neutral in social science research during my first fieldwork in 1991. A linguist in Lviv expressed dismay when I indicated my interest in bilingualism: "First the Soviets imposed bilingualism, now the Americans!" At first I was taken aback: bilingualism un-

---

6. Silverstein (2000, 2003) presents the case for viewing languages and nations as ideological constructs. On the historical and contemporary complexities of standard English, see Bonfiglio 2002, Parakrama 1995, and the articles in Bex and Watts 1999; on French, see Schiffman 1996, 75–147; and on Russian, see Radchuk 2000b.

7. While news reporters, after the fall of Soviet power, have tended to be less sloppy about confusing Russia with the former Soviet states, this practice has not yet died out. For example, in the British newspaper the *Globe and Mail* an article of October 3, 2003, by Mark MacKinnon on Ukrainian president Kuchma listed "Kiev, Russia" as the reporting location; the *New York Times* of July 2, 2004, in its rubric *World Briefing*, page A6, placed the Ukrainian city of Donetsk in Russia.

doubtedly existed in Ukraine, so why shouldn't I study it? The Lviv linguist explained that the term "bilingualism" had become a mask for Russification and that, through the years, policies of "bilingualism" were increasingly directed toward insuring proficiency in standard Russian, at the expense of other languages such as Ukrainian. In the first year of Ukrainian independence my desire to pursue an academic study of bilingualism was controversial; indeed, it was tantamount to a legitimation of the role of Russian in Ukraine, since for so long that role had been to undermine and replace Ukrainianness. My academic interest in the mixed language *surzhyk* was even more problematic, in that it legitimized as worthy of serious study a phenomenon that many saw as a disease or a product of Ukrainian self-hate and self-denigration (Bilaniuk 1997b, 2004; Serbens'ka 1994; Stavyts'ka 2001). For the rest of that year and in later field research I found it difficult to conduct research without being assigned a particular "side," either pro-Ukrainian or pro-Russian (the latter sometimes conflated with "bilingualism"). If I wasn't supporting one side, then I must be against it.[8]

As a Westerner I had the luxury of being able to distance myself from the situation I studied, but this did not amount to neutrality inasmuch as any social scientific work invariably can become a basis for legitimizing or delegitimizing a group's claims. As argued by Silverstein (2003, 554), "there is, in the long run, no neutrally dispassionate, disinterested linguistic or ethnographic collecting and describing, whatever the explicit intent of the linguist or anthropologist." Indeed, the work of linguists and ethnographers has been integral in nation building and the legitimization of ethnicities (Anderson 1991; Gal 1995, 2001; Gal and Irvine 1995; Gal and Woolard 1995; Irvine and Gal 2000; Ssorin-Chaikov 2003). In Ukraine many linguists and ethnologists I met expressed a responsibility (whether explicit or implicit) that their work should contribute to the formation of their country's social and political future in whichever direction they believed was right.

So where did I stand? While my own background was Ukrainian, I had found the idealist and purist narratives of Ukraine's history, culture, and language that I learned in childhood (at home, in community Saturday school, and in scouting events) limited and limiting once I went to Ukraine as an adult. College-level

---

8. The implications of my research focus did not necessarily fit the agenda of one camp or the other; other sociopolitical aspirations are also possible. For example, in the United States in 2001 I encountered two academics from Ukraine who explicitly wanted to harness my research on *surzhyk*, the "mixed Ukrainian-Russian language," to a Herderian-type ideology of linguistic legitimation. They seemed eager to find scientific support for the legitimacy of the variety of northeastern Ukrainian most native to them and were frustrated that I did not provide a traditional bounded structural-linguistic definition of surzhyk that could be the basis for a legitimacy parallel with other codified labeled languages. Instead, I analyzed the ideological aspects of this labeled category, which encompasses a diversity of structural features, as discussed in chapter 4.

РУССКИЙ ЯЗЫК

УКРАЇНСЬКА МОВА

V. Lazunko
Bcecmix@sympatico.ca

Unequal bilingualism: cartoon by the artist Vasyl' Lazun'ko, from Zaporizhia, depicting русский язык (*russkyj jazyk*) 'Russian language' engulfing українська мова (*ukrajins'ka mova*) 'Ukrainian language'. The Russian word for "language" is identical to the word for "tongue."

study of Ukrainian literature and music was also enlightening, as I learned of tensions, contradictions, and struggles in the country's traditions. In my field research in newly independent Ukraine I was intrigued by the complexity of identities that were both familiar and unfamiliar to me. My interests in ethnolinguistic politics and language mixing in Ukraine were surely influenced by my own experience of a multiethnic, multilingual upbringing. So while I have resisted professing a political agenda, the focus of this work is definitively a product of my internalization of contemporary social science discourses and my own Western diasporic identity. I recognize that different approaches bring different kinds of understanding; my own analyses of the interpersonal and sociopolitical struggles that have shaped the language situation in Ukraine seek to answer different questions than do studies that prioritize the aesthetic, spiritual, or applied and prescriptive concerns.

This book has three goals: first, to examine language ideologies and language politics in Ukraine, including historical context to the extent that it is critical in understanding contemporary dynamics and developments during the first decade of post-Soviet independence. I take into account official language policies, and, whenever possible, I present the everyday ideas and impressions of people regarding linguistic uses and values. The second goal of this book is to shine the spotlight on "mixed language" practices in Ukraine that have generally been either ignored or reviled, tracing the history and social implications of such mixing and the ideologies of correction that have accompanied it. I argue that the current preoccupation with linguistic correction evident in Ukraine is similar to the situation at the inception of the USSR: in both cases, abrupt social changes led to heightened anxiety about the symbolic markers of authenticity, culturedness, and social legitimacy. Through a focus on mixed language, I examine the power dynamics of the practices of linguistic and cultural correction, through which people seek to either confer or deny others social legitimacy. My third goal is to build on general theories of language and social power that so far have been based mostly on the analysis of relatively stable social situations, through this study of the rapid transformation of systems of symbolic values in Ukraine.

1 # Language Paradoxes and Ideologies of Correction

The word as the ideological phenomenon par excellence exists in continuous generation and change; it sensitively reflects all social shifts and alterations.

V. N. VOLOSHINOV, *MARXISM AND THE PHILOSOPHY OF LANGUAGE*

Ukraine in Cultural and Linguistic Transition

For seventy years the Soviet regime perpetuated a system of cultural planning and ideological control buttressed by a cumbersome bureaucracy and ruthless secret service. When Gorbachev's reforms unexpectedly destabilized the system in the late 1980s, the existing prescriptive paradigms for behavior and belief suddenly seemed to lose currency. The fear that had been a prime instrument of maintaining power slowly evaporated. People were thrown off balance by the barrage of new information and open expressions of ideas, as they experienced incredulity, elation, hope, disenchantment, anger, and a new fear of an unknown future.

As freedom of expression burgeoned within the former USSR, the borders to the rest of the noncommunist world were opened. This unleashed curiosity and a yearning for new ideas and products. Even before independence, in 1988, the first pageant was staged to choose a "Miss Ukraine." Once Ukraine became independent, the Ukrainian Parliament chose and ratified an official national flag and insignia, choosing national symbols from pre-Soviet times. Accompanying the return to historic Ukrainian national traditions was the modernization of technologies and commodities as people aspired to make their country a full-fledged member of the modern community of nations. It was not long before cities were studded with Western establishments—restaurants, discos, supermarkets, and photocopy shops. Kiosks proliferated throughout cities and spread into distant villages, their shelves carrying random assortments of imported products such as Lycra leggings, novelty condoms, candy bars, *Playboy* magazines, syringes, and rosaries. Athletes won gold medals for Ukraine at Olympic events, bolstering people's confidence in their country's place in the world.[1]

To many, the fall of the Soviet Empire was cause for celebration. It was a chance to resuscitate nations and identities that had been cruelly stifled, to vindicate relatives and friends who had perished for openly cherishing non-Soviet traditions or not conforming to the "correct" ideology. The injustices of the Soviet period were brought out into the open, and pre-Soviet Ukrainian history was invoked to support a return to the path of national development. This effort to reclaim the past was a form of cultural correction.

Some former Soviet citizens found it difficult to believe in the new governments and their plans for the future. To others it seemed that nothing substantial had changed—as one Ukrainian friend put it, politicians still put forth the same old propaganda slogans, with a few different words substituted. Many of the people once in power remained in power but proclaimed new convictions. Feelings of freedom were dampened by changes in the bureaucracy of everyday life, when inscrutable new rules replaced familiar (albeit cumbersome) procedures regulating housing, employment, and pensions, and the economy deteriorated and everyday survival became more difficult for many.

Numerous studies have shown how histories, identities, and economies were revised and reinterpreted, as people sought to exalt, reject, or combine the contending pre-Soviet, Soviet, Western, and newly invented traditions.[2] Some people did not waver as they asserted their national identity, religious convictions, and political beliefs. For others, the course of action was less clear, as they were torn between nationalism, Westernization, and the legacy of Sovietness. Daily behavior, including language use, took on new symbolic meanings as values were renegotiated.

During the era of perestroika from 1988 to 1991 each of the USSR's constituent republics had rushed to enhance the legal status of its "own" language (Arel 1993, iii, 4–8). This legislation, along with increased freedom of discussion in the media, made language a central issue in social and political conflicts of this time. In Ukraine a 1989 Law on Language named Ukrainian the sole official state

---

1. Particularly significant was the first gold medal won for Ukraine, in 1994, by the figure skater Oksana Baiul.

2. On European Russia, see Ries 1997 and the articles in Barker 1999; on Siberian and Far Eastern Russia, see Grant 1995 and Humphrey 2002; on gypsies in Russia, see Lemon 2000; on Ukraine, see Wanner 1998; and for a comparative study of Latvia, Estonia, Kazakhstan, and Ukraine, see Laitin 1998.

language. Until then, Russian had been the de facto official language throughout the USSR. A diglossic situation existed in Ukraine, with Ukrainian in the role of "low language," associated with the peasantry and having low prestige, and Russian as the "high language," considered prestigious, cultured, and authoritative.[3] The legislation making Ukrainian the state language, subsequently ratified as part of independent Ukraine's constitution in 1996, spurred a striking rise in its status, but changes did not proceed evenly or unidirectionally.

Opposition to the promotion of Ukrainian came from people of various ethnic backgrounds who favored Russian, who argued that it was an infringement of their rights to be expected to use Ukrainian at work or to have their children schooled in Ukrainian. Some viewed Ukrainian as inferior by nature to Russian and felt that their children would be disadvantaged by not maintaining close ties to Russian culture. In the urban areas of eastern Ukraine where Ukrainian was not widely used publicly, these regulations spurred only limited institutional use of Ukrainian, which risked giving it the connotations of a shallow bureaucratic language. People who did not have strong political or cultural convictions argued that it was impractical in times of economic crisis to expend effort to change language use. These discourses of practicality also had political implications; for they strove to mask the fact that the definition of a social order and cultural values was at stake in the determination of language statuses.

Contextualizing Correction: The Legacy of Soviet Language Policies

Attempts to legislate language use have had a long history in the USSR, and construction of Ukrainian as the state language of an independent nation had to contend with the legacy of Soviet linguistic planning and manipulation. In Soviet times the projected ideal for the future was a socialist society that transcended ethnic divisions. National languages were expected to die out, as the creation of a single world socialist economic base would be accompanied by a single world

---

3. Diglossia usually entails two languages that coexist in a society but that have different statuses and functions or spheres of usage (Ferguson 1959; Fasold 1984, 34–59). The "high" language is considered prestigious and appropriate for literary, scientific, official/governmental, formal, and elite usage. Usually the high language is standardized, codified in grammar books and dictionaries, has a literary heritage, and is seen as requiring schooling to master. In many cases the "low" language is not standardized, or not written at all, and not taught through any formal schooling. People commonly say that it "lacks grammar." In other cases (as with Ukrainian during the Soviet period) the low language is standardized, codified, and has its own literature, but it is ideologically construed as backward and associated with lower classes. The low language is seen as limited in use to informal contexts, with or among people with little formal education. It may also be considered particularly appropriate for expressing humor or satire.

language in the superstructure (Goodman 1968, 729). Early theories proposed that the language would be a new composite of elements from existing languages. In the early Soviet years the policy of *korenizatsiia*—"nativization" or "indigenization"—supported the development of non-Russian languages (Liber 1991; Martin 2001). This policy was meant to counteract the legacy of Russian imperialism and to draw non-Russians to support Soviet rule but also to facilitate the introduction of Russian which would lead to greater centralization of power. Nativization was unevenly implemented and short-lived, and Stalin ultimately established the primacy of modern standard Russian as the language for all Soviet peoples (Smith 1998, 73, 169; Martin 2001, 451–461). Central government came to see a greater threat in the empowerment of non-Russian groups through nativization than in the "Russian great-power chauvinism" that had been identified as the main threat in the 1920s (Liber 1992, 21). This change lead to the vigorous institutional promotion of Russian throughout the republics.

In addition to traditional means of promoting one language and subjugating others through institutional control, Soviet domination was unique in its policies of linguistic interference through which the orthography, morphology, and grammar of other languages were to be gradually transformed to become more similar to Russian. According to the Soviet linguist Marr, "Mankind, proceeding toward economic unity and a classless society, cannot help applying artificial means, scientifically worked out, in order to accelerate this broad process" (quoted in Goodman 1968). Local non-Russian intelligentsia who worked on linguistic coding and standardization were criticized for creating puristic or "bourgeois nationalist" local languages, and in the early 1930s dictionaries were purged of local values, replaced with terms more similar to Russian ones (Karavans'kyi 1994; Kocherga and Kulyk 1994; Masenko 2004; Pachlovska 1998). The linguistic manipulations, which were often experienced by non-Russians as symbolic violations of their language and identity, were enforced with physical punishment, particularly under Stalin. Many of the cultural elite who worked on nativization were later purged (Masenko 2004, 31–38; Martin 2001, 269, 305, 345–352, 363). The perpetrators justified the violence as serving the goals of strengthening the cohesion of the Soviet Empire and promoting the establishment of Russian as a world language.

Not only was Russian to be the language of Soviet people, but it needed to be *correct* Russian. Authorities became concerned with correctness early on, as lower-class Russians assumed positions of public authority following the eradication of the nobility after 1917 (Smith 1998, 36). Even though revolutionary communist ideology officially rejected elite culture and promoted the celebration of proletarian values, the new Soviet elite, Lenin among them, campaigned to promote linguistic purism and conservative values and tastes among the masses in order to elevate them to what was considered the "high cultural level" of Great Russian literature (Smith 1998, 43). Linguists deemed that teaching from newspapers was harmful because they were full of dialectisms and street language, and that language should be taught through the nineteenth-century literary classics. Pronunciation was to be based on the Moscow dialect, which was seen as the most highly cultured, and radio later helped to further propagate this standard (Smith 1998, 113, 151; Woolhiser 2001, 103). The shift away from revolutionary values toward materialism, bourgeois styles, and the reverence of pre-revolutionary classicism became particularly marked in the mid-1930s under Stalin (Hoffmann 1994, 177–179).

The incorrectness of language, which was a problem with Russian peasants and workers, was even more of a problem with non-Russians; for deviations from the standard threatened central control and the construction of cultural unity and value. As Smith recounts, language had lost value, becoming "tattered and worn":

> As more and more of the non-Russians came to speak and write the Russian language, it appeared more truly as something of their own: not the language of Pushkin or Gorkii, but an awkwardly colloquial Russian koine, a tattered and worn currency of the new Soviet Union. As soon as the Russian language campaign started in 1925, educators publicly voiced their alarm over the poor mastery of the Russian language by non-Russians. (Smith 1998, 55)

The perceived incorrectness of the Russian language in non-Russian regions was often the result of the mixing of Russian with non-Russian linguistic elements. In Ukraine the blending of features of Russian and Ukrainian merited its own label, "surzhyk," originally a term for a low-grade mixture of wheat and rye flour (Bilaniuk 1997b, 2004). In Belarus the mixture of Belarusian and Russian was called *trasianka*, which had originally referred to a mixture of hay and straw (Woolhiser 2001, 105–106). Smith writes of a similar phenomenon in the North Caucasus, based on reports from 1927 Soviet education committee reports, that he refers to as "mountaineer-Russian speech," "neither native nor Russian but 'something in between, a kind of jargon, cutting to the ear'" (Smith 1998, 56). Such mixtures were marginalized, reviled, and derided, for they were considered emblematic of backwardness and limited education.

The forces that led to language mixing in Ukraine began under Russian tsarist rule and continued under the Soviets. Such language mixing was typical of peasants who came to the city and used their native Ukrainian linguistic forms while trying to speak the more prestigious urban Russian, a language they did not know well. In the late 1920s the great influx into cities of a new generation of "promoted ones" (*vydvyženc'i* in Ukrainian), replacing purged cultural elites and stepping up urbanization, "created a strange hybrid of city life, an 'urban peasant subculture'" in which rural and urban linguistic and cultural practices were combined (Hoffmann 1994, 182–189; Smith 1998, 143). In Ukraine these conditions led to the formation of regularized syncretic languages (combining standard Ukrainian, Russian, and local dialects), used by populations in suburban areas and small towns, and in villages with close ties to urban areas. During the period of support for nativization Mykola Skrypnyk (People's Commissar of Education and Member of the Central Committee of the Communist Party of Ukraine, 1927–1933) focused on the mixed nature of language to argue for stronger efforts at Ukrainianization: "His education policy was based on his theory that russified Ukrainians spoke a 'mixed dialect' whose syntactical base was Ukrainian. Therefore, they should study in Ukrainian-language schools even if their parents declared their native language to be Russian. Skrypnyk was exceedingly fond of his theory and repeated it as late as the fall of 1932" (Martin 2001, 353). Skrypnyk's policies, and their reversal in 1933, illustrate how interpretation and labeling of nonstandard and mixed languages can be used for socio political agendas; as argued earlier, it is not the empirical reality of language that counts but rather how it is perceived and labeled. Criticism of Skrypnyk's theory was accompanied by "a strong sense that Russian honor had been slighted" (Martin 2001, 354). In 1933 nativization had fallen into disfavor and Soviet language policies increasingly came to favor the propagation of Russian. As a result Skrypnyk was removed and his theory denounced as "forced Ukrainianization" and "de-Russification."

The preponderance of language mixtures and deviations from standard literary Russian made linguistic correction an issue at the Seventeenth Party Conference of 1932, in which the central Soviet government committed to fight for cultured speech. Not only was the government pushing for a narrowly defined standard but the newly elevated urbanized peasants and workers also aspired to "high culture" in language and "quickly became proud guardians of the Russian language" (Smith 1998, 146, 150). In embracing traditionally established cultural and linguistic values, the "promoted ones" solidified their own claim to higher status. World War II and its aftermath reinforced the identification of Russian language and Russian nationalism with Soviet class values, and pure Russian was venerated and again vigorously promoted (Smith 1998, 161, 164). Proper study of other languages was appropriate inasmuch as it also strengthened the study of Russian, but concerns with the purity of these languages were muted because they risked seeming bourgeois nationalist or separatist. As far as non-Russian languages were concerned, linguistic processes were meant to lead to the "flowing together" of peoples into the fold of Russianness. Concern for the maintenance of standard literary Russian and the "struggle against the emergence of local variants" continued into the 1970s and 1980s (Woolhiser 2001, 103, citing Desheriev and Protchenko 1972, 10, and Ivanov and Mikhailovskaia 1982, 10).

Changes and Continuities in De-Sovietizing Ukraine

Just as regulation of language was key in the crafting of Soviet power, so, too, has language been central in its dissolution. The disintegration of Soviet power in the 1980s, and the declaration of new nations and new state languages in the 1990s, disrupted the hegemonic semiotic system in which Russian was elevated. This did not cause Russian to lose status immediately, for its value was ingrained in institutionalized practices and in people's attitudes, but its privileged position was openly questioned and rejected by some who saw it as a colonizer's language. The social and political turmoil of independence brought issues of language values and statuses to the fore, and people's dispositions to favor Russian competed with newly legislated and practiced behaviors favoring Ukrainian. Language issues entered awareness and became a ubiquitous topic of heated discussion.

The elevation of Ukrainian and the other non-Russian languages to the role of official state languages of newly independent nations potentially raised the social status of the ethnic groups associated with these languages. This situation evoked many of the same concerns as had the elevation of the peasants and workers to positions of social power at the inception of Soviet rule after 1917. Parallels may also be drawn to the linguistic struggles that accompanied the French and American revolutions, and rapid urbanization in Britain (Bonfiglio 2002; Milroy 1999, 188; Schiffman 1996; Thompson 1991, 6). In all cases there emerged an increased awareness of class- and regionally based linguistic differences, with the elevation of a "pure" or "most refined" variety. In post-Soviet Ukraine the language situation was transformed not only because the previously disenfranchised suddenly had access to social power. Many of those who remained in positions of authority, men and women who had previously conducted professional business in Russian, attempted to establish their legitimacy in the new nation by speaking Ukrainian. Since many of them lacked training in Ukrainian, or their experience was limited to childhood summers with village relatives, the varieties of Ukrainian language that they spoke had connotations of backwardness. Incomplete knowledge and lack of practice in standard Ukrainian also led to the mixing of Ukrainian and Russian forms, which evoked criticism of impurity, inauthenticity, and the damning labeling of their language as surzhyk.

A heightened concern for linguistic correctness was one response to the skepticism about the legitimacy of Ukrainian and of the new regime, and particularly about those Communist Party functionaries who were remaking themselves as nationalists. Over the course of many of our conversations, some people voiced doubt that true, pure Ukrainian existed at all, thereby withholding their support of the nation-building project. Judgments and choices of language use became key means by which people strove to shape the emerging social order. By judging that someone's language was good and pure, people could accord that person social authority; criticizing someone's language as impure served to undermine their authority. Likewise, in choosing which language to speak in particular situations, people asserted the legitimate domains of that language.

Concern with linguistic and cultural correction took unique forms in the post-Soviet Ukrainian context, but its roots lay firmly in Soviet practices and ideologies as they did in all twentieth-century modernizing projects. Even though revolutionary communist ideology officially promoted a leveling of cultural and linguistic hierarchies, critical awareness of correctness and social hierarchy had been inherent in Soviet society from its inception, since Soviet practices prioritized the conservative goal of achieving a "high level" of (preexisting) cultural and linguistic values. The efforts to police correctness that flourished in independent Ukraine were not really new but had been fostered since the initial efforts to construct communism in the USSR. Cultural and linguistic conservatism promoting Russian, which took hold in the 1930s, built upon the well-established and institutionalized traditions of Imperial Russia. In Ukraine the institutionalization of standard and prestigious linguistic values was far less homogeneous or established, making more complex the post-Soviet pursuit of legitimacy through correction of illegitimate forms.

The conflicting attitudes about language statuses were complicated by the existence of social and regional varieties of Ukrainian, Russian, and the syncretic Ukrainian-Russian languages known as surzhyk. New forces leading to language mixing emerged after independence as urban Russian speakers who knew Ukrainian poorly found that they needed to speak it. The forces leading people to mix standard languages (occasionally) or to speak syncretic languages (as a native language) were varied, but surzhyk served as an umbrella term to label various transgressions of purity. As the ideology of linguistic purism resurged in public discourse, the term "surzhyk" was widely used to criticize and discredit other speakers. I frequently found that people who were more accustomed to speaking Russian were inhibited from using Ukrainian, fearing embarrassment that their language would be labeled surzhyk. A few people advocated the use of mixed language as a positive step toward standard Ukrainian, but this view was marginalized.[4] Portrayals of surzhyk in popular culture largely reinforced its image as a degradation of Ukrainian language and culture. Even people who preferred that Ukraine be officially bilingual (Russian and Ukrainian) tended to argue that the languages must be correct and pure.

The concern with linguistic purity corresponded to the maintenance of ethnonational divisions fostered by Soviet social theory and the system of central-

---

4. In my participant-observation fieldwork, and in the more than one hundred interviews I conducted in 1991–92 and 1994–95, I very rarely encountered the idea that surzhyk could be considered positively. I found a lone printed example of this view in a tiny local newspaper in Dnipropetrovsk (Stepanenko et al. 1995).

ized command. The promotion of Russian as the language of the Soviet people accompanied a shift in the 1930s from viewing nations as historical social constructs to seeing nations as having deep primordial roots (Martin 2001, 442–443). Later, in the 1960s, building on the ideas set forth by Stalin in his writings of the 1940s and 1950s, this primordialist view persisted in Soviet social theory, focusing on "ethnos" as a stable basic category dividing humanity, which took on different forms depending on socioeconomic development (Bromlei, in Dunn 1975, 65; Cheboksarov 1970; Slezkine 1994; Ssorin-Chaikov 2003, 189). The basic unit of ethnos was believed to correspond to natural language units. The tendency to think of named languages as being naturally delimited relegated mixed languages to low visibility in both academic and folk ideologies. Little is written on language mixing in the USSR, although we can expect that it was common, given the extensive varied contact between languages in all the regions of the Union (Lewis 1972, 275–282, 292).[5] Institutional practices were largely in line with academic theories, since ethnic, national, and linguistic categories were established and reinforced through administrative practices, such as passports and censuses, in a system that originally had outwardly condemned them (Arel 2002; Hirsch 1997; Motyl and Krawchenko 1997; Slezkine 1994; Smith 1998; Verdery 1996, 83 ff).

Post-Soviet Practices

The Ukrainian nation may be envisioned as multi-ethnic or ethnically Ukrainian, multilingual or monolingual, modern and Westernized or having a uniquely Ukrainian non-Western, non-Soviet identity. These alternative visions have roots in historical constructs and social ideals. Some people envisioned the unity of the East Slavic nations—Belarus, Russia, and Ukraine—as the natural path to the future (as advocated by Solzhenitsyn 1990, 1991).[6] For others the demise of the Soviet Union was finally the chance to remedy a perceived disenfranchisement of the Ukrainian nation, to revive the Ukrainian language and identity while rejecting other languages and ethnic identities that were seen as impositions of the colonizing rule of other states. This path could entail the rejection of Western influences, seen as yet another interfering imposition on Ukraine's national development. Yet others sought to embrace Western influences as evidence of Ukraine's membership in the international community, Europe in particular.

---

5. A notable exception, discussed in chapter 4, is Chizhikova (1968).

6. The unification of Belarus, Russia, and Ukraine was seen as a move away from the "unnatural" Soviet efforts to unify cultures and languages that were too diverse. East Slavic unity was also perceived as reaffirming of common cultural values that were at risk of being overwhelmed by globalization. This paradigm tended to continue the privileging of Russia as the largest, most "advanced," and politically and economically most powerful of the three.

Still others rejected any major reconstruction of social or linguistic identities, particularly those that prioritized one identity above others, as a negative continuation of Soviet practices, embracing instead the Western ideals of pluralism. General appreciation for Western goods, technologies, and living standards, along with contingencies of Western aid, lent support to the latter approach. Following this paradigm, the Ukrainian government in 1995 decided to eliminate the "nationality" category in Ukrainian passports, a controversial move that sought to facilitate the integration of people of various backgrounds as citizens of a newly independent Ukraine, indeed to establish Ukraine as a multiethnic nation.[7]

In the early years of the twenty-first century tensions still existed between different visions of the Ukrainian nation. The general trend appeared to be toward acceptance of European standards for the protection of minority rights, concurrent with institutional bolstering of the use and status of Ukrainian language. While bilingualism had been widespread in the Soviet era, a decade after independence a new nonreciprocal bilingualism was gelling in some public spheres and the media, which gave Ukrainian a much more prominent role than before. Nonreciprocal bilingualism entailed each interlocutor speaking his or her preferred language and not accommodating to others, sometimes resulting in conversations being carried on in two languages. Such interactions had become acceptable in public in Kyiv, where in 2002 one could comfortably speak either language in public. At that time many nationally televised talk shows and game shows instituted this kind of bilingualism by having two hosts, one speaking each language, while guests or contestants spoke their preferred language with little or no switching by individuals. Nonaccommodation became the norm, as the two languages were treated as equal and equivalent, with the expectation that everyone would be understood. This represented a significant change from ten years earlier, when Russian was dominant and Ukrainian rare in the public spaces of the city. In 2002 the reinforcement of bilingualism coexisted with continuing struggles over the statuses and spheres of use of each language. Nonreciprocal bilingualism helped to depoliticize language because interlocutors could adhere to their preferred language, with either language choice equally acceptable at least in theory. This paradigm of interaction could serve to defuse and submerge ethnolinguistic struggles, but they would be implicit in linguistic practices as long as linguistic forms correlated with social differences such as ethnic, regional, urban/rural, and educational background.[8]

7. The term "Ukrainian" still carries definite connotations of ethnic identity, so here I do not use this term by itself to mean "an inhabitant of Ukraine"; instead, I specify "Ukrainian citizen." I use "Ukrainian" and "Russian" by themselves to refer to people who identify their nationality as such.

8. See Irvine and Gal 2000, for a discussion of the ideological processes through which linguistic and social values are correlated.

More than a decade after independence Russian still had an important presence in the newly independent states of the former Soviet Union, especially in countries such as Ukraine where many citizens spoke it as a first language and bilingualism had broad support. Russian still had the status of a world language, but English emerged as a competing alternative and had a growing presence in education, business, and government as a result of new economic and political contacts with the West. The English language and associated Western, especially American, values were seen as an antidote to Soviet ideologies, policies, behaviors, and styles (as was also the case in Russia; see Ries 1997, 174–176). True, already in the 1990s and into the early 2000s, some negative aspects of Westernization were remarked upon (such as the flourishing of fast-food establishments and the associated rushed, impersonal eating habits, increased economic differences, and decreased hospitality and generosity). Nevertheless, efforts to avoid mixing Ukrainian and Russian contrasted with the increasingly frequent mixing of Slavic and English elements which I observed in advertising and popular culture. English was sometimes even chosen as neutral ground between Ukrainophone and Russophone speakers, who thereby avoided ceding the "upper hand" to either native language.[9]

Language Paradoxes: Ideology and Power in the Construction of Languages

Language is paradoxical, at once individual yet social, stable yet fluid. It is both a conveyor of information and a creator of social realities. In times of social turmoil people argue about it fervently, but most linguistic processes go on without speakers' conscious involvement. And while languages are referred to and distinguished by simple labels, actual linguistic practices blend and blur into one another, showing almost infinite variability and mutability. Nonetheless people will fight for the "purity" of "their language" (Williams 1989).

Nation building everywhere has involved ideologies that focus attention on a labeled ideal, privileging a specific language and identity and consequently disadvantaging others. While overt discrimination on the basis of race, ethnicity, and regional or class background is generally no longer acceptable in the international community, the marginalizing of some groups and the privileging of others continues on the basis of language, a discrimination that is justified by an ideology that naturalizes a linguistic standard (Blommaert and Verschueren 1992; Lippi-Green 1997; Stroud 2004).

---

9. Fishman (1975) argues that English can be ethnically neutral in some contexts, but Flaitz (1988) disagrees, contending that it is always ethnically marked. I agree with Flaitz, since neutrality is also a social construct that obscures relations of power. However, the use of English can connote the desire for neutrality, an avoidance of ethnolinguistic opposition by appeal to an external, impartial authority. The cases of English being used to avoid choice between Ukrainian and Russian were related to me in interviews in 2002.

Language ideology has recently become a focus of anthropological and sociolinguistic research, bringing together the previously disconnected areas of social theory and linguistic studies of variation.[10] Language ideology can be defined broadly to include the wide range of phenomena (ways of thinking, logics, beliefs, and discourses) that all serve to mediate between social forms and forms of talk (Woolard 1998a). The social forms that are shaped in part through language use according to a given language ideology include social formations and forms of status (such as nations, labeled languages, class, ethnicity, "culturedness," and social power) and personal character traits (such as intelligence, poise, and personal authority). The forms of talk that are ideologically linked with particular social forms may be labeled languages, lexical choices, grammatical constructions, or "accents" (phonetic and phonological features). Language ideologies may be conscious explicit statements by institutions or individuals, or they may be implicit in interactional behaviors or policies. The links may take various forms; for example, Irvine and Gal (2000) have identified iconization, fractal recursivity, and erasure as key semiotic processes linking linguistic and social differences. Whereas some have treated ideology as a neutral phenomenon, here I follow a critical approach, considering how given ideological stances serve to empower some people and disadvantage others. My goal is to bring to light how ideological processes on many levels lead to the construction, maintenance, or blurring of named language units ("Ukrainian" and "Russian") and how language is implicated in negotiations of social power. This approach is new to Ukrainian studies, but similar studies have been conducted elsewhere, for example, in Catalonia (Woolard 1989; Pujolar 2001), Corsica (Jaffe 1999), Kenya (Parkin 1994), Indonesia (Errington 1998), Mexico (Hill and Hill 1980, 1984), Peru (Mannheim 1991), and the United States (Lippi-Green 1997; Bonfiglio 2002).

The reification of language units dominates lay attitudes, and many researchers continue to treat languages as discrete units whose reality lies outside ideology, following the theoretical traditions of Saussure, continued in modern linguistics by Chomsky and his followers.[11] Even studies that examine language

---

10. For overviews of the field, see Friedrich 1989, Irvine 1989, Woolard 1992, 1998a, and Woolard and Schieffelin 1994. Several edited volumes of articles represent the range of recent research on language ideology: Blommaert 1999, Kroskrity 2000, Kroskrity et al. 1992, and Schieffelin et al. 1998.

11. The reification of language units is the theoretical legacy of the Swiss linguist Ferdinand de Saussure, who posited that the imperfect *parole* 'speech' is secondary relative to the system of *langue* 'language'. Saussure used these terms to distinguish the variability and messiness of actual utterances from the ideal grammatical and phonological systems that define a language. One can see parallels in Noam Chomsky's formulation of "performance" as the messy rendition of the organized "competence" that lies in the mind. In this tradition, individual behaviors are only of interest as evidence of an underlying unified social phenomenon. Since "competence" is seen as functioning unconsciously, conscious assessments and ideologies of

contact have tended to assume the underlying existence of ideal distinct languages, whose influences may be clearly separated (Gardner-Chloros 1995). The division of language into labeled units appears to be even more deeply naturalized than the division of people into nations. In Anderson's argument that national languages were constructed as part of print capitalism, this construction is seen as a fait accompli and homogeneous national languages are viewed as tangible realities (Anderson 1991; Irvine and Gal 2000, 76; Silverstein 2000, 2003). Nations may be "imagined communities," but few see languages as "imagined" entities.

There are no objective linguistic criteria that determine precisely what a distinct language is. All that is necessary is that a group of people consider a linguistic variety to be distinct and legitimate. Preferably these people should have the resources and power to institute the legitimacy of their linguistic variety in education and government, and in dictionaries and other publications. As the familiar adage goes, the only difference between a language and a dialect is that a language has the backing of an army and a navy. However, in some cases a linguistic variety may even be denied the status of "dialect." For many people in Ukraine, dialect connotes some kind of scientific, historical legitimacy—if not actually respectable, it is at least viewed positively as being folkloric and quaint. The term "dialect" is often reserved for languages that are seen as having retained an "authenticity" untouched by the modernizing world, spoken by older people and documented by linguists. People may deny that term to the many languages that have more recent histories of formation as a result of the influences of languages of dominating regimes. Such more recently formed languages are often viewed as impure, corrupted, and mixed. They may be reviled as a constant reminder of injustice and shame. As is the case for both surzhyk in Ukraine and nonstandard varieties elsewhere, many people deny these languages the status of "language" or refer to them as "bad language," "broken language," or "slang." While there are structural linguistic processes that govern language mixing, the time and conditions necessary for a linguistic variety to become a dialect or language is determined not by linguistic rules but by the sociopolitical climate (Winford 2003, 24–28, 313).

Languages and their histories are molded to justify sociopolitical orders, just as histories are re-created and traditions invented (Hobsbawm 1983). In Soviet times the prevailing theory of linguistic origins posited the one-time unity of Russian, Belarusian, and Ukrainian as a justification and reinforcement of the Soviet project of cultural and linguistic unification and homogenization. Pachlovska (1998, 91) debunks this theory as "a myth supported by clear ideological inten-

---

language have generally been dismissed as irrelevant, secondary phenomena. For further discussion, see Bourdieu 1991, 43 ff.

tions." In the evidence she brings forth, she highlights the historical connections between Ukraine and Europe that were overlooked by Soviet researchers. The etymological evidence advanced by Radchuk (2000b), discussed earlier, also undermines the theory of exclusive East Slavic unity. Pachlovska's and Radchuk's scientific arguments are part of the struggle to redefine the sociopolitical order after the fall of Soviet power.

How different or similar a linguistic form is to other varieties does not determine whether it is politically distinctive. For example, Serbo-Croatian used to be viewed as a single language, but its varieties are now divided and considered to be three distinct languages (Serbian, Croatian, and Bosnian) (Bugarski 1992; Jahn 1999, 330). At the opposite extreme, spoken languages that are mutually unintelligible even at rather basic levels may be officially considered the same language, especially if they do not have a legitimate distinct written form (as within Chinese—Mandarin and Cantonese; German—Swabian and Platt-Deutsch; and Italian—Calabrese and Milanese). As Haugen (1972, 215–236) has shown, mutual intelligibility is influenced by ideological and political factors, not just linguistic similarity or difference.

The legitimacy of a language as a discrete entity is often linked to linguistic correctness, which is ideologized as an immutable essence. Whether correctness is defined as purity, antiquity, culturedness, or adherence to a particular codified norm, it is a social construct (Thomas 1991). The processes of correction that work to maintain a language of power are present everywhere. They become more visible in times of social turbulence, as judgments and discussions of the values of linguistic forms become more frequent and prominent in public discourse. The variations in language, some of which may be judged to be deviations from correctness, are not superfluous but are suffused with meanings embodying regional, class, ethnic, and other differences. Both institutions and informal practices serve to maintain a symbolic system linking linguistic forms to social factors. As Bourdieu has argued,

> The legitimate language is a semi-artificial language which has to be sustained by a permanent effort to correction, a task which falls both to institutions specially designed for this purpose and to individual speakers. Through its grammarians, who fix and codify legitimate usage, and its teachers who impose and inculcate it through innumerable acts of correction, the educational system tends, in this area as elsewhere, to produce the need for its own services and its own products, i.e. the labour and instruments of correction. (Bourdieu 1991, 60)

When people struggle to elevate and legitimize their identity through their language, they reaffirm the system that links linguistic forms with social statuses in the first place. By striving to alter their language, and thereby participating in the race for refinement, people are "maintaining, precisely by running the race, the disparity which underlies the race." Disagreements over the merit or demerit of specific forms, whether particular pronunciations, lexical items, or syntactic forms, mask the fact that in their disagreements people are agreeing to the rules of the game by which legitimacy is defined (Bourdieu 1991, 58, 64).

It is not just linguistic forms but also the social statuses of those who use them that shape relations of symbolic power (Bourdieu 1977b, 652). Symbolic power consists in the practices that establish beliefs about the world, and what is and is not valuable in it. These beliefs are part of what Bourdieu calls a person's *habitus*, the dispositions instilled in each individual through their upbringing and myriad aspects of daily life in their society, as a result of which they come to accept certain practices and ideas as "natural" and "correct." Habitus generates "common-sense" behaviors that are harder to challenge and are thus more powerful than any formal rules and explicit norms (Bourdieu 1990, 54–55). Symbolic power correlates to physically enforceable and economic power, but it operates more subtly and thus is more difficult to resist: it is "that invisible power which can be exercised only with the complicity of those who do not want to know that they are subject to it or even that they themselves exercise it" (Bourdieu 1991, 164). Symbolic power and symbolic capital (access to the trappings of symbolic power) is convertible to other forms of power and capital (for example, having a degree from an exclusive educational institution and wielding a prestigious language can lead to lucrative employment). However, it is key in the functioning of symbolic power that it be misrecognized, that is, disguised as something other than power and basis for social inequality (Bourdieu 1977a, 171–183). Thus social power takes form in phenomena such as tact, good taste, respectability, culturedness, refinement, erudition, honor, and prestige—all of which emanate from commonsense judgments that are enactments of an individual's habitus, masking the rootedness of these values in systems that privilege one group of people over another.[12]

The ideology of the naturalness and necessity of the existence of an ideal national language is one of the most important aspects of habitus in the modern state. Mastery of what is judged to be this prestigious linguistic variety comprises symbolic capital. Regardless of just how the prestigious language is defined, people usually do not question the necessity that there be such a standard. While having a single standard language has functional advantages for states, the value of this language is usually not justified in terms of its functionality but rather in terms of its inherently superior clarity, refinement, or spiritual linkage to "a people." Once established, the standard language is naturalized and not easily discerned as a particular social language; it is pervasive because of its legitimization by linguists, government, and media (Barthes 1989, 107–108).

---

12. See Bourdieu 1977a and 1990 for an analysis of symbolic capital, honor in particular, among the Kabyles of Algeria, and idem 1984 for analysis of social tastes in France.

Standardization is never a completed process, even for the most well-established languages of power, such as English.[13] It is an ideology of standard—what
Lippi-Green (1997) calls the "myth of standard language"—that leads people to
consider actual speech as being closer to or further from a given idealized language. In this ideology the written word is often given more weight than spoken
practices. People tend to believe that correctness can be determined objectively
by referring to dictionaries or grammar books, as if these books were not the em-
bodiments of social inequalities to begin with.[14]

Since we are predisposed by our habitus to misrecognize domination through
our complicity in the functioning of symbolic power, where is the possibility of
individual agency and change? Bourdieu focused his theory primarily on the
means by which stable social situations are maintained, in which hierarchies of
linguistic value are widely accepted and institutionalized. His goals were to uncover the practices and processes that continuously enable social and linguistic
hierarchies to exist, which appear as given commonsense structures. In his writings he emphasized the constancy, resistance to change, and self-perpetuation of
habitus, in which aberrant practices are unthinkable, because objective, external
structures (institutions and material correlates of social inequality) and internalized structures (feelings, beliefs, and dispositions) coincide, providing "the illu-
sion of immediate understanding" (Bourdieu 1990, 26, 54, 58–61; 1991, 44–49).
Bourdieu stresses the homogeneity of habitus among individuals of a given class,
which developed in the same objective conditions, based on similar histories.

In this totalizing portrayal of a self-regulating system of symbolic domination there seems to be little room for agency. Bourdieu acknowledged that *habitus* is paradoxical in this respect in that it entails neither determinism nor
freedom: "Because the *habitus* is an endless capacity to engender products—
thoughts, perceptions, expressions, actions—whose limits are set by the historically and socially situated conditions of its production, the conditioned and con-
ditional freedom it secures is as remote from a creation of unpredictable novelty
as it is from a simple mechanical reproduction of the initial conditionings"
(1977a, 95).

We do find some room for agency in Bourdieu's discussion of the uncertainty
of outcomes of practices, particularly in how they are timed, and the possibility
of actors choosing to act ambiguously, maintaining uncertainty of meanings and
playing on equivocations while they gauge how to proceed (Bourdieu 1977a, 9–
10, 14; 1990, 98–111). These practices, according to Bourdieu, still do not escape

13. The articles in the volume edited by Bex and Watts (1999) present a wide range of debates surrounding the definitions and implications of standard English.

14. See Davis 1999 for a discussion of speech versus writing in the determination of standards in the case of English.

or disrupt a stable system of symbolic domination. Thus an area that remains undertheorized is what underlies rapid social change and the disruption of language hierarchies, with people elevated from low social positions to positions of social authority. The creation and the dissolution of the USSR have involved such cases.

To develop a theory of change in systems of symbolic domination it is useful to scrutinize what Bourdieu sees as the "objective externalized structures" that are shaped by practices and in turn serve to reinforce them. I argue here that the power of these structures is not objectively fixed in them, even in apparently stable situations, but lies in how they are interpreted and internalized. Thus we need to view these structures in a more complex and dynamic way than portrayed by Bourdieu. Because my focus here is on language, the structures I examine in more depth are word meanings and the social values of language varieties. For example, if a particular language is institutionalized as the standard prestige variety, in order to function as symbolic capital it must still be recognized as such by individuals working in the institutions who have power to hire, admit, or otherwise grant efficacy to that embodiment of language. In practice, a standard language is never objectively fixed.

It is useful here to draw on the ideas of Bakhtin and Voloshinov, and to view meanings and values as heteroglossic or multivoiced, thus locating ongoing struggle and dialogism in both practices and the conditions of their production.[15] This approach embraces the fact that each use of a word adds to the word's history and modifies it slightly, and thus it embodies different voices and reflects "all the transitory, delicate, momentary phases of social change" (Voloshinov 1973, 19). Each individual has a different acquaintance with a given word—he or she has heard it in different contexts and so each has a somewhat different understanding of it. At stake are not only referential meanings but also connotations of prestige, qualities of character, or associations with particular social or ethnic identities. Linguistic anthropologists have developed the concept of language as dialogic and heteroglossic in studies of language ideology worldwide (e.g., Argentier 2001; Hill and Hill 1984, 388–400; Limon 1998; Makley 1998; Pujolar 2001; Tedlock and Mannheim 1995).

Social context "has assimilative power which forces a word to have only certain functions and colors them with the tone of the activity in which they participate" (Tynianov 1981, 71). The context is always ideological, saturated with attitudes, intentions, desires, and power relations. The "countless ideological threads running through all areas of social intercourse register effect in the word"

---

15. The congruence and complementarity of the ideas of Bakhtin and Voloshinov are not surprising given that they interacted in the same circles. There has been controversy over authorship, with some scholars arguing that, because of political issues, Bakhtin was actually the author of some works published under Voloshinov's name (Clark and Holquist 1984; Todorov 1984).

(Voloshinov 1973, 19). In speaking we are always implicitly citing other instances in which our words were spoken, and thus invoking ideological stances. There are never ideologically neutral utterances: "All words have the 'taste' of a profession, a genre, a tendency, a party, a particular work, a particular person, a generation, an age group, the day and hour" (Bakhtin 1981, 293). No two people have the same experiences of contextualized utterances, so cumulatively we could say that no two people share exactly the same language, and even one person's language changes through time. The differences in meaning that speakers and hearers bring to an utterance may be microscopic, but infinitesimal variations build up over time, leading to greater differences. Translation is necessary for "one social group to understand another in the same city, for children to understand parents in the same family, for one day to understand the next" (Emerson 1984, xxxi).

In times of social instability the rifts between ideological stances in language become more pronounced and more often consciously expressed. This is congruent with Bourdieu's statements that the more stable the social conditions, the less consciously relations of domination are practiced, while times of crisis lead to more conscious awareness of the construction of these relations (Bourdieu 1977a, 80–83, 165–166, 169, 170; 1977b, 665). Also, people are more vividly aware of recent social and cultural developments, as they have not had the time to become habituated (Bourdieu 1990, 56, citing Durkheim). Bourdieu further argued that, until a system is set up, the dominant class has to work constantly to reproduce the conditions of domination (1977a, 190). It is here that we need to realize that this constant work is ongoing even in seemingly stable situations, in the everyday momentary struggles inherent in the definition of meanings and values. Rather than stable situations being maintained unconsciously and crisis situations consciously, I argue that the potential for conscious individual manipulation is always present and implemented to varying degrees. In times of rapid social change the strategic manipulations are just more visible.

The multiplicity of voices is not haphazard but rather is molded by ideologies immanent in social relationships. Bakhtin describes the structuring of heteroglossia as "the (relatively) protracted and socially meaningful (collective) saturation of language with specific (and consequently limiting) intentions and accents" (1981, 293). It is to the advantage of those in power to maintain the dominance of their language, and so "the ruling class tries to impart a supraclass, eternal character to the ideological sign, to drive inward the struggle between social value judgments which occurs in it, to make the sign uniaccentual" (Voloshinov 1973, 23). The degree to which various languages become saturated with authority changes with time and varies across a population. A single variety may emerge as dominant while another may be devalued, in which case we can speak of the existence of diglossia. But when the hierarchy of languages becomes destabilized, the very definition of the language units that constitute the hierarchy can come into question, as is the case in Ukraine.

The unity of a dominant language referred to with a simple label is a social construct that must be constantly maintained by political, ideological, and administrative means, or it will be pulled apart into the writhing reality of living language by the centrifugal forces of heteroglossia (Bakhtin 1981, 418). Labeling a language implies stability and obscures the dialogic tensions that are always present. Bakhtin and Voloshinov portray the unity of a dominant language as more fragile and slippery than Bourdieu's formulation, and they grant greater agency to individuals who exert ideological intentions in every use of language. As Bakhtin states:

> Various tendencies (artistic and otherwise), circles, journals, particular newspapers, even particular significant artistic works and individual persons are all capable of stratifying language, in proportion to their social significance; they are capable of attracting its words and forms into their orbit by means of their own characteristic intentions and accents, and in so doing to a certain extent alienating these words and forms from other tendencies, parties, artistic works and persons.
>
> Every socially significant verbal performance has the ability [. . .] to infect with its own intention certain aspects of language. (1981, 290)

The social significance of an utterance will to some extent depend on the backing of wealth, education, or institutionalized structures. Some authors are more authoritative than others (Bourdieu 1991, 58).

By viewing external structures as dialogic and inherently mobile, we should not lose sight of the power of habitus as a conservative force. In the changes in post-Soviet Ukraine some aspects of habitus have indeed remained constant. Despite drastic struggles over and shifts in the symbolic values of particular linguistic forms, the belief in the necessity of a prestigious standard persists. While the defining features and political statuses of Ukrainian and Russian are disputed, it is key that the notions of "correctness" and "purity" are being upheld. These concepts are part of the "myths of homogeneity" of a nation, which are equally, if not more, critical to nation building than choice of language (Williams 1989, 429). Bourdieu (1977a, 169), just as simply, called this "orthodoxy," literally, the straightening of opinions.

The social significance that lends power to bend language to one's benefit does not necessarily have to be based in prestigious hegemonic society. Groups seen as passively accepting the order of authority are also inventive in responding to it and capable of opposing it in their solidarity, creating spheres of alternative norms (Woolard 1985, 744–745). Different aspects of power may be associated with different language forms. For example, in his research in New

York City, Labov (1972b, 295–296) found that listeners rated a middle-class speaker more likely to be suitable for a job but judged a working-class speaker more likely to win a fight. Trudgill (1974) refers to the positive value of the nonstandard variety among working-class men in Norwich, England, as "covert prestige." In my research some informants celebrated the unique expressive capabilities of surzhyk and criticized "pure language" as being "dead" and stifling in interpersonal interactions. This heterogeneity in symbolic valuation is another source of tension and change in a symbolic system. Heterogeneity may be found not only in informal and disempowered communities but also in institutions, complicating hierarchies of linguistic and social value.[16]

In analyzing the dynamics of social change in Ukraine after the fall of Soviet power, we must consider the historical conditions that shaped contemporary ideologies: habitus is "embodied history, internalized as a second nature and so forgotten as history—it is the active presence of a whole past of which it is the product" (Bourdieu 1990, 56). We must also be attentive to the struggles inherent in practices of dominant symbolic values, and to their varied and sometimes conflicting sites and definitions. "Pure" languages are always already mixtures, suffused with the conflicting intentions of their users. The following chapters delve into both the larger historical context and individual life histories to illuminate the processes shaping linguistic habitus in Ukraine.

Linguistic Solutions and Dissolutions

While some of the cultural elite perished in the 1917 Revolution and in the early years of Soviet power or went into exile, others took central roles in the new Soviet regime and continued to propagate conservative Russian high cultural and linguistic standards. Thus while individuals shifted social position, many of the old cultural and linguistic hierarchies held fast, particularly as policies promoting non-Russian culture fell into disfavor and Russian was again venerated. As Smith (1998) documents, anxieties regarding the correctness and culturedness of language use prompted concerted efforts at intervention, supported both from above and below. As in post-Soviet Ukraine, some aspects of habitus remained constant through the revolutionary changes.

Regulation of language by government institutions was key in the crafting of Soviet power, and likewise language has been central in its dissolution. The dismantling of Soviet power, accompanied by the abrupt legislated change in the status of the local non-Russian languages along with the new independent

---

16. This point is argued by Haeri (1997), who shows that in Egypt conflicting systems of valuation of symbolic capital are espoused by different institutions (religious, educational, and business).

nationhood of the republics, challenged the place of Russian at the pinnacle of cultural and linguistic hierarchies. This challenge destabilized linguistic hierarchies, and, again, anxieties regarding legitimacy led to a pervasive tension and conservatism in efforts at correction. It was, after all, a widespread conservative political paradigm—the nation—that was being instituted.

Ukrainian legislators updated the Herderian model of nation with the more recent paradigms of multiculturalism and individual human rights in order to conform with international standards. The latter sometimes competed with nation-building projects, discrediting the "one nation–one language" ideal as discriminatory, even though this was the ideal according to which many of the European nations had originally been constructed, an ideal still upheld by many institutions and policies in Europe. For example, in order to improve international ties with Europe, the Ukrainian government was under pressure to adopt the European Charter for Regional or Minority Languages (Council of Europe 1992) and consequently to recognize Russian as a minority language that needs protection, an ironic move given its historic role as an imposed dominant language whose forms were grafted into the non-Russian languages with the express goal that these other languages should eventually die out.[17] The new international expectations, along with the historical forces leading to a multiethnic population, complicate the creation of any simply conceived symbolic order.

Post-Soviet transformations created new conditions of upward social mobility for people who could identify themselves with the local non-Russian languages or identities. It was ethnolinguistic groups, not social classes, that became potentially mobile, although in the Soviet system ethnolinguistic groups often displayed some of the correlates of classes.[18] In independent Ukraine, for many people Ukrainian continued to be associated with the peasantry and Russian with the urban elite even after Ukrainian became the official state language. Awareness and anxiety over symbolic values and legitimacy became widespread as politically repressed and marginalized individuals publicly asserted their opinions, politicians put to use their often rusty Ukrainian, and more people started using Ukrainian in public.[19] Many people voiced insecurity and skepticism regarding

---

17. The Ukrainian situation has parallels in the Baltics, which faced pressure to accommodate rights of Russian speakers prior to joining the European Union, an issue that continues to incite conflicts (Jacobs 2004; Laitin 1998).

18. Martin (2001, 273 ff.) details how class and nationality became conflated during Stalinist terror.

19. Part of the punishment for political dissidence in the USSR often included blacklisting an individual so that he or she could not reside in cities and could only obtain employment in the least desirable blue-collar jobs. Soviet-era dissidents who came forward to become leaders after the fall of Soviet power often had lived many years secluded from social power and high culture, although they usually strove to maintain the "correct" linguistic standards that

the value of Ukrainian, inasmuch as their habitus predisposed them to reject it as not suitable for a language of power and high culture. Even people who consciously favored the ascendance of Ukrainian restricted it to their narrow definition of a distinctive Ukrainian, thereby striving to dissociate it from low connotations.

The case was made more complex by the structural closeness of Ukrainian and Russian, the existence of mixtures of the two, and different regional variants of each, which made more vivid the symbolic, ideological nature of the struggle over valuation of linguistic capital. The Soviet policies of Russification, which maintained Russian purity but "polluted" other languages with markers of domination by trying to make them more like Russian, resulted in the desire for clear separation between the two languages as a precondition for legitimacy. Thus, in newly independent Ukraine, value corresponded to purity, and language mixing was stigmatized, at best limited to low carnivalesque humor. Symbolic values were bound to imperatives of maintaining ethnic and social distinctions, and the policing of linguistic values most often took the form of criticism of mixing. The closeness of the two languages (similar to the bilingual situations in Belarus, Corsica, and Catalonia)[20] did not diminish the significance and consequences of mixing. The politics surrounding purity and surzhyk highlighted the ability of language to sensitively register social nuances in linguistic detail, and the inclination of people to make the most of linguistic details as markers of social status and allegiance (Irvine 1985; Thomas 1991).

In Ukraine social turbulence after the fall of the Soviet system made heteroglossia more obvious than it had been in the late Soviet period, and the definitions of "authenticity," "purity," and "correctness" of language and identity became passionately disputed. As with any nation-building project, people strove to (re)create categories and fill them with meaning. The "ideologies we call nationalism [...] result from the various plans and programs for the constructions of myths of homogeneity out of the realities of heterogeneity that characterize all nation building" (Williams 1989, 429). In the post-Soviet context, these efforts entailed unmaking Soviet linguistic interventions, which had propagated a hybrid high-cultural and proletarian Russian cultural imperialism. In central and eastern Ukraine people also had to contend with the pre-Soviet history of Russian, and in western Ukraine the Polish cultural domination before World War II. The historical closeness and empirical similarities between Ukrainian, Russian, and

---

they had acquired before being repressed. In addition to this blacklisting, more serious transgressions were usually punished by years in hard labor prison camps in Siberia or forced psychiatric treatments or both. The rise of dissidents to positions of authority underscored the overturning of the old social and political hierarchies.

20. See Woolhiser 2001 on Belarus, Jaffe 1999 on Corsica, and Woolard 1988, 1989 on Catalonia.

Polish posed a special challenge to ideological constructions of Ukrainian nationhood.

The antithesis of escalated ethnolinguistic tensions, a relaxation of tension, could be facilitated by an acceptance of the coexistence of the languages in the same spheres of use. Such a move toward the reduction of tension was evident in the nonreciprocal Ukrainian-Russian bilingualism that I documented in Ukrainian media and in public use Kyiv in 2002, where each speaker stuck to his or her preferred language in a given conversation, and neither accommodated to the language of the other. This bilingual practice was shaped by the combination of continued concerns with purism and correctness, and the need for a compromise and peaceful resolution between Ukrainian and Russian speakers. It created the conditions for the depoliticization of language, since it became acceptable to speak either Russian or Ukrainian in most contexts, and to receive responses in either language, without the expectation of linguistic accommodation.

Language is the site where social tensions take form. It is the paradoxical nature of language that we cannot discuss the language situation without using categories such as "Ukrainian" and "Russian." The categories are salient because they are the ideological reference points according to which people make judgments and institutional arrangements. And yet the unlabeled variations in the enactments of languages are key in the negotiation of social power and cultural correctness, as these variations come to be indexically or iconically linked to social status. Major social changes in Ukraine weakened the links between linguistic forms and social positions, as the institutionalization of standards fell into disarray and new voices clamored for authority. It is this turbulence that makes visible the perduring ideological parameters that are essential in defining languages, and how these are intertwined with political, economic, and social interests. The emerging new order is being determined by the accumulation of people's daily decisions of what to speak and how to judge other speakers, decisions that are shaped by the countless threads of meaning between speakers present and past, a web that has grown larger and more complex with Ukraine's independence.

2 **Lives of Language**
Individual Motivations, Practices,
and Symbolic Power in a Changing
Social Order

It is in our autobiographical acts, contextual, provisional, per-
formative, that we give shape to, and remake ourselves through,
memory, experience, identity, embodiment, and agency.

SIDONIE SMITH AND JULIA WATSON, *READING*
AUTOBIOGRAPHY

Contexts and Corrections in Individual Linguistic Choices

The construction of social values and relationships through language is a multi-faceted process. Families, residential groupings, regions, social classes, and ethnic allegiances all come into play in language politics, and the pull of these group-ings is embodied in individuals and refracted by their personalities. Often people struggle with conflicting ideologies and must make choices to balance their de-sires and the practicalities of their lives. The historically shaped values of lan-guages and definitions of correctness are internalized but then also reinterpreted and changed. The life stories of individuals presented here give a sense of how lan-guage politics are experienced, how and why corrections are enacted, and what shapes the emergence of ethnolinguistic awareness. Language, heteroglossic and saturated with ideology, lives in people, fueled by their beliefs and molded by their aspirations.

The four biographical narratives presented in this chapter were collected in 2002. I asked acquaintances to tell me their life stories in terms of language, to de-scribe the kinds of linguistic environment they grew up in, and the forces that affected their language use and attitudes. Although I knew the individuals to some extent, I was surprised by the richness and complexity of the stories they told, particularly for people whose ethnic and linguistic affiliation seemed clear-cut prior to the interviews. These life histories underscore the limitations of census statistics that simply list ethnicity and language as indexes of people's identities (Arel 2002). Underneath the choice of labels lie realms of beliefs, hopes, and desires as people strive for self-affirmation, power, love, and fairness. The things people strive for are, in part, products of their socialization in a particular historical context—their habitus—but people choose how to interpret and assign values from a range of heteroglossic meanings.

The biographies reveal the many ways in which linguistic forms and social roles are interrelated, shaped both by the historical circumstances that formed individuals' predispositions regarding language values and the conscious concerted efforts of individuals at correction. Some of the broad patterns in language politics that characterize the situation in Ukraine are evident in the narratives. These can be considered elements of a relatively stable habitus, where the multivoicedness of meanings is muted and a dominant symbolic order well established. One such relationship that recurs through all the narratives is the association of Ukrainian language and culture with the rural sphere, and Russian with the urban sphere. Further correlates of this relationship include the association of Ukrainian with provincialism, lower education, unculturedness, and weakness versus Russian with centrality, better and higher education, high culture, and strength. These associations exemplify the process of iconization through which linguistic features linked with particular social groups come to represent them, "as if a linguistic feature somehow depicted or displayed a social group's inherent nature or essence" (Irvine and Gal 2000, 37). Thus, for many people, speaking Ukrainian evoked low culture and little education whereas speaking Russian evoked high culture and better education.

While this stereotypical pattern is borne out to some degree in all four life histories presented here, there are also relationships that defy the stereotype, revealing heterogeneity in practices and ideologies. We learn of a Russophone from a provincial city who discovered high elite Ukrainian culture and language in Kyiv, and developed admiration for it, at a time when Ukrainian was being increasingly marginalized and excluded from prestigious urban spheres. Another interviewee was oblivious to the supposedly higher status of Russian during his childhood, and, once he encountered it in Kyiv, resented and rejected what he saw as its unfair privileging. People's relationships to the stereotypical pattern (Ukrainian/rural/low status versus Russian/urban/high status) changed throughout their lives as they at times believed in and re-created the pattern, and at other times directly challenged it. The existence of cases defying the dominant pattern were key in allowing for the shift that began to take place visibly with Ukrainian independence, establishing Ukrainian as a prestigious state language and dissociating it from its low connotations. The narratives show that this shift was not a process that began abruptly but was rooted in the heterogeneity of individual practices and beliefs that were always actively supporting or resisting a given symbolic order. With independence and institutionalized nation building we can speak of a more defined effort to enact a shift, but it is important to point out that there was shifting under way even within the seemingly stable Soviet-era context.

The situation becomes more complicated when we delve beneath the simple categorization of Ukrainian and Russian to consider linguistic variability and people's awareness of it. Here there is also evidence of a dominant ideology in the narratives, the "standard language myth" discussed in the previous chapter, according to which an ideal, pure, correct language is valued while nonstandard, mixed languages are devalued. All the interviewees discussed their discrimination of what was "good" versus "bad" Ukrainian and Russian, but their interpretations of what was good and bad varied.

The two interviewees who grew up in villages reported becoming aware of differences between the Ukrainian literary standard and the vernaculars they heard spoken in public during their youth. This awareness led to conscious choices regarding which language variants to use, choices that at times were conflicted between the belief in the need for correction (speaking standard) and accommodation (speaking a local nonstandard). Furthermore, the linguistic ideal can be elusive: one interviewee described her appreciation of the "pure" Ukrainian language but later rejected what she saw as the overly pure language of radio and television announcers who did not use the language in daily life. She felt that their language was sterile and artificial. Correction for her meant contradictory processes: striving for "pure" literary language but also struggling to retain the authenticity of nonstandard vernaculars.

The interviewees also distinguished different values of varieties of the Russian language. The Russian language originating in Russia (especially Moscow) was generally considered the most authentic and prestigious, as opposed to the local "Ukrainian-accented" version. However, one of those interviewed rejected the Moscow standard in favor of the urban Ukrainian-Russian standard that was native to him, both in his childhood and later in life. This was an expression of local pride and self-confidence, and also an assertion of the place of Russian language in Ukraine. The identification of Russia as the locus of true Russian implies that Russian is not native to Ukraine, an implication he rejected. He did distinguish between "good" and "bad" Russian, but he drew the boundary differently than the other interviewees: the Russian that was spoken as a second language by Ukrainophones he viewed as low and degraded, while, for him, the Russian learned as a first language by people in Ukraine was legitimate and good, if different from the Russian language of Russia.

In the preceding examples we see the operation of another process linking linguistic and social forms identified by Irvine and Gal, termed "fractal recursivity" (2000, 38). Fractal recursivity refers to the replication of similar kinds of relationships on different levels, as we see here in judgments of degrees of correctness and authenticity of Russian: nonnative Ukrainian-accented Russian versus the Russian language native to people of Ukraine versus the Russian language of Moscow. In the narratives we find similar relationships of fractal recursivity regarding degrees of provinciality as evident in cultural, linguistic, and educational values: village/small provincial city/oblast; capital/republic capital (Kyiv)/USSR capital (Moscow). These relationships replicated at different levels reinforce a hierarchy of symbolic power, and contesting the system of symbolic power entails reinterpreting the recursive relationships, for example, rejecting the subordination of Kyivan standards to Moscow Russian standards.

Another general pattern of sociolinguistic practices in Ukraine is the regionalism resulting from historical conditions and demographics. Ukrainian language and nationalist inclinations were prevalent in western regions and the percentage of ethnic Russians there was relatively low, although western cities were linguistically Russified to a degree. Meanwhile, in the east of the country, nationalist sentiment was low, the ethnic Russian population comprised a relatively higher percentage, and public city life was conducted almost exclusively in Russian. Ukrainian still prevailed in rural areas in the east but it had significant Russian influence, particularly in villages closer to cities, more so than in rural regions in other parts of the country. In the four life histories presented, some evidence of this pattern became apparent but also examples that contradicted it. One interviewee who spent part of his youth in a western region told how it was a friend from eastern Ukraine who made him aware of injustices toward Ukrainian cultural and linguistic rights and influenced him to become an activist. Another interviewee insisted that his mother's village in northeastern Ukraine had "good" Ukrainian language, that it was not Russified (as dialects of the area often were). This last case may be an example of erasure, another key process that mediates links between linguistic forms and social processes, and entails ignoring facts inconsistent with a given ideological scheme (Irvine and Gal 2000, 38). The judgment that people in his mother's village spoke "good Ukrainian" was part of a belief that these people, and hence the interviewee's background, were legitimately and authentically Ukrainian. If there were any Russian influences in the language, pointing them out could undermine the legitimacy of Ukrainianness in this border region close to Russia. Regardless of linguistic features that are impossible to ascertain now, the positive judgment of quality defied stereotypes of the region as being Russified in order to assert the legitimacy of the interviewee's ethnic background.

The accounts also illustrate the institutionalization of language practices, such as the dominance of Russian in the military and the increasing Russification of education during the 1970s and 1980s. Better and higher education tended to be in Russian. More powerful administrative roles were also generally carried out in Russian. But this patterning was not categorical, and Ukrainian was still present in higher education and administration. In the Ministry of Foreign Affairs, in contrast to other republic ministries, Ukrainian was used for paperwork and spoken by about half the personnel. Thus conflicting practices coexist in different institutions within a country, potentially facilitating change, in contradiction to Bourdieu's portrayal of state institutionalization of language power as stable and homogeneous (Haeri 1997).

Many of the motivations and choices related here can be seen as efforts to correct perceived linguistic and social inadequacies or anomalies. In terms of the broad categories, we learn how individuals corrected practices both from Ukrainian to Russian, and Russian to Ukrainian, in constructing themselves as ethnic and social beings. The narrators also described efforts to correct village Ukrainian, or surzhyk (Russified Ukrainian), into standard literary Ukrainian.[1] While one narrator was concerned to correct provincial Russian to good Russian, another struggled to define what some may have seen as "provincial" as in fact "good." A third saw bilingualism in a child's upbringing as problematic, something that should be corrected to "natural, organic" monolingualism, but then his family's practices returned to bilingualism to correct for the unjust exclusion of his wife's native Russophone self-expression. Corrections on many levels pervade the life histories, including corrections of interpersonal linguistic practices, institutional practices, and ideological definitions of which linguistic practices are "normal" and "good." It is these personal corrections that add up to larger social shifts in the statuses of languages.

The following narratives are based on taped interviews, which I translated into English. I present them as they are told in the first person by my interviewees, but they are not exact transcriptions. I have retained much of the narrative structure and wording chosen by the tellers but have edited the narratives for a smoother presentation as written texts. I occasionally include my questions when these are necessary for the flow of narrative, but otherwise I omit my own side of the conversation. All names are pseudonyms except for Borys Tarasyuk, foreign minister of Ukraine from 1998 to 2000, and appointed again to this post in 2005. Between his appointments as foreign minister, Mr. Tarasyuk served as a member of the Ukrainian parliament and president of the political party Rukh (People's Movement of Ukraine). Mr. Tarasyuk's profession as a diplomat, minister, and prominent politician are key elements of his linguistic story. I felt that much

---

1. As discussed in chapter 1, "surzhyk" is the label given to language that is perceived as impure or mixed, in particular a mixture of Ukrainian and Russian. For a more detailed analysis of surzhyk, see chapter 4 in this volume, and also Bilaniuk 1977b; 2004. Further, "literary language" is the terminology used to refer to "standard language" in Ukrainian.

would be lost by eliminating these indicators of his identity, and so, with his permission, they are retained. For all the others, I have omitted or changed nonessential details to mask individuals' identities, the usual practice in anthropology.

Sofia: Negotiating the Rural/Urban and Ukrainian/Russian Divides

Sofia was in her fifties at the time of the interview in 2002. She grew up in the Poltava oblast, a region frequently named as the site of the purest Ukrainian, but her village was marginal—both linguistically, as far as purity is concerned, and geographically, being situated on the edge of the oblast. In her late teens Sofia had moved to Kyiv for further education and remained there, working as a philologist and literary scholar. Her story embodied the struggle between rural and urban, Ukrainian and Russian. In some aspects of her life, such as her marriage, this struggle had found resolution: she married a man from Russia, and they had a bilingual household in which each spoke one's preferred language; she spoke Ukrainian, he spoke Russian, and their son spoke both languages at home. I encountered this pattern among several other interethnic married couples: during the first period of acquaintance there was often accommodation on the part of one of the partners, but, later, marriage and comfort in the relationship entailed each being at ease speaking one's native language. In other aspects Sofia still faced conflict regarding the two languages and identities: she clearly wished for her son to use Ukrainian more than Russian, and she invoked the ideologies of correctness to justify her inclinations, criticizing his Russian as being a Ukrainianized form that was not truly legitimate.

> *Sofia:* I was born in the mid-1950s and grew up until age sixteen in Poltavshchyna. I grew up not in the Poltavshchyna most people know, but right on its border, the next village over was in Kharkivshchyna [Kharkiv oblast]. So I see this as a typical part of Slobozhanshchyna [northeastern Ukrainian cultural region]. I had this image that beyond my village there were dark forests, the villages beyond had strange names, the world ended there. I grew up in the village until age sixteen, when I finished ten years of school, and after that I went to Kyiv. I've lived in Kyiv for about thirty years now. So it's hard for me to remember those times in the village, those are really memories of childhood.
>
> At home we spoke the language that is spoken in that area. Now, when I visit, the way I perceive this language is what one could call the most typical surzhyk. Some words are funny. For example, I remember that the word *koridor* [corridor] is pronounced *kalidor.* I remember we would sometimes make fun of my grandmother, that she couldn't pronounce normally, but then what is the norm? In my memory she is associated with this word—the word *velysoped* [bicycle], let's say. My grandmother said *lisopeta.* It wasn't just my grandmother who spoke that way, other people did, too. But most people there said *velisopet.*
>
> For me, during my school years, there existed, in fact, two Ukrainian languages.

One was the language spoken there; this was really Ukrainian language but with some Russianisms and some twists like I've already mentioned. And along with that there was the literary language, which we tried to speak. I don't remember how exactly the teachers spoke, but I think that indeed they were closer to the literary language. The literature, books, and textbooks that we read—that was a completely different language, the one that was spoken on the radio, for example, of course I felt that there is a difference. And I tried to make myself, in school or somewhere like that, to speak this language, this language of books, this pure Ukrainian—people would call it *chysto po-ukrajins'komu* 'purely in Ukrainian.'[2]

I have to say that even now, when I visit home, there are words that disgust me, because they are so far from the literary language. But then I feel that when I start to speak in the pure literary language, it's not that people don't understand me, but in any case I look like a white crow [oddball] among these people. And so I try to use some of the words from the language that is spoken in the village. I've forgotten most of it, but there are some little words that I use. I think that the first language that you learn is retained somewhere there in your subconscious. You can still remember something.

My parents were Ukrainians from the area. My father spent some time in Odesa, and then he came back here [to the village in Poltava oblast]. He worked as a technician at the radio station. We had a radio program for the village, for all the village issues. And I was chosen as an announcer, I think it was when I was thirteen or fourteen. A teacher wrote the text and I read it, and maybe I prepared something of my own sometimes. There was something on school issues, about the students who got bad grades— they were called *dvičnyky*.[3] In the evenings after the radio shows I would be afraid to go home, because on our street there lived such a *dvičnyk*, and some of the things I read were against him. So I remember trying to sneak home because I was afraid of him, he was older than me. He probably did hear the program—in the village every house had the *radiotočka* [hard-wired radio] and it was almost always left on all the time, no matter what people were doing. It was called the *brexunec'* [the little liar].

LB: Did you have television, too?

Sofia: No, until someone in our village got one of the first televisions in the area, and then everyone would gather from all around, filling the house to watch this television. Sometimes it was a movie, and everyone loved ice skating, and then a mass of people would gather, they would barely fit.

LB: Was Russian taught at school?

Sofia: In school, yes, we had Russian language and Russian literature. My mother worked in a hospital, and one of the doctors there had a Russophone wife. I think that they were actually Jewish. That was the first time I encountered the fact that there are Jewish people. This wasn't negative, just they were different in that they were Jewish.

---

2. Ironically the phrase itself is not altogether standard or "pure," as the adjective "in Ukrainian" has the masculine ending implying the Russian noun for "language," *jazyk*, which is masculine. In standard Ukrainian "language" is a feminine noun: *mova*.

3. *Dvičnyk* literally means "two-er," someone who is given the low grade of 2 out of a maximum of 5 points, which was the standard grade scale throughout the USSR.

My mother was friends with them and they met frequently, so I heard Russian from them. But Russian in school, I can't remember clearly when exactly I differentiated that there was Ukrainian and Russian. It must have been when I started to read. Aside from all that, people got used to Russian from childhood, because we would frequently hear Russian on the radio. So it wasn't a language that I didn't know at all. To read is one thing, but when you listen to it all the time, you start understanding it.

As far as separate words, my mother and grandmother were from another village, about twenty kilometers away, and so from childhood I was used to the fact that there are different villages with different traditions. When I spent time in that village with my grandmother, everything seemed different. They prepared food differently, they spoke differently. I remember that some of the words, especially things from everyday life, were different from the words in our village.

Then I came to Kyiv to go to the university. Kyiv was then very Russified. This was in the early 1970s. Just before that there had been a lot of arrests.[4] At the university students were expelled—there was a whole process in which students were expelled for what was called "nationalism." So that was the first time I encountered the fact that a lot of people spoke Russian. It was always difficult for me to speak Russian. I loved Russian literature, and in the village school the teacher had me read whole texts aloud in class. But to converse, that is something completely different. I remember that I had to speak Russian most of all when I was dating my future husband, and when I got married. When we first met I tried to speak Russian, since he had just come from Moscow and he didn't know Ukrainian at all. But for me this always felt false and awkward. I had been used to feeling myself free in language, with language being like my body. And when I spoke in Russian with him, I had to put a lot of effort into this, it was hard for me, I lacked words, I didn't know how to construct sentences correctly. He made fun of me a bit, said I didn't know how to talk—even though I was a philologist! But this didn't get in the way—we dated for two months and got married right away. This was after graduate school. I don't remember when it happened, that I decided I don't feel right when I'm not myself, and I switched to Ukrainian. But he continued with Russian, and so that's how in the family we have this situation. I don't notice now that I don't speak like him and he doesn't speak like me. We speak like each of us wants to.

I felt clear alienation when I came to Kyiv, inasmuch as I had come from the village. I didn't have any family there, and I lived in a dorm. It was hard to get used to daily life, to the studies, to the almost completely Russian-speaking Kyiv. Even when I went to the store I had the impression that the shopkeepers either wouldn't pay attention to me or would put me down when I spoke Ukrainian. I felt that I really should speak with them in Russian. That was my experience. In my closer group of friends it was different; we spoke Ukrainian. And all our courses were in Ukrainian except for Russian language and literature.

LB: Did you also have to study ideology? Was that taught in Russian?

Sofia: Oh, for the first three years that was integral. The history of the KPRS [Commu-

---

4. Under Khrushchev in the 1960s there was some easing of restrictions that led to a Ukrainian cultural revival, as exemplified by the prolific group of Ukrainian poets and writers known as the *Shestydesiatnyky* 'sixties'. However, in the 1970s, there was another crackdown on people involved in Ukrainian cultural activities (Pachlovska 1998, 862–868; Subtelny 1988, 506–508).

nist Party of the Soviet Union], that was the worst. We had to do more work for that than for anything else. They made us prepare summaries of Marx, Lenin, Brezhnev, and these summaries were checked. Passing the exams was an ordeal because we had to learn everything—which year which congress happened, what they did. And this was in Ukrainian. I think that the courses were adapted for the discipline, and for us they were in Ukrainian since most of our studies were in Ukrainian then.

As far as the Russian language, I remember having to put in great effort and to force myself to get used to Russian when I was writing my dissertation. Because in those years, at the end of the 1970s, all dissertations had to be written in Russian, even if you were writing about Ukrainian literature in Ukraine. You had to write it in Russian, and it was sent to Moscow, and there they would decide on the granting of degrees. I happened to be doing this in the period when it was obligatory to write in Russian, maybe it was allowed in Ukrainian earlier. And can you imagine, all the work that you have written, say 180 pages, you have to translate into Russian. Some students found someone else to translate for them. Or they wrote it in Ukrainian and translated themselves. At some stage I decided, why do the job twice, I will write in Russian from the start. At first this was hard for me; it was strange for me.

I had thought that everyone more or less can speak both Ukrainian and Russian. And then at the institute I met a man from Zakarpattia [southwestern region], who made an impression on me. We had to go order some tickets for a trip at a special agency. And I came with this man, and he said, "you go and do the talking." And I said, "why should I do the talking?" And he said, "because you can speak Russian, and I can't. If I speak, they will make fun of me." I was surprised to encounter this.

At some stage, perhaps since I myself constructed my language, this literary language, I consciously tried to separate myself from the language that was spoken in the village. It took some effort to forget, to start speaking a different, literary language and not use the village words. But at a certain stage I developed a kind of aversion to pure language. I knew that the announcers I heard on radio or television, who were speaking supposedly pure Ukrainian language, would switch right away off the air and use Russian at home and in their daily lives. This emphasis on purity, this linguistic sterility, God forbid to use some surzhyk word, or some simple word, for me this was the sign of a dead language, an artificially cleansed language, not a live language. After that, when I heard people in Kyiv from the village, I was nostalgic for the village. I feel this most vividly with the village grannies that you meet somewhere in Kyiv, on the bus, or at the train station, and they start to talk a lot, to tell stories, and I really like this, how they look and everything. I also still feel that I lack words, especially for daily life things. I've retained the words from my childhood, and I haven't found replacements for them. I haven't learned the purely literary Ukrainian counterparts or gotten used to using them. For example, *opolonnyk*, that is what we call the large spoon that you can ladle soup with.

LB: I call it *koxl'a.*

Sofia: Well, it's this word *koxl'a* that I heard much later, and I never switched to it. In Russian it's *polovn'ik*, so again this is some kind of twist, some kind of surzhyk form, I don't know. I don't really like this word *polovnyk*, and I avoid it, but then I say "that *ložka* [spoon]."[5] So sometimes I feel that I lack these words for daily life. I think that if

---

5. To clarify the lexicon discussed by Sofia, at issue is the terminology for "ladle." The stan-

my husband were from another region of Ukraine, and used these words, then they would graft themselves onto me more quickly. I am the main carrier of Ukrainian language in the family, and I have taught my son, and he learned from me and also from school and from books. Now he also keeps track of language, and sometimes he'll tell me some interesting Ukrainian word. But our daily home life was not a creative environment, so the language of everyday life gelled at a certain stage. As far as intellectual language, of course I have countless opportunities; I talk with people and I read, and when I write I develop this language myself.

LB: What happened after you defended your dissertation?

Sofia: I stayed on to work at the institute where I still work; I have also taught at the university.

LB: And how did you meet your husband?

Sofia: I have to tell you, for me, when I later analyzed this, I thought that my marriage is an example of an imperial romance or love of the empire or some kind of attraction to the empire. I had met a lot of boys—philologists, at parties and get-togethers. All the boys I was acquainted with, I had the impression that they were all weak. They all needed to be pitied. They were not just looking for a friend, a lover, but for someone who would elevate them, who would tell them how great they are, who would compensate for their lack of confidence or strength—strength or social status, I don't know. And this always bothered me somehow. I didn't want to carry out this role— you know, to be such a mother, let's say.

LB: Were they all Ukrainians?

Sofia: Yes, they were all Ukrainians. And then I met my husband, and, for me, he was completely different. He came from a completely different background. He had just come from Moscow, he had studied in Moscow. He was born in a city in Russia, his parents live there—a completely different cultural environment. He had studied in a very prestigious institute in Moscow, and then he got assigned to work in an institute in Kyiv. We lived in the same dorm, and we met there. At a New Year's party we were sitting next to each other, and we started to talk, and he told of Moscow and of all his adventures. For me, this was so different, and he had no hang-ups, he didn't want to be pitied. I listened to him wide-eyed, it was so interesting for me, all the things that I associated with "the center." And he started telling me all these stories of how he and his friends went to restaurants, or their dorm life, and this was such a masculine world. It wasn't weak. I found it attractive because it was so masculine. We ended up meeting a lot, going to concerts, and so our romance began and very soon after that we got married.

At first I tried to speak Russian with him, but I don't remember when it happened

---

dard Ukrainian term is *koxl'a,* and the standard Russian term is *polovnik.* In the village where Sofia grew up, the term used was *opolonnyk,* which appears to be based on the Russian root but modified and expressed in Ukrainian phonology. Sofia also mentions the possibility of saying *polovnyk,* which is the standard Russian morphology expressed in Ukrainian phonology. Because of her unfamiliarity with the standard Ukrainian *koxl'a,* and her discomfort with using the nonstandard or Russified forms, she avoids them, using instead the less specialized term *ložka,* 'spoon'.

that I reverted back to Ukrainian. Whether it was before or after we were married, I don't know. But this happened imperceptibly somehow. There was no specific conversation or decision or contract between us—I don't remember anything like that.

After a couple of years our son was born. My husband convinced me to go give birth in Russia, where his parents live. He said that there they could help me out, help take care of the child in the beginning. And now what I regret the most is that, in my son's passport, the place of birth is listed as Russia.[6] In fact, his birthplace and place of residence is Kyiv, except for the first month, but his passport says Russia, and I find this very unfortunate. If I'd had the foresight to register him in Kyiv, once I returned when he was a month and a half old, I could have done it then. But I had been afraid that we have to register him right away. I was there for a total of three months, I gave birth there, and now he has a stamp that says he was born in Russia, in a foreign land.

LB: What language did your son grow up with?

Sofia: I remember that when he was about a year and a half old, for the summer I took him to my mother in the village, because I had to work. And then Chornobyl happened, and so he stayed with my mother for a whole year.[7] When he started walking and talking, during a stay back in Kyiv, I remember I tried to teach him French. I read him books and played a record for him, and tried to get him to pronounce words. And aside from that I told him that there are different languages in the world, and there was a poem about different languages. Of course, when he was with my mother all that time, he would forget us a bit. And I remember one time when we visited, he said, "My papa is a Frenchman"—because papa speaks a different language! He knew that French is a different language, and his father spoke differently than the rest of us [he spoke Russian], and so my son called him French.[8]

Now my son is a teenager. In Kyiv the situation is such that very few children can surmount the very strong influence of the environment and continue speaking Ukrainian. These kids feel very uncomfortable. I just know from the example of my son and his friends. One boy, much more than my son, resisted the influence of the environ-

---

6. Sofia's concern with the listing of her son's birthplace is, as far as I know, purely symbolic and does not correlate to any practical or institutional implications. Rather, place of birth connotes connections to homeland and ethnic identity according to a Herderian model of the unity of language/culture/homeland. Since her son only spent a month and a half in Russia, she feels that his birthplace, in the sense of his homeland, really is Ukraine, and she could have registered him thus back then. This is an example of how an administrative detail undermines a desire to construct a unified "natural" identity, and is also an expression of the desire for correction.

7. While, in Ukrainian, the city name is transliterated as Chornobyl, most English readers will be more familiar with the transliteration from Russian, Chernobyl. Chornobyl is approximately 130 kilometers from Kyiv, and the capital city suffered significant levels of radiation exposure; so, when possible, parents sent their children away to relatives in safer regions.

8. This anecdote illustrates the incipient awareness of a young child of the categorical difference between Ukrainian and Russian languages before knowing the appropriate labels. In a similar incident during her first month in a Kyiv preschool, my own five-year-old daughter (who knew Ukrainian and English) told me she thought that a Russian-speaking teacher was speaking German.

ment. He spoke Ukrainian among the Russian-speaking kids who can be very cruel about anyone speaking a different language and made fun of him, he withstood all this. My son, whether it is because he is morally weaker or because of my husband and me, he gave in to the influence of the street more easily.

My son went to a Ukrainian-language school. After he came back from the village he couldn't speak Russian. After all, he had spent most of his time with me and with my mother, so his early efforts at Russian were funny—he tried to use Ukrainian words to speak Russian. I also tried to "clean up" his Ukrainian language, because he brought with him the language of my mother's region. He would speak this surzhyk here in Kyiv, and I tried to clean it up.

My son always liked to play with words. He speaks both Ukrainian and Russian at home—Russian with my husband and Ukrainian with me. And as I sometimes tell him, his Ukrainian is much better than his Russian. It's more refined, he uses it more fluently. I tell him he should realize that if he wants to make a good impression, his Ukrainian language is "cool." It is not something to be ashamed of. But he is ashamed. I don't know when, but at some point he said that, in Kyiv, anyone who speaks Ukrainian is regarded as a village hick. A mark of belonging to the city is when you speak Russian, and this hasn't changed. He does listen to a few Ukrainian groups, Okean El'zy, Vopli Vidopliasova. But mostly he listens to English-language music.

Recently, when he was taking his university exams, we hired a tutor, a university lecturer, to help prepare him. I know that this tutor is Ukrainophone in his personal life, but he insisted on tutoring in Russian. I found this sad. This subject is now taught in Ukrainian, but he tutored in Russian. He gave my son a Russian textbook, even though I had already gotten a Ukrainian-language textbook earlier. Even when we asked, the tutor wouldn't agree to teach in Ukrainian—he was just too used to teaching in Russian. Even though it's hard with the different terminology, I told my son, listen, if you want to make a good impression on the commission and to speak well and to speak more fluently, you should speak Ukrainian. I always had the impression that my son's Russian has some kind of Kyivan accent. My husband who speaks the normal Russian language, not a Ukrainianized language, he speaks in a completely different manner than Russian speakers in Kyiv. It is really a big difference. My son doesn't speak the real Russian, he speaks Kyivan Russian. I really don't like it, it's a Ukrainianized variant. I can't pinpoint it, but I feel it. My son said it was his business, but later he did choose to do his oral exams in Ukrainian, which I was happy about.

In his tastes my son appreciates sophisticated Ukrainian literature and theater. He meets my friends who are Ukrainian-speaking scholars. His tastes aren't low, but still he can't overcome the idea that in speaking Ukrainian with his age-mates he loses in status, that this is a sign of hickness. It is all so complicated. I try to convince him otherwise.

Yurij: Embracing the Ironies of Ukrainianness

Yurij was about forty years old at the time I interviewed him. He was from an industrial region of Ukraine that is often grouped culturally and politically with Eastern and Southern Ukrainian regions.[9] Yurij did not agree with this classifi-

---

9. Arel (1993, 94–98), based on Szporluk (1975), presents an explanation of the rationale for the subdivision of Ukraine into East, West, Central, and Southern regions, based mostly on

cation and preferred to think of his birthplace as Central Ukraine. He bolstered his classification with the fact that key events in Ukraine's history, in the Cossack period, were centered in his home region. Yurij's desire to see his region as central mirrored his claim to Ukrainian authenticity, but in his claim he embraced the ironies he saw in this identity. He grew up speaking Russian in the home, and it had been central in his life. He described himself as having had a "normal Russophone life" until 1989, when he was in his late twenties. His wife's preferred language was also Russian, and even after independence Russian continued to be the primary language in their home. Also, their daughter studied in a school with Russian as the primary language of instruction. After independence, however, Ukrainian took on a larger role for Yurij, both in his professional life and in his sense of personal identity. He was critical of diasporic influences on the Ukrainian language that were then in fashion but that he felt were incorrect and alien to his own practices. Implicit in his narrative was an awareness of the legitimacy and authority that a claim to nativeness of language conferred. But Yurij's vision of Ukrainian authenticity was not simply a promotion of the kind of Ukrainian more familiar to him but entailed embracing the ironies of this identity.

> *Yurij:* My father was born in a village in Dnipropetrovsk oblast and lived there until he was sixteen, when his mother sent him to the city of Dniprodzerzhynsk to study.[10] She did this so that at least someone in the family would survive the famine of the time [it was 1946]. While he had only spoken Ukrainian until then, in his technical education his teachers spoke Russian. So he learned the Russian language along with his trade. My father later got a job at a large factory and was proud that from among the village boys he was able to get ahead in life. He was the oldest of his four siblings. When he came back to the village he would speak Russian with his brothers but Ukrainian with his mother, who only spoke Ukrainian.
>
> My mother is originally from the northern part of Luhans'k oblast, in the Slobozhanshchyna region of northeastern Ukraine. From what I remember from my visits to my grandparents, people there spoke a good Ukrainian language—I don't remember anything particularly Russian about it. My mother came to work at the same factory as my father in Dniprodzerzhynsk, and they met there and were soon married.
>
> I was born in Dniprodzerzhynsk in the early 1960s, and, as early as I can remember, my family only spoke Russian at home. But sometimes, when I came home from school and recited Ukrainian poems I had learned, my parents would recite with me. I remember that my uncle could speak both languages easily without an accent, and he would cite passages from literature. The village population was drawn to culture. After all, when a villager starts to recite poems or to use citations from literature in daily language, this makes an impression.

---

historical (both pre-Soviet and Soviet) regional differences. According to this classification, Dnipropetrovsk falls in with other eastern industrial and mining oblasts, namely, Donetsk, Luhansk, Kharkiv, and Zaporizhia.

10. Dniprodzerzhynsk is a small city in the Dnipropetrovsk oblast, named after its regional capital of Dnipropetrovsk, which lies on the Dnipro River. Dniprodzerzhynsk was the birthplace of the USSR Communist Party leader Leonid Brezhnev.

My older brother still only speaks Russian, no Ukrainian, except for some phrases when he visits relatives in the village. He didn't do as well in school as I did. We both went to Russian school. There were few Ukrainian schools in the area; we kids had heard about them and spoke of them as of a curiosity. For us it was normal that we studied in a Russian school. Everyone in the city spoke Russian, and Russian is the first language we learned to speak. It seemed like a misunderstanding: you didn't hear Ukrainian anywhere, so what would be the point of learning in Ukrainian? Since we lived pretty much in the city center, there were no Ukrainian schools there in principle. The Ukrainian schools were in the outskirts, where the city transformed into suburbs, and people there were Ukrainian-speaking. There they lived in little two-story houses, and we lived in a multistory building, which we were proud of since that was truly the city.

We studied Ukrainian in school starting from second grade. I learned it well, and it went easily for me. A lot depends on the teacher. In the fourth and fifth grades we had a good teacher of Russian language and literature, and she also taught Ukrainian. Starting in sixth grade, we had different teachers of Ukrainian. Ukrainian teachers in the provinces—and here I mean everything beyond the bounds of Kyiv, and so I call myself a real "provincial"—were filled with a sense of responsibility. I could see this. First, theirs was a beautiful language, and they were good, gentle, and never pressured students. Maybe it's a difference in time, maybe it's a different attitude toward the subjects—now I just don't see teachers like this. Or maybe this is a symptom of old age—earlier everything was better. But something is different now.

LB: If Ukrainian wasn't used anywhere, how did the children feel about studying it in school?

Yurij: The children were pretty disciplined—there is a subject of study, you need to study it. What's the problem? At Ukrainian lessons, you speak Ukrainian and write dictations. This was the attitude in the fourth and fifth grades.

LB: Were there any students who knew Ukrainian better from having spoken it at home?

Yurij: All my classmates were Russian-speaking from the start, so no one stood out as knowing it better. The only problem was when students arrived from Russia, and there were quite a few since this was a zone of active colonization for Russians. Russians from Russia wanted to come to Ukraine—it was a good career move that required connections, because Ukraine was seen as "more civilized" and pleasant than most other regions in the USSR. When Russian kids came they didn't have to take Ukrainian classes, and all the other kids were jealous of them because they didn't have to take exams or get graded in that subject. Sometimes they would just sit in the class without having to participate, and if it was the last class of the day, they would get to go home early.

I remember filling out some kind of forms in school, in the first or second grade, where we had to write down our nationality. The kids would look at each other's forms to see "and who are you?—I'm a Russian—and you're a Ukrainian." Russians would be the most proud of their identity. I felt odd—because I spoke Russian, but I wrote down that I was Ukrainian. My parents had told me that I was Ukrainian. Well, if Ukrainian then Ukrainian, so be it.

I remember the moment when I first felt myself to be Ukrainian. Guests were over at my house—a get-together of my parents' friends. I was seven years old, just before starting school. Everyone was drinking and making toasts, which created the ambience of a holiday. Since I wasn't allowed to sit at the table with the adults, I went into the kitchen, poured myself a cup of compote, and the only toast that came to my mind was "Let's drink to Ukraine" [said in Russian]. My father, who was an ardent Communist, had been standing behind me and had overheard this, and he went back to the guests and told them what he heard. It made everyone laugh. I didn't like the fact that my father had told the guests about this, I felt a little betrayed. But this only emphasized the significance of this moment in my consciousness.

Later, when I was studying the Ukrainian language at school, it seemed less understandable in terms of rules than Russian. Russian grammar was very formalized and 100 percent clear. There were irregularities that were enumerated and categorized, and I was able to learn them all by heart, and I still remembered them long after school. Ukrainian didn't have that. You had to learn all the complex cases one by one—they were not categorized. This bothered me. What I saw was that the languages were similar, but the rules and the way they were taught were different. Some Russian rules correlated with Ukrainian, and so I used them. And when I didn't pay too much attention to Ukrainian grammar and got lower grades, this annoyed me. Well, come on, I thought, I know it, and it annoyed me that I would get lower grades for it.

My first familiarity with Ukrainian was during visits to my father's village, and also thanks to my mother. When I was five or six she would sometimes read to me in Ukrainian, and she made me read in Ukrainian. But I didn't like this much, because Russian came more easily to me. Until second grade (when we started studying Ukrainian in school) I only had practice with Ukrainian in the village, but we went there almost every week. Kids find a common language easily. There were pretty girls in the village, so I tried to speak their language—before I knew that Russian was prestigious. I didn't think about it much, I just wanted to speak the way the object of my passions spoke, and so I came down from my urban cloud onto the ground.

On her own my mother read in Ukrainian and Russian, mostly low-quality novels about love and war that were geared toward women, but also some Ukrainian classics. Generally, though, "recognized" literary works were not to her taste. At home we had the *Russian Soviet Encyclopedia*, which was better than the shorter, more provincial Ukrainian one. My father subscribed to editions of the Russian classics, but he didn't have time to read them. Acquiring books was both a sign of culture and reflected a better standard of living, even though this was sometimes just for show.

My mother's Russian was not the best, and it went down in quality especially at the end of her career. She retired in the mid-1970s. While my parents worked at the factory, their Russian was very good. But now that they are retired, Ukrainian is coming back to them, not in long clauses but just short phrases and words from Ukrainian. They have no more of the interactions at work that demanded the use of Russian. Now most of their interactions are at the dacha where there are simpler, less educated people.[11]

My father was an avid Communist internationalist. He had good language abilities, and for a while he knew Russian perfectly. I hated him when he came back from his stays in Moscow and spoke with a Moscow accent. This nauseated me and disgusted me, this *moskal'n'a* 'Moscow talk.'

---

11. A dacha is a summer home, usually located in a rural area.

In summer in the late 1960s, when I was eight, after the end of first grade, I had my first visit to pioneer camp in the Crimea. Most of the camp belonged to my father's factory. But Moscow had its section, and some other closed cities from Udmurtia, Siberia, and elsewhere could also send their quota of children. There were kids from the *poštovi skrynky* [post boxes], cities that were secret and unnamed because they were engaged in military production. But most of the kids were from Dniprodzerzhynsk.

So there we were, the "xoxly"—Ukrainians—and the rest were "moskal'i";[12] we basically considered non-Russian ethnicities from within the Russian Republic to be Russian. When campers arrived and left they had assemblies where the numbers of participants from each group were announced. The numbers from Dniprodzerzhynsk were always the largest, on the order of twelve hundred compared to fifty from Moscow and handfuls from other cities. We all spoke Russian, but of course with the Dniprodzerzhynsk accent. I thought that ours was the normal Russian language, but for some reason the Moscovites spoke differently, and we made fun of the way they spoke. We all said "h" for the Russian "g," and it annoyed me when people said "g." At school, in my class two girls from Russia always said "g" during the Russian language and literature classes, which set them apart as Russians, and this only annoyed me. At camp I felt set apart from the Russians, perhaps because of regionalism. I felt that here in Dniprodzerzhynsk everything is great, not like your bedraggled Moscow, and we are the ones whose speech is normal.

This was our small-city patriotism that is typical for Dniprodzerzhynsk, a city that is the origin of many important people, like Leonid Brezhnev, the Soviet leader from 1964 to 1982. We felt that our region is desirable—people were coming to us to make money. This is the reason that people from Dnipropetrovsk oblast, and especially the city of Dniprodzerzhynsk, don't feel lower than Kyivans. People in Kharkiv have a chip on their shoulder because their city was the capital for a while and then the capital was transferred back to Kyiv.

LB: And Donetsk?

Yurij: That's not Ukraine at all—just kidding! There is very little Ukrainianness there.[13]

After school I went to University in Kyiv. I had ambitions, and there were more opportunities in Kyiv, more possibilities for studying what interested me than in Dnipropetrovsk. I started Kyiv University in 1977. Kyiv was a totally Russian-language city. Nothing in the first year was in Ukrainian. There was only one teacher who spoke a strange language: Russian but with a very strong Ukrainian accent. Even in Dniprodzerzhynsk we made a great distinction between grannies that came and *balakaly* [spoke

---

12. *Xoxol*, literally the tuft of hair on an otherwise shaven head, worn by Ukrainian Cossacks, is usually a derogatory term for Ukrainians. *Moskal'* is a derogatory term for Russians, whether or not they are from Moscow.

13. Donetsk is a major urban center in the southeastern industrial Donbas region. In contrast to Dnipropetrovsk, Donetsk did not play a major role in Ukraine's pre-Soviet history. Also, Donetsk has had a much higher proportion of ethnic Russians (according to census data, 44 percent of the population declared themselves ethnic Russians in 1989, and 38 percent did so in 2001) compared to the population of Dnipropetrovsk (24 percent ethnic Russians in 1989, and 18 percent in 2001). Aside from Crimea, Donetsk and Luhansk oblasts have much higher proportions of ethnic Russians than any of the other regions of Ukraine.

in nonstandard language], which was very amusing to us, versus the "normal" Russian language we spoke. One other course, on Russian history, was taught in Ukrainian by a talentless teacher. The only tests requiring Ukrainian language were on the history of Ukraine—or was it called feudalism? This created certain difficulties because I didn't use the language at all. Having to take exams in Ukrainian—this depressed me.

Students were differentiated by language, and the few who spoke Ukrainian hung together. This correlated to a geographic division. The Ukrainian speakers were from the right bank [west of the Dnipro River, which divides the country in the middle from north to south] and small villages and cities, with maybe a few from Slobozhan-shchyna [north-eastern Ukraine]. Otherwise, the Kyivans and students from large cities spoke Russian. I hung out with Kyivans, and they didn't suspect that I wasn't from Kyiv. It helped that I didn't live in a dorm but had a room with family friends. I didn't hide my background, but I didn't advertise it either. Everyone spoke Russian, especially in sports, and I participated a lot. It was a normal Russophone life, without any problems.

My wife is also a Russophone Ukrainian. She is from Kyiv, raised on Russian litera-ture. Her grandfather was a mid-level party secretary. Her father was crazy about Dos-toyevsky, Tolstoy, and all those Russian classics. He had studied in a Ukrainian school, and he was proud of knowing Ukrainian but regarded Russian as higher, so what was the sense of studying Ukrainian? My mother-in-law is from central-western Ukraine. She grew up with Ukrainian, but then in Kyiv she only spoke Russian except when she was on the phone with her sisters.

Language was not an issue in my relationship with my wife; there were no prob-lems. I spoke without an accent, and this saved me, a provincial. At that time I can't imagine my wife to have found a common language with someone who speaks with a Ukrainian accent. People who spoke that way were from completely different worlds, they didn't communicate.[14]

LB: But what about your Dniprodzerzhynsk accent?

Yurij: That was still the normative Russian language of Ukraine, very different from the accent of someone whose first language was Ukrainian. Russophone Kyivans say "h" for "g," too.

In 1989 the language situation changed. At work I was preparing a large body of documentation, and until then it had needed to be in Russian. But in 1989 I had to translate this into Ukrainian. Twelve years after school I had not used Ukrainian at all, and so this was difficult. But I managed to rewrite it in Ukrainian myself, without needing to use a dictionary—the Russian terminology translated easily to Ukrainian. But I did have to tune my "language device." The writing in Ukrainian was an obliga-tion—I had to do it, but my soul wasn't in it.

Ukrainian language became a necessity for me when I transferred jobs to a differ-ent department in 1989, where the head was Ukrainophone. Most people in that divi-sion spoke Ukrainian, and documentation had to be written in Ukrainian. But my progress was very fast. At the end of that year I became acquainted with people in my profession from the West, the diaspora, who were Ukrainian speakers. Because of these contacts I got more and more into Ukrainian. At the time it was not a choice of Ukrain-

---

14. Yurij's account of provincial language as precluding the possibility of romantic interest echoes the account in the 1930s play *Myna Mazajlo,* discussed in chapter 4.

ophone or Russophone environment; this was secondary to my professional interests. Now I am more conscious of language and of my responsibility for the development of Ukrainian language. Language is a symbol, the flag of our Ukrainian team who has to prove its ability to thrive in Ukrainian. We clearly need to exit from Russian influence, create our own cohort, and it is good to have our own language for this. I want to show them—Moscow—that we can do it on our own and even do better than the Russians. We feel our separateness from the Russians—language is like our team flag.

LB: What about your daughter?

Yurij: She goes to a Russian school. Ukrainian was designated the priority in Ukraine, but I remembered my own experience of studying Ukrainian, and it was through Russian that I had mastered the principles of linguistics. So we decided to send our daughter to a Russian school, because the teaching in Russian was traditionally much better than the teaching in Ukrainian. The school we chose is one of the most prestigious schools in Kyiv, and it is still Russophone. There are other schools that are Ukrainophone that are supposed to be very good even closer to where we live, and they also specialize in English. It's been said that they are crazy for America, which we didn't like because to us it meant that they are superficial and phony.

Good education was in Russian. Prestigious universities were Russophone. Provincial universities were Ukrainophone. So all the Ukrainian-language teachers are from the provinces. Who from a prestigious university is going to go teach an unprestigious subject like Ukrainian language? But now I feel burned anyway, because in my daughter's school neither Ukrainian nor Russian is being taught very well. My daughter complains that she has to memorize things rather than have them come freely. I remember studying Russian as an easy game. But there has been a complete degradation of teaching in Kyiv in general. One of my daughter's former Russian teachers made egregious errors in Russian. My daughter's homework, written correctly, would be marked up incorrectly. This was just the teacher's low level of education. As for Ukrainian, the promotion of a diasporan way of pronouncing annoys me, especially when my child speaks that way. She does this because of teachers who are ignorant of pronunciation standards. They teach dialect variants, in many cases western Ukrainian ones—for example, the harder "č" [as opposed to the more palatalized sound that Yurij uses]. I really don't like this. This is not the Ukrainian language that I speak. The transition to Ukrainian language has been too sudden; teachers are not prepared for it.

LB: One last question before we end. I've noticed that you often prefer to say *xoxol* rather than "Ukrainian." Why do you do this, since a lot of people take this word to be derogatory? How do you choose which word to use?

Yurij: When I want to present the idea of the competition of Ukrainians with Russians I like to use *xoxol.* It has two meanings—the first connotes fighting, competition—it is a term that is cocky—it has a coiled spring in it. *Xoxols* are not submissive. They might be stubborn fools, but when they get together in force they can do something grand.

The second connotation is ironic and self-ironizing. On the one hand, I may not like what Ukrainians do, but then I regard myself as part of this denomination and I feel a responsibility to enlighten it. I consciously fulfill my role. I also support Ukrainian language, but I am disturbed by how this is done now. It begins with the teacher. I know my Ukrainian language and its grammar from my teacher, not from my parents. Prepare teachers first, and then send them into the classroom. Teachers are now in the classroom being sent without adequate preparation, and teaching quality and the quality of the language has gone down.

Taras: National Ideologies and Their Consequences

Taras was in his late thirties when he gave this interview. He grew up in villages in northern Ukraine, where he came to be aware of local language specificities that differed from the literary standard used in school and at home (his mother was a schoolteacher). During the first part of his life Russian was a distant foreign language from which he did not experience any pressure. He encountered Russian more when he went to a boarding high school in Kyiv, and then, when he began attending a university, he became acutely aware of language conflicts, influenced, in part, by a friend from eastern Ukraine. His protests against Russification and criticisms of the unfair treatment of Ukrainian led him to be expelled from the university and blacklisted by Soviet authorities. Taras then managed to find work in a factory, which had its own linguistic and political dynamics. After several years Taras was able to return to evening school, complete a university degree, and obtain a white-collar job. When perestroika got under way, a specific event triggered in Taras a new commitment to speak only Ukrainian—a correction, he felt, that allowed him to be true to himself. His strong Ukrainian national beliefs, bolstered through suffering the harsh sanctions of the Soviet regime, then conflicted with the bilingual realities of language use in his family and in the city. He found himself torn between wanting to impart true Ukrainian consciousness to his son and wanting to be fair to his wife whose native language was Russian. Taras ultimately accepted a degree of domestic bilingualism, but tensions over parental authority were often expressed in linguistic struggles between him and his son. Taras faced another source of linguistic frustration when he found that his mother's language had begun to include Russian elements, becoming surzhyk, once she retired from her job as a teacher. Taras describes these linguistic "degradations" as "taking away [his] mother tongue" and chipping away at his relationship with his mother. In Taras's life story, his language ideology was both the basis for bonding and for becoming alienated in interpersonal relationships.

> *Taras:* I was born in a village in northeastern Ukraine. It wasn't a regular village, because my mother was a teacher in a boarding school and many teachers' families and school workers were concentrated there. So our community differed somewhat from neighboring villages in language—it was mostly correct Ukrainian with maybe some phrases patterned on Russian and some local surzhyk, but not much. I lived there until first grade. My parents were both Ukrainian, but they separated when I was very little, so my father had little influence on my life. Then in second grade, when I was eight years old, we moved to another nearby village, a regular village. There, I remember, the dialect had very strong *akanie* [a pronunciation feature of Russian] and some of its

own words, and I remember I picked this up on the street and brought it home. It was normal for me to speak like others were speaking; I tried to accommodate to them so they would accept me into their group. Being new and a teacher's child it was hard to relate to other kids. Of course I had the desire to integrate.

I remember that when I brought this dialect language home my mother and older brother laughed, especially my brother since he was older and had outgrown this desire to imitate the language. I don't quite remember, but probably on the street I continued to accommodate to the way the local kids spoke, but at home we spoke normally as we had before. So we kept our own language when we moved. I did very well in all the subjects in school, including language.

Of course, I had no idea about the existence of Russification or the existence of different varieties of Ukrainian language, all those interdictions. But the language was Ukrainian, and in my world at the time nobody oppressed it. We studied Russian as a foreign language. I spoke it only in classes and, or course, with a terrible accent. We read it, there was no problem; we heard both languages on the radio, and I didn't feel a conflict between them. But in that world everyone spoke Ukrainian. The most important institution was the village council, and everyone there spoke Ukrainian. It was not a limited language. There was the sense that this is Ukraine, that everyone here speaks Ukrainian, and that somewhere there is Russia, and people speak Russian there. Russian is the language of the Union. This created no problems.

My mother is from northwestern Ukraine. We occasionally visited grandparents there, and so, in coming through Kyiv, I heard Russian, but it was more of an adventure, it was entertaining rather than a painful experience.

In the northwest, when visiting my grandmother, the language there was completely different, a different dialect, but I understood it. It was somewhat weird or funny when I was learning it. I tried to speak like them, and being a child, it was easy for me to imitate the way they spoke.

When I was ten years old I moved to northwestern Ukraine, but to a different village than my grandmother's. This was a different zone; again, the dialect there was completely different. They would say "je" instead of "ja"—*jebluko, jemka*.[15] I understood that I couldn't speak exactly like them—different people speak differently—and the school environment to an extent forced us to stick to more normative language.

When my mother retired her language quickly started to degrade, it quickly started to dialectize and then, once she came to Kyiv, it *surzhykified* horribly. Russian words keep creeping in, and I find this embitters me. This is ruining the connection that our family ties are built on. They are taking away my mother tongue, the language my mother once spoke to me. Of course, I can't follow her path, I can't speak the language she speaks now. And I try to correct her so that she doesn't spoil my kids by speaking a spoiled language to them.

I lived in northwestern Ukraine for three years, and then I moved to Kyiv to attend a boarding school during the late 1970s. The school was organized so that each year there were four classes, two in Ukrainian and two in Russian.[16] This was recogni-

---

15. The standard Ukrainian forms are *jabluko* 'apple' and *jamka* 'small pit'.

16. In the Ukrainian educational system, individuals grouped into classes generally stay together through the years of a given institution, whether elementary, high school, or the course of study at the university. Thus there is the concept of *odnoklasnyk*—a classmate who would have been in one's class group for many years.

tion of the reality that Ukraine had Ukrainian and Russian speakers. But this had been changing. I later found out that five years earlier there had been three Ukrainian classes and one Russian one.

There was not so much contact between classes. In our class we all spoke Ukrainian. For Kyivans there was a different school, and boarding school kids were mostly from elsewhere. I knew of one boy who was from a Ukrainian village and went to a Ukrainian school but ended up in a Russian class at our school because of lack of room or something, so he had to adapt to that situation and his Ukrainianness was suppressed. But for me, nothing was suppressed, everything was normal, it was Soviet-Ukrainian; you needed to praise the party and Brezhnev but everything was in Ukrainian. I think in ninth grade we got one lecturer in Russian. No one asked us what we thought of this. We didn't make an issue of it; he was considered a good teacher. When a substitute came who spoke Russian, for the most part kids answered in Russian. We had the sense that you should use the language in which you were addressed.

LB: Was Russian considered more prestigious?

Taras: In the boarding school, on the outskirts of Kyiv, the prestige of city Russian was not an issue. We only had a few trips to the city. I finished school in the late 1970s. I had no sharp feelings about language, it was just not an issue. There was no lack of Ukrainian books, and sometimes I read in Russian, but I had no sense of lack. Theater also, it was socialist realist, but in Ukrainian. Announcements in the public transportation were in Ukrainian. Some people spoke Russian—well, that was just up to them, and this didn't bother me.

When I was entering the university, I really wanted to go to Moscow—it had the reputation of being the best. But I decided to go to Kyiv; Moscow seemed so far, so foreign. My brother was in Kyiv, and it was closer. My mother dissuaded me from studying journalism, she said it meant traveling to heaps of manure to gather lies. As a teacher, she had to teach lies about the party, although the teachers could be cynical among themselves.

When I was at the university, contacts with Russian speakers were much more intense than at school. In my first year most of my courses were in Ukrainian, in the second year they started to change rapidly toward more Russian courses, and by my third year almost nobody was lecturing in Ukrainian. Sometimes a teacher might come in and ask, "In which language is it better to proceed?" and everyone would call out, "In Russian." I didn't really like this because my opinion didn't count, but still at the time language was not a poignant issue.

The political formation of my language behavior was influenced by my roommate, who was from eastern Ukraine close to the Russian border. He had a lot of anti-Soviet ideas. He put the glasses on me through which I started to see what was happening around me, to see it as discrimination, or limitations, and unfairness. Until then, I didn't see that. My friend had gone to a Russian school, so maybe that experience was more painful for him, and he felt the limitations. His Ukrainianness was completely repressed in contrast to mine. In our micro-world we spoke Ukrainian.

In our second year, this friend and I started talking to other students about Russification and the idea of an independent Ukraine. We felt that the regime had fouled up communist ideals and enslaved Ukraine, and that Ukraine needed to be free so that an unblemished communism could be created. Three or four months later we were turned in by fellow students. So the KGB took us and interrogated us about what

influenced us. It was funny, because I was influenced by works that everyone read in
school. The most subversive thing I had read was a Bible, in Russian though. But we really had no subversive literature or contacts. Still, we were expelled from the university with a public auto-da-fé [public punishment of heretics in the Inquisition].

All those discussions with the KGB, even though they were demoralizing and
broke me to some extent, at the same time they also reified my nationalism. Because
then, with their dumb lying arguments, they said there is no problem, everything is in
Ukrainian—they were saying what they had to. This taught me that I couldn't talk
about the injustice, this is something I had to hide.

I was expelled immediately, and they tried to take me into the army. Their policy
was to expel you and send you away, so that you could be reforged into a real Soviet
person. They had distinct orders to take me into the army: there you will be reedu-
cated, there they will break your nationalism. But because of my health problems, this
didn't happen. I had to get medical attention, so I didn't end up going into the army.

After some treatment in the hospital, I then tried to find a job. I didn't want to go
back to the village where my mother lived, since it would be impossible to get a
"white" [white-collar] job there—just farm work. And, more important, my story
would sully my mother, which could be especially problematic—catastrophic—for a
teacher. Later, the KGB did inform her school principal about this, but he kept it private and did not disseminate this information through the whole school.

It was very hard to find a job in Kyiv. My record noted that I was expelled for an
act that was incompatible with being called a Soviet student, so then I had to explain
what had happened. I didn't lie because I knew they would find out sooner or later.
And I didn't have a *propyska* [residency registration (*propiska* in Russian)]. Nobody
would take me until finally one place—a factory—took me on. The division manager
who hired me told me that they can take people from prison who had committed violent crimes but that they can't take nationalists. But she felt sorry for me. So she told
me, if anyone asks, you told me that you were expelled for getting 2's [low grades].

So I was hired. This was in the early 1980s. I lived in the workers' dorm. For the
most part the workers spoke surzhyk. There were some Russian speakers who had
come from the Donbas [southeast Ukrainian industrial region] or somewhere similar.
But for the most part these were people from nearby villages. I didn't speak surzhyk
like everyone else, which did set me apart a bit. Some noticed this, but it was explained
away as a result of my status as a student. They thought I was still planning on studying, and so I was not like them. Being a student didn't give me any authority, but nor
was it disrespected. Some thought of it more highly, but these people didn't have
higher education except for one engineer I became friends with. We were brought together by our education. People who came from the village got the blackest work, even
those who spoke Russian were not any higher than anyone else. Among the workers
nobody switched to Russian with each other, the surzhyk speakers spoke surzhyk with
everyone.

Most of the management spoke Russian, both those who were from Russia and
those who were Ukrainian. With them, many workers switched to Russian, and with
the director everyone did. Because of my medical condition I couldn't do heavy physical work, and I ended up getting a physically easier job. The manager of my division
spoke Russian but clearly with a Ukrainian accent, and the workers spoke with him in
various ways. I spoke only Ukrainian with him, but Russian with the director and
other higher-ups.

Finally, the KGB caught up with me, and I had to come to weekly discussions. I suspect these were supposed to be part of my reeducation. I kept trying to figure out what they wanted from me. I would be told that I would find out some day, but I never did. The first agent spoke Russian, then came one who spoke Ukrainian. He even gave me "politically correct books" to read.

Because of my education I could excel and help with the paperwork. I worked at the factory for five-and-a-half years. I started having more contacts with other departments and better-placed [white-collar] workers who mostly spoke Russian but among them were those who could speak Ukrainian, and I was comfortable speaking Ukrainian with them. There is one incident I remember well. It involved a woman engineer from central Ukraine who spoke Ukrainian well. As a rule, people with higher education didn't speak surzhyk but spoke either Ukrainian or Russian. Even when talking with surzhyk-speaking workers, this woman spoke a literary Ukrainian that in my eyes elevated her prestige. She and I usually spoke Ukrainian, and I could identify with her more. At one point when we were with a senior Russian manager, we were speaking Russian but reverted to Ukrainian when the Russian woman left the room. When the Russian manager returned and heard us speaking Ukrainian, she said, "In front of me, in Russian please!" This gave me a pang of injustice, but I didn't make an issue of it.

In a year I tried to reenroll in the university, and I needed a character description [a personal recommendation] from my workplace. By the way, before I got expelled from the university, I was thrown out of the Komsomol [Communist Youth Organization]. And then when I came to my new workplace, they found out I was not in the Komsomol, so they thought this was good because they could fulfill their plan and get a new member.[17] I had nothing against (re)joining the Komsomol, since I knew it was one of the prerequisites for getting back into the university. No one had asked if I had been in it earlier. They thought I had never been, so I was accepted quickly.

Once everything became clear about my history, they felt I hadn't been forthright with them. But they hadn't asked! So then they felt that I hadn't quite worked long enough and wouldn't give me the recommendation yet.

The news about the real reason for my expulsion changed how I was perceived. I wasn't ostracized—we had already developed a relationship—but I got labeled a nationalist, a "Bandera."[18] Easterners see Banderas as having some strange streak, that you need to be careful with them but that they are otherwise fine. This was a partial disqualification: by certain parameters I was not adequate. But the solidarity of the workers of a certain division was stronger than ethnic or linguistic or ideological divisions. Workers covered for one another.

---

17. "Fullfilling their plan" refers to the administrative imperative to increase enrollment in the Komsomol, much like the Soviet practice of establishing plans for levels of productivity of goods by farms and factories.

18. *Banderivec'* refers to followers of Stepan Bandera, who was the head of the Organization of Ukrainian Nationalists in the 1930s and the founder of the Ukrainian Insurgent Army which fought the Soviet and German forces during World War II. *Banderivec'*, or the shorthand version *bandera*, became used as an epithet for Ukrainian nationalists or for any western Ukrainians who were often stereotyped as nationalists. Often the terms were used lightly and jokingly, but they could also be offensive. In another interview a woman from western Ukraine told me that she was hurt and insulted when relatives at a wedding in eastern Ukraine called her and her sister *banderivc'i*.

After one more year I managed to get into evening classes at the university.[19] I kept working at the factory during the day and took classes in the evenings. It was then that I met my first wife, through my brother. I was very lonely, and so I had tried to keep in touch with my brother. He was sympathetic—he didn't approve of my extreme measures, he thought I had been stupid to have ruined my life like that.

LB: What language did your brother speak?

Taras: Before his service in the army, my brother had switched to Russian in the city; he had adapted and had no trouble. But from the army he came home very clearly feeling that he was Ukrainian. So then he spoke more Ukrainian, and his wife and my wife both spoke a surzhyk-ful Ukrainian. My wife and I spoke Ukrainian from the beginning. She also used Russian at her work.

When we had our daughter, there was a little bit of conflict since I wanted us to speak *normal* Ukrainian with her. My wife didn't speak Russian but spoke a surzhyk with her. The first serious conflict emerged when my wife refused to refer to me as *tato* [Ukrainian for "daddy"] when speaking to our daughter and instead said *papa* [Russian]. To me this was awful. Now my daughter calls me *tato* to my face and *papa* when speaking to her mom or her friends. So I spoke Ukrainian with her, and my wife spoke Ukrainian with *surzhyk*.

When I was finishing university through evening courses, by then the courses were all in Russian, which I accepted even though I knew it was unfair. In the late 1980s I left the factory after getting my university degree. My wife then got the apartment for which she had been on the waiting list. This meant I got a city *propyska* [residency registration]. So then I had the two requirements for getting a good job in Kyiv, a degree and a *propyska*.

But my wife and I separated soon after that. This meant that I had much more free time, and I reconnected with my university roommate who had also been expelled. He had managed to enroll again a bit later than I did and was still studying for a degree. In the spring of 1988 we became involved in cultural revival activities. By then the situation had changed, and more was permitted. There were still conflicts; the party organization still impeded our activities. To commemorate the fiftieth anniversary of a famous dissident poet's death we had been promised a meeting hall at the university, but then we were denied the hall at the last minute, so we held our meeting and poetry reading on the university steps in bitter freezing weather. This group consisted of all sorts of activists for Ukrainian culture, for example, speaking out against the destruction of an archaeological Cossack site during a construction project and working on the restoration of monuments. Many people who are now well known were involved in our activities. They reflected the relegitimization of being Ukrainian. But then, when Rukh was founded, our group became less important, but still it was important in the transitional period.[20]

---

19. Admission to an evening degree program was not as competitive and prestigious as admission to a daytime university program.

20. Rukh (literally "movement" in Ukrainian), known in English as the People's Movement of Ukraine, was founded in 1989 as a popular civic movement whose goal was to establish an independent democratic Ukrainian state, and by 1991 it had been transformed into a political party. The final interviewee in this chapter, Borys Tarasyuk, was elected president of Rukh in May 2003. See the Rukh website at http://nru.org.ua/en/.

One of my groups of friends from the university were Russian speakers. I had spoken Russian with them all along, because I wanted to belong with them and they all spoke Russian. But then very suddenly in 1987 I decided I was going to speak Ukrainian with them. It was funny. We went to the theater, and there was a play about the renewal of truth, a play by Yurij Bondarev translated into Ukrainian from Russian. He later became a proponent of Russian nationalism, but this particular play was very Soviet. When we arrived at the theater we were speaking Russian, during the intermission we spoke Russian, but at the end I spoke Ukrainian, since I realized that language was one of the truths I needed to renew. My friends were surprised. I explained that to be true to myself, I needed to speak my native language. The two girls I was with reacted very differently. We talked about it later. One girl (who later became my second wife) said that she was fine with it, but the other was offended; she said she didn't want to see me anymore. What was most astounding was not that she didn't want to have anything to do with me anymore but rather the different reactions of the two—why two people who were very similar would react so differently.

The girl who reacted negatively was a Russian, born in Russia, who later came to Kyiv to study. She was very Soviet in her identity, and later she sent her kids to Russian school. We've kept in touch, and only recently has she become less negative about my speaking Ukrainian. The other girl (whom I later married) was half-Ukrainian, half-Russian, born in Ukraine. She went to a Russian school, but she had studied Ukrainian there. She accepted the idea of the country's independence and cultural rebirth. So right around then in 1988, I started making my transition to only speaking Ukrainian with everyone. Some people answered me in Ukrainian right away; others took more time before they switched to Ukrainian.

There are two situations I remember. I was writing an official request at work. I took it to the secretary to pass it on to the director, and she disagreed with my use of "-ovi" [an option in Ukrainian for the male singular dative ending that is more distinctive from an alternative ending that is closer to Russian]. She said it should be the "-u" ending. She then asked if I could write it in Russian instead, but I didn't want to. A colleague later told me that it was a good thing times had changed. A few years earlier, writing a request in Ukrainian would have sealed its fate, guaranteeing a negative answer just by the fact of being written in Ukrainian. But in this case the Ukrainian request went through, and I got a positive reply.

Now the second case. I went to see a superior at the organization where I worked. He was an "underground Ukrainian," from the Donbas [southeastern industrial region] but with an affinity for Ukrainianness. He only rose to a high position after perestroika. I was summoned to a meeting, and there was the director, and two other higher-ups, and they were all speaking Russian with one another. This was after the Ukrainian Language Law, the end of 1989, early 1990. When I came in I spoke in Ukrainian, and the director looked at the vice directors and said, "Well, then, should we switch to the state language?" And they then went on to speak Ukrainian just fine. So here, with the arrival of someone whose status is not so high, these highly positioned people switched to Ukrainian. What stuck in my mind was their ability, and also their readiness, to switch to Ukrainian, even though I was lower-ranked than they. This was evidence of a little nudge of change, and soon these people started to speak Ukrainian all the time, and worked to convert all the proceedings to Ukrainian. So there were no problems with language there.

The next stage was the Ukrainianization of my circle of interaction. When I left my first marriage, I went to live in a dorm. Many spoke Ukrainian there, the majority. My friend, who later became my wife, lived in an apartment nearby, and we spent a lot of time together. I can't remember when she switched to speaking Ukrainian with me, but this happened by the year 1990. She hadn't used Ukrainian much in her life till then, so it was hard for her at first; it took time, but after a while it happened. There were a lot of factors that helped her. At the time there were lots of rallies, all sorts of poetry-reading evenings, and there was the spirit of fairness: that Ukrainians had experienced subjugation, so it was fair to speak Ukrainian, to try to undo some of the damage, and there was a sense that those who spoke Russian had been participants in the Russification of Ukraine. I know many others who felt this way. There were a lot of Ukrainian-language social activities of various political leanings, but all for Ukrainian independence and Ukrainian language. I was cut off from my factory friends, from my former wife's surzhyk-speaking friends, and I found myself in a wholly Ukrainian-speaking sphere. This all felt so normal, so organic, and it felt very natural to expand this into the family.

When we got married we only spoke Ukrainian by then. We actually married when our son was a year old—we waited because I hoped to get an apartment as a single person through my work. But before that, in fact once we started living together and she got pregnant, I don't remember when we talked about using only Ukrainian, but for me it was the only possible way. She was aware of this lack of alternatives. But also there was an acceptance that Ukrainian was going to be the state language. I think at the time I was so stuck on this, so single-minded about it, that if she had suddenly said she doesn't want to speak Ukrainian I don't think I would have married her. For me this was a prerequisite, to create a *normal* Ukrainian family. I was then very deeply convinced that all those families that have two different languages are not normal. I know, I acknowledge how essentialist my views were then. I felt that this leads to a divided person, a stilted consciousness, that a person will then fight with their own self.[21] I wanted to give a child a normal family, where everything would be whole, organic, only Ukrainian, so that from the outset the child can grow up whole, not deformed, not crippled, not bilingual.

This path was easy for me, and I didn't see the reverse at the time, I didn't see things from my wife's point of view, that her transition to Ukrainian is also giving up her Russian. For her it was not simply rejecting an ideologically imposed language but giving up her native language. And for a long time I didn't understand this. There was the problem that she didn't speak Ukrainian very well, that she sometimes mixed words. But it seemed that this would be fixed with practice. I tried to correct her delicately, but sometimes this came out the wrong way, since my knowledge of Ukrainian was obviously better than hers.

My wife didn't make a total transition like me; she continued to speak Russian with her Russian-speaking friends and colleagues at work. She spoke with people in the language they preferred. I didn't really like this, but I figured that, as time went on, the street would become more Ukrainianized, all the spheres of daily life, the stores, the bazaars, and the buses, and that she would become Ukrainianized along with them. In 1991, 1992, 1993, one could still expect this. What became for me an indicator that this is not wholly positive but also negative, that this is not just an acquisition for her but a loss, that this is not just voluntary but also something I imposed on her, was

---

21. For similar negative views on the effects of bilingualism, see Handler 1988, 168.

when she told me sadly that our son would never know what a *neval'aška* was [a traditional Russian weeble-wobble toy]. She couldn't impart this in Ukrainian, she couldn't
impart her cosmos to him. By establishing the right to impart my cosmos I barred her
right to do so. So then I said, well, if you want, speak Russian to him, but by then she
also thought it was better to use one language at a time, and that it was better now to
have him learn Ukrainian first, so she didn't use Russian with him. But then, from time
to time, I felt her discomfort. She told me, the child will remember you as eloquent and
me as linguistically hobbled.

And then she did try to speak Russian with our son, first when she scolded him. At
first he couldn't say anything, but by the time he was four he responded by telling her:
"Don't speak Russian." So by then he knew of the existence of the two languages, and
he said the phrase in good Ukrainian.

Besides scolding in Russian, my wife sometimes read to him in Russian. When
I read, even Russian books, I translated them on the go into Ukrainian, which I could
do easily. But my wife read in Russian. We didn't translate poems, and on television he
got some Russian. He understood that Mom can't translate so well for him, so he accepted it in Russian. Then when he was six, he realized that Russian gave him solidarity with his mother, and it constituted resistance to my strictness, since I was much
more strict than my wife. He felt that I set more limitations for him, and as a form of resistance he would use Russian with me. What I did in turn was to then respond to him
in English, which he could understand hardly at all. He understood that this was a disqualification of him, that while he had tried to disqualify me, his father, I was more
effective because I could understand him, but then he couldn't understand me. So after
two minutes this led my son to beg me to speak Ukrainian, and he would speak Ukrainian himself. So then I agreed. But this experience taught my son that this subject is
important to me, that I don't like him speaking Russian, that this can get to me. So
sometimes at dinner he would say to his mother, "Let's speak Russian." And my wife
would say, "Well, your dad is here now, let's wait till he isn't and then we can." But, of
course, this wasn't what he wanted, because he knew it would bother me more to
speak Russian in my presence.

So once my son asked, why don't you like the Russian language? And I answered,
why not, I like it, see here, I read all these Russian books. We even listen to Russian music more often than Ukrainian music, since we especially like the Russian bards. I explained that, as Ukrainians, we speak Ukrainian, just as other nations speak their
language. "But it is not Mom's native language." Yes, but she decided to speak Ukrainian with you. In any case, there was evidence that he was trying to figure out this linguistic problem.

My wife's parents—her father is from Russia. His was a typical Soviet Russian
style of life in that he never learned to speak Ukrainian, aside from a few Ukrainianized words he uses like *ohirjochky* [little pickles]. My mother-in-law makes a lot of
effort for me—her *banderivs'kyj* [slang for "nationalist"; see note 18] son-in-law—her
language is good; she is also of a mixed [ethnic] background but grew up with Ukrainian. My son thought that his Russian-speaking grandfather was eccentric in that he
didn't speak Ukrainian. But later on he started to use Russian with his grandpa. Again,
I felt that this is something alien to me, why is my son doing this? The grandfather un-
derstands Ukrainian just fine! But for my son, he felt that—this is my grandfather, why
should I do something that distances us?

Another issue was my son's interaction with friends. He at first knew only Ukrainian, but then when he was about five he realized that among kids Russian was the language to speak, that it was more "cool." My son is more of a follower, and he felt that part of his marginalization among kids was because of language, and so he started to try to speak Russian. He came up with a comical mix at first, but then with time and the influence of television he learned Russian well. So now he predominantly speaks Russian with his friends, even though he is in a Ukrainian school. That is the going trend. There are only a few kids who have the character to withstand this.

My older daughter speaks Ukrainian in a somewhat *surzhykified* way, despite all my corrections. Only now that she is about to enter the university she's speaking a more literary language with mistakes, rather than a mixture. We haven't put much effort into finding Ukrainian-speaking friends for my son; we should probably do that more. One playmate, who is from a Russian-speaking family but was raised by grandparents in Ukrainian, thanked my son after a visit to our place: she said "Thank you for a Ukrainian day."

Borys Tarasyuk: Crafting Identity in the Image of a Nation

Borys Ivanovych Tarasyuk was born in 1949 in a small central Ukrainian city.[22] His ethnic background was part Ukrainian, part Russian, and Russian language prevailed in the first half of his life. Typical of urban Russophone children in Ukraine, he learned Ukrainian during summers spent with village relatives (as was also the case with Yurij). This pattern of language acquisition reinforced the rural connotations of Ukrainian, but, for Mr. Tarasyuk, the memories of his village experiences also served to solidify his sense of Ukrainian roots, and connections to the land and traditional Ukrainian culture. When he moved to Kyiv to pursue higher education, he encountered the usual dominance of Russian language in the city but also an urban elite Ukrainian culture. Even before perestroika, his profession as a diplomat led him to use Ukrainian much more than most other government professions would have. This was because of the need to interact with diasporic (Ukrainophone) Ukrainians abroad, and also a result of the relatively high degree of use of Ukrainian in the Ministry of Foreign Affairs of the Ukrainian SSR. That Ukraine had its own UN seat even in Soviet times helped to foster a sense of the legitimacy of its separateness for those who represented it.[23] When Ukraine became independent, Mr. Tarasyuk and his family

---

22. As mentioned at the beginning of the chapter, although I have used pseudonyms for all the other narrators, I have retained the actual identity of Borys Tarasyuk, with his permission. Mr. Tarasyuk's professional roles are key elements in his linguistic story, and thus I felt much would be lost by masking these identifiers.

23. Under pressure from Stalin, Ukraine and Belarus, along with the USSR, were included among the forty-seven founding states of the United Nations in 1945. Stalin's motives have been explained as a desire to get more UN votes, and also as a response to the pride of Ukrainians in defeating Nazi Germany. Ukraine became a member of twenty international organizations and concluded sixty-five treaties on its own by 1950, although it always adhered to

switched to only using Ukrainian language at home. Through this major corrective measure, his family underwent a change of linguistic regime that reinforced the change in the political regime on an everyday level. Thus he brought his personal life in line with what he felt he represented as a diplomat for Ukraine. From 1998 to 2000 Mr. Tarasyuk served as the foreign minister, from 2002 to 2005 he served as a member of the Verkhovna Rada (parliament) of Ukraine, and in May 2003 he was elected president of the political party Rukh, the People's Movement of Ukraine. In February 2005, Mr. Tarasyuk was again appointed foreign minister by the newly elected president Viktor Yushchenko. His life story illustrates the many interconnections between institutional structures and personal choices in processes of correction.

> *Borys Tarasyuk:* I grew up in a bilingual environment in which Russian prevailed, in Novohrad-Volyns'kyi, a small city of fifty thousand people in Zhytomyrs'ka oblast in central Ukraine, just west of Kyiv oblast. It was there that I was formed as a conscious individual.
>
> My parents met at the front during World War II. They were married after the war, and my Siberian Russian mother came to Ukraine with my Ukrainian father. Russian prevailed in our home since my mother didn't speak Ukrainian, but frequently Ukrainian would break through, and my father would speak Ukrainian. My parents were both government workers, which entailed using Russian, but my father's job as a financial inspector required him to travel to villages where he had to use Ukrainian more.
>
> Like most Ukrainian cities, Novohrad-Volyns'kyi was steadily becoming Russified. I attended a Russian-language school, and my friends and I spoke predominantly in Russian. At that time, almost every summer my brother and I went to my father's village to live with my father's parents for three months each summer. When we would first get to the village, from inertia we would still speak Russian. There were no unfriendly attitudes, but our age-mates would call us *kacapy* [slang term for Russians]. But in time it all evened out, and we were indistinguishable from the village kids. We became fully integrated into village life, interacting with all our relatives and age-mates—all this in Ukrainian, of course. We took the cows out to pasture and did the household chores just like everyone else. After three months we returned to the city fully Ukrainian-speaking, and it took time to adapt to a Russian-language environment again.
>
> I never had problems with the Ukrainian language. From my Ukrainian roots I got not only love for the language but also for the traditions, the culture, and the songs. In the evenings after hard work everyone would get together after dinner to sing. This enchanted me—the Ukrainian songs they sing so beautifully in the village. I think this was a significant influence on my formation. I love to sing. No one taught me especially but I remember the songs from the village. The river there is the Roztavytsia—these are ancient lands of Kyivs'ka Rus'.
>
> Growing up I didn't have this question of which language to speak, Ukrainian or Russian. In the neighborhood where I grew up there was a relatively low income level.

Russian predominated, even though there were families that used other languages. There were no problems, no taboos, no sense that one must speak only one language. It was just the reality, and there was no ostracism.

After eight grades of primary school, I left for Kyiv to attend four years of technical school in communications. Like in my hometown, Russian predominated in Kyiv. But here I encountered a Ukrainian elite that supported Ukrainian culture, especially later at the university. This didn't change the fact that Russian was dominant in daily life. But there was a national elite that supported developments in literature and history—highly educated people with an elevated Ukrainian consciousness, who yearned to spread knowledge about Ukraine. For these people it was a matter of principle to only use Ukrainian.

After technical school I fulfilled my two years of army service. Even though I was stationed in western Ukraine there was not even any question of using any language other than Russian in the army. It was during an army leave that I met my future wife, a native of Kyiv. We communicated in Russian, even though she also knew Ukrainian and her family had some village roots. It was she who encouraged me to enter the competition to study in international law and international relations at Kyiv University. I doubted that they would take an applicant from the provinces, and one just out of the army. But I was accepted.

At first my university studies were conducted half in Russian, half in Ukrainian. Then when I specialized in international relations, of my cohort of one hundred students about eighty were from other countries, mostly third-world. Then most classes were conducted in Russian, since the foreign students were prepared to study in Russian and not in Ukrainian.

In 1975, after five years in the university, I was offered a starting position in the Ministry of Foreign Affairs in Kyiv. I had to go through interviews in which my knowledge of two languages was tested—English and Ukrainian. I was surprised that I was tested on Ukrainian. I must say that even then in the 1970s, in contrast to other ministries, in the Ministry of Foreign Affairs Ukrainian prevailed in documents, and I would say that about half of us communicated in Ukrainian, about half in Russian. We were a small ministry, less than one hundred people. Why? Ukrainian diplomats in contrast to other government workers had to interact with the Ukrainian diaspora when they were overseas. Of course, in that case you had to show that you're not just a Ukrainian diplomat but that you know Ukrainian. But the character of the ministry was also shaped by ministers who had a particular affinity for Ukrainian culture.

I had a rule that I would speak in Ukrainian if spoken to in Ukrainian. I had great respect for people who spoke beautifully in Ukrainian. One such person was a senior colleague, who died a tragic death in a car accident. He was in the Writers' Union, wrote poems, and did translations of literature and poetry from Bengali to Ukrainian—a very highly educated person.

One event that made a significant impression on my awareness happened during one of my first diplomatic trips abroad, as a representative in the UN delegation from the Ukrainian SSR. The Ukrainian SSR had its own UN seat, like the Belarusian SSR, in addition to the USSR as a whole, which was part of Stalin's bid to get more UN votes. During this mission I had a casual conversation with the head of the USSR delegation, a Russian. This man talked of how beautiful he found Ukraine on a drive from the north to the Black Sea in Crimea. He said, Ukraine is beautiful, but you are all nationalists there. I asked him what he meant by this, and he said, well, you use Ukrainian there on all your signs. What for? And I said, do you ask yourself why in Georgia or Estonia or Latvia they use their own language on signs? And he replied, well, that's Georgia or Latvia or Estonia, but this is Ukraine, after all, how can this be! The fact that it was offensive to him, that Ukrainian language would be used in Ukraine instead of Russian—this made a very strong impression on me.[24]

That was in the 1970s. In 1990, when the declaration of state sovereignty was accepted, there were rather pointed discussions about national identity and about independence in the new parliament. I was decidedly on the side for independence—most people in our ministry were. In 1990 I personally worked on the main Ukrainian-Russian agreement, and also on the Ukrainian-Hungarian and Ukrainian-Polish documents. I already felt like I was working for an independent state even when it wasn't there yet.

And then my wife and I decided to switch to speaking Ukrainian in daily life at home. I have to say that, once we decided, there were no discussions, and we demanded this of our children, too (who were then eighteen, ten, and six years old). At first it was strange for them, but then they got used to it. It was harder for our friends to get used to us speaking Ukrainian, but slowly they also switched to Ukrainian. Now it no longer calls forth any surprise. There are a few friends who stick to Russian. But most use Ukrainian with us and then switch back to Russian when they're on their own. I must say that there are not many families that would speak Ukrainian at home and not just out of obligation to state duties. This is not a widespread phenomenon.

I am impressed by General Morozov.[25] He took independence not just as some job, but he took it to his soul, his heart. He felt this internal need, and he learned Ukrainian. He is a great example. Many, many people who started to work for Ukraine found that they could not do this job in any other language.

My children really embody the changing tides of language in their education. Our oldest daughter studied only in Russian-language schools, our middle daughter at first was in Russian- and then Ukrainian-language school, and our youngest son has only been in Ukrainian-language school. He hasn't even studied Russian at all, but even he speaks Russian—which he learned informally—with his friends outside class. Some dynamics remain the same: Russian is still the "cool" language among Kyiv's youth.[26]

Another recent incident [in 2001] shows that some dynamics haven't changed.

---

24. The Russian diplomat's statements are reminiscent of Solzhenitsyn's arguments (1990, 1991).

25. General Kostiantyn Morozov was a key figure in the establishment of the independent Ukrainian military. He had no Ukrainian language education until independence, but by 2002 he was generally speaking only Ukrainian in public and with his family. See Morozov 2000.

26. In 2002 Russian was still the most widely accepted language among Kyivan youth, resting on the persisting connotations of Ukrainian as provincial or backward. After Ukrainian independence, as schooling was increasingly conducted in Ukrainian with particular stress on correct language use, speaking Ukrainian outside school came to connote a submission to school policy that was not "cool," especially among adolescents. However, Ukrainian also began to take on countercultural values attractive to youth with the popularity of Ukrainian-language hip-hop, rock, and other forms of popular culture. These Ukrainian cultural productions were themselves products of young people choosing to embrace Ukrainian as "cool," to stand behind independent Ukraine as their own country, and to make the Ukrainian language their own (not always adhering to standards of purity in the process).

A relative of mine from the village who grew up in a Ukrainian-language environment called me when he moved to Kyiv. When he called he tried to speak Russian, and the Russian language was such that he'd do better not to speak it at all. I was surprised and offended, and I asked why he was doing this. I told him to speak Ukrainian or else I didn't want to talk to him at all. So then he switched to Ukrainian. But the next time he called he tried to speak Russian again! You see, a person from the village thinks that if they come to the city and start speaking Russian, then right away they'll become a city person, right away they'll become *stoličnym čelov'ekom* [in Russian; 'a person of the capital city']. The dynamic that existed earlier continues. That relative of mine is young, about twenty. He fits into a category of people who are not very educated and without any serious markers of national consciousness. This is not a mass phenomenon. For example, I know a man from a village in my home oblast, Zhytomyrshchyna, who is very, very nationally conscious.

Some examples are close to my heart. The first ambassador of Norway, Nord Slattern, impressed everyone. He spoke at Parliament in Ukrainian on issues of gender, and this was met with ovations. It was another grounds for criticizing those deputies, predominantly deputies on the left, who used only Russian. See—he is a foreigner, he could learn to speak in Ukrainian, and what is it that gets in your way? The ambassador from Great Britain, before appearing officially, he came and lived in Ukraine with his family for a month and studied Ukrainian. So then in his public appearances he spoke Ukrainian. Now no one is surprised that U.S. diplomats can speak and even conduct a debate in Ukrainian.

I served as Ukraine's Minister of Foreign Affairs from 1998 to 2000.[27] When I was minister I visited a lot of regions, including in the east. And I often faced the question—Should I speak Ukrainian?—which made sense to me as a member of government, or conform to my audience who will understand me better in Russian. I came to the conclusion that I must speak publicly in Ukrainian, since I was not the minister for Kyiv but for all Ukraine. On the other hand, I feel that, outside formal appearances, if public servants are addressed in Russian, they should answer, if they can, in Russian, since it is they who serve the citizen and not the other way around.

LB: What do you think about the Law on Languages?[28]

Borys Tarasyuk: The Law on Language has proceeded very slowly, but I have had occasion to apply it. Once I gave a diplomat an official reprimand for not using Ukrainian in his paperwork. Another time we had an applicant for a position, but he refused to speak Ukrainian or to be tested on his knowledge of the language. So he didn't get the job. I do not believe force should be used, but the Law should create conditions in which people will choose to speak Ukrainian, and also choose to have their children educated in Ukrainian so they will be more competitive.

More and more people are switching to Ukrainian, in both their public and personal lives. It is hard to imagine that three years ago Yulia Tymoshenko [a well-known politician, leader of a parliamentary faction named after her, and appointed prime min-

---

27. Mr. Tarasyuk was reappointed to the post of foreign minister in February 2005, in the government of President Viktor Yushchenko.

28. The 1989 Law on Language in Ukraine named Ukrainian the sole official state language but allowed for the official and institutional use of Russian and other minority languages in some contexts, such as in regions with compact minority populations.

ister of Ukraine in February 2005] only spoke Russian, even when I spoke to her in Ukrainian. Now she speaks only Ukrainian. Inasmuch as the Ukrainian language was suppressed by tsarist Russia and Bolshevik rule and that this process took centuries, we can't expect that right away in a few years everyone will speak Ukrainian. Look how long they tried to poison the Ukrainian language out of us, and they didn't manage to root it out—but still a large portion of Ukraine was Russified. So for this we need time, we need patience, and a delicate attitude toward these people [Russophone Ukrainians]. They are not enemies of Ukraine. We should not condemn those Ukrainians who don't speak Ukrainian, but we should try to understand why this happened and do everything possible to create conditions that will encourage use of Ukrainian. Because in a democratic society we can't force anyone like in tsarist times, force only repels people—we just have to create favorable conditions. Many people who used and still use only Russian, even businessmen, more and more they send their kids to Ukrainian-language schools. There is no longer any doubt about the existence of the Ukrainian state, and the Ukrainian language sooner or later will be the dominant language. They want their kids to be ready to be linguistically competitive in life.

Every conscious Ukrainian, no matter how well he wields the Ukrainian language, should try to use Ukrainian. We can't expect perfect Ukrainian language from him. Let it be imperfect, but he should use it, and with time he will make it better, but if he's going to wait for it to come to him itself, while he's sleeping, then that is naïve; it won't come on its own, you have to use it. Without any criticism of those who don't use it well, people should be encouraged.

Coherence and Correction in Life Histories

The life stories of Sofia, Taras, Yurij, and Borys Tarasyuk capture many facets of Ukraine's recent history, particularly concerning language choice and correctness, the urban-rural dynamic, regional variation, institutional control of language, Soviet systems of subjugation, and linguistic changes after independence. The narratives provide a sense of how Ukrainian and Russian languages and identities coexisted sometimes in harmony, at other times in tension, as people worked to adjust linguistic ideologies to linguistic practicalities, enacting corrections on multiple levels.

The definition of categories, particularly what constituted "good" and "bad" languages, was a key part of the narrators' choices and their definition of symbolic power. For all four narrators, correction of language was an important concept but in different ways, as specific life events shaped linguistic values. For Sofia, it is the imperfection of Kyivan Russian that made it less desirable than Ukrainian, while as an adult she enjoyed some of the nonstandard variations in Ukrainian that she associated with her childhood. Taras was most frustrated by the impurity of surzhyk-Ukrainian as spoken by close relatives, and also struggled to balance familial bilingualism with a construction of cultural integrity. Yurij was dissatisfied with the quality of both languages as they were taught in schools but ultimately saw both as part of Ukrainian identity. Meanwhile, Mr. Tarasyuk appreciated "cultivated, beautiful" Ukrainian but argued that fear of incorrectness must not be a hindrance, that people must first choose to speak Ukrainian in order for the country's independence to develop. For him, correctness of language choice, in line with national identity, takes precedence over grammatical correctness, although the latter is important as well.

The very telling of a life history is also an act of correction, as individuals strive to tell their past in a way that makes sense today, thus creating coherence in their lives (Linde 1993). As the interviewer I was party to the construction of this coherence, since I asked questions that directed my interviewees on a more or less temporally linear path, and also asked for explanations as to why and how a particular change in linguistic practices occurred.

In telling their stories, people constructed themselves and others as agents. Sometimes the causality for certain attitudes was located wholly within individuals, when, for example, they felt a legitimate claim to an identity or a calling to fight for a cause by making changes in their own linguistic practices. Such was the case with Mr. Tarasyuk's shift from using Russian to Ukrainian language both inside and outside the home. Although the inclination to make this change was conditioned by his experiences as a diplomat and also by the country's independence, Mr. Tarasyuk described this decision as an event for which only he and his family were responsible.

At other times the inner drive to act was awakened or caused by another person or event. For instance, it was Taras's friend who opened Taras's eyes to injustices and set him on a path of activism that cost him dearly but which he did not regret. Later, a play by Bondarev about the "renewal of truth" led Taras to choose to speak Ukrainian exclusively. According to Taras, his brother came to feel decidedly Ukrainian only after his experience in the army (a causality I encountered in other interviews as well). Mr. Tarasyuk credited a Russian diplomat who negated Ukraine's right to its own language as effecting a key shift in his awareness of injustice in cultural politics. Yurij was influenced by increased contacts with colleagues from the Ukrainian diaspora to shift to using Ukrainian more in his professional life.

In telling their stories, the narrators constructed understandings of themselves and others as agents in the world. On the one hand, they were enacting their habitus, explaining their lives according to the parameters of normalcy and common sense which they had internalized throughout their lives. On the other hand, in their narratives they were participating in establishing definitions of categories and models of legitimate being. These categories and models, momentarily fixed in the interviews, continued to circulate as these individuals interacted with others. Sometimes they would influence, sometimes they would be influenced. With time the individual linguistic ideologies and activities add up to larger social tendencies, constituting a history of language politics.

CHAPTER **3** **Language at the Threshold**

**A History of Ideological Categories
and Corrections**

Чи знаєте, між іншим, чого наша мова у порога
віки вистояла? Бог про неї забув, як мішав язики на
вавилонській башті. Крім того, Дух Святий зійшов
на апостоли всіма мовами, забув тільки про нашу
українську. На це РНК звернув уже свою увагу, та
тільки без мене навряд, щоб що вийшло.

*Do you know why our language has stood at the threshold
through the ages? God forgot about it when he mixed languages
at the Tower of Babylon. Furthermore, the Holy Ghost came to
the apostles in all languages, but he forgot about our Ukrainian.
The Council of People's Commissioners has already taken note
of this, but without me, it's not likely that something will come
of it.*

— MYKOLA KULISH, *NARODNYJ MALAXIJ*

An Overview of Ukraine's History

Ukraine's new status as an independent nation in 1991 prompted many people,
from politicians and poets to workers and peasants, to look to history for a validation of their right to nationhood, as was the case in many other post-Soviet
states (e.g., Smith et al. 1998).[1] This entailed a reevaluation of historical events,
which paralleled the reevaluation and correction of cultural and linguistic val-

---

1. For historical overviews that are concise but more detailed than the one presented here,
see Motyl and Krawchenko 1997 and Reid 1997.

ues. This chapter traces the historical trajectory of Ukrainian language as an ideological and political construct, and highlights the historical events that people invoked after independence to justify their stances toward language and institutional measures.

Ukrainian historians commonly locate the roots of the Ukrainian state in Kyivan Rus' (ninth century to thirteenth century A.D.), when Kyiv (the current capital of Ukraine) was the center of a powerful principality. Descendants of Kyivan princes eventually founded principalities in the northern areas that later became Muscovy and then Russia. For this reason Russia can also trace its roots back to Kyivan Rus'. This dual national referent poses some conflicts, since many Ukrainians feel that Russia's claims are efforts to "steal" Ukraine's history and thus to undermine its nationhood. At the same time, many Russians interpret this history as the basis for ethnic and political unity between Ukrainians and Russians. In 1988, the year marking the millennium of the adoption of Christianity as the state religion for Kyivan Rus' by Prince Volodymyr the Great, many Ukrainians felt that the Russian Church had no right to celebrate this millennium as its own. They argued that the rightful descendant of Kyivan Rus' is Ukraine, with Kyiv its capital. Some people also view Russia's claim to a name so similar to that of the early state Rus' (originally a Norse name) as another way to co-opt history. A scientist in Kyiv explained her belief that choosing the name "Russia" for his state at the end of the seventeenth century was a way for Peter I to acquire eight hundred years of history for his relatively young country.[2]

The centralized power of the Kyivan Rus' principality had already begun to decline when it fell to the Mongol invasion in 1240, and other regional principalities took on importance. The Galician-Volhynian principality in what is now western Ukraine is considered by some historians to be the continuation of independent Ukraine (e.g., Subtelny 1988, 105). However, in the mid-fourteenth century, the last prince of Galicia-Volhynia died without leaving a successor, and these lands fell under the rule of Poland and Lithuania. Lithuania also incorporated the Kyiv and Chernihiv regions, which are now in central Ukraine, as well as regions that are now in Belarus and Russia. The language of administration, law, and diplomacy used in the Lithuanian Grand Duchy, called *rus' ka mova*, is considered by some to be old Ukrainian, a development of the language of Kyivan Rus', while others refer to it as "Belarusian with a substantial infusion of Ukrainian"—evidence of the complexity of justifying later national identities with the past (Markus and Senkus 1993, 46; Pachlovska 1998, 96).

In 1569 the Union of Lublin incorporated Ukrainian territories into a Polish Lithuanian Commonwealth. Within this Commonwealth, most of the current Ukrainian territory was administratively united within the Kingdom of Poland,

---

2. On the history and politics of toponymy of Rus'/Ukraine, see Pachlovska 1998, 78ff.

apart from other former Rus' lands. This period marked the beginning of Polonization and discrimination toward the *rus'ka* (old Ukrainian/Belarusian) language (Pachlovska 1998, 97). After Poland and Lithuania were joined into a Commonwealth, most of the Ukrainian lands continued to be united under separate (Polish) administration. Despite the supremacy of Polish, this fostered the cultural and political integration of eastern and western Ukrainian areas.

The central-southern areas of Ukraine remained a borderland at this time, occasionally fought over by the Polish, Russians, and Tatars.[3] There the Ukrainian Cossacks emerged, composed mostly of peasants fleeing their lords, and disenfranchised adventure-seeking burghers and noblemen. The Cossacks first appeared at the end of the fifteenth century and became a larger and more organized presence with the development of serfdom (and hence fleeing serfs) in the sixteenth and seventeenth centuries. Many Ukrainians consider the Cossack society, led by a Hetman (and called a "Hetmanate"), as another embodiment of independent Ukrainianhood, and consider Cossacks to be symbols of freedom and defiance of feudal oppression. Reid argues that as "outlaws and frontiersmen, fighters and pioneers, the Cossacks are to the Ukrainian national consciousness what cowboys are to the American" (Reid 1997, 30). In the seventeenth century, the Cossacks occasionally entered into agreements of military cooperation with Poland, Muscovy, the Crimean Khanate, Transylvania, and Sweden, but they attempted to maintain their independence.

An alliance between the Ukrainian Cossacks and the Russian tsar established by the Pereiaslav Agreement in 1654 ultimately led to the subjugation of the Cossacks and the partition of Ukrainian Cossack lands between Russia and Poland along the Dnipro River in 1667. Poland held most of what is now western Ukraine, except for a few regions that were under Ottoman and Hungarian rule. All the current Ukrainian lands would not be united until after World War II, in the form of a Soviet Republic.

After the partition of the Cossack state in 1667 the Cossack Hetmanate continued to exist within the Russian Empire, and in 1709 attempted to gain freedom from Russia by allying with Sweden in its war with Tsar Peter I. This failed attempt led to the ultimate demise of the Hetmanate under pressure from the tsar and the abolition of the separate political existence of Ukraine within the Russian Empire. At the end of the eighteenth century, when the Crimean Khanate came under Russian rule and the Polish Kingdom was partitioned, Russia acquired most of what is now central and southern Ukraine, while western areas fell under Austrian rule. Ukraine remained thus divided between Austria and Russia until

---

3. The Tatars had arrived with the Mongol army in the mid-thirteenth century, and they ruled over the Crimean peninsula as a semi-independent khanate under Ottoman protection until the late eighteenth century, when Russia annexed the peninsula (Reid 1997, 175–177).

World War I. While under the Russian Empire there were efforts to efface Ukrainian language and identity, the Austrian constitution specifically recognized the rights of Ukrainians as a distinct ethnic group and Ukrainian as their language (Bider 1997, 24).

After tsarist rule was overthrown by the Russian Revolution of 1917, various Ukrainian governments successively asserted independence for their country between 1917 and 1921. However brief, this resurgence of Ukrainian nationhood had great symbolic importance for nation building in the 1990s, as the most recent precedent for an independent democratic Ukraine. In the early 1920s eastern and central Ukraine came under Russian rule once again, as a Soviet Republic. Western Ukrainian lands fell primarily under Polish rule, with some regions under Romania, Hungary, and Czechoslovakia. This division remained until after World War II when western Ukrainian regions were joined with central and eastern Ukraine, forming a larger Ukrainian Soviet Socialist Republic. The borders of Ukraine have remained basically the same to this day, with the annexation of Crimea in 1954.

This brief historical overview highlights the complexity of Ukraine's political trajectory. One journalist has referred to Ukraine's development as "an identity crisis lasting centuries" (Perlez 1994, 3). Motyl and Krawchenko (1997, 239) summarize it thus: "For some 400 to 500 years, Ukraine was the site of attempts at annexation, plunder, and buffer maintenance by Poles, Ottomans, Tatars, and Muscovites. The constant incursions of all four into the no-man's land separating them destabilized Ukrainian society and made indigenous Ukrainian attempts at concerted state-building exceedingly difficult." Indeed, the concerted efforts to subjugate and eradicate Ukrainianness were key in defining it, and continue to be central in most historical narratives.

Pre-Soviet Restrictions on Ukrainian Language

Under various foreign regimes, the Ukrainian language was often devalued and persecuted as part of strategies to assimilate ethnically Ukrainian territories. Cultural and linguistic subjugation was the most extreme and prolonged under Russian rule. Overt suppression of Ukrainian by Russian decrees is documented as early as the 1620s and through the late 1980s under Soviet Russian dominance. Decrees in 1627 and 1628 ordered that books printed in Lithuania in the Ukrainian variant of Old Church Slavonic were to be confiscated and burned. In 1721 Tsar Peter I's decree prohibited the publication of books in Ukraine, with the exception of Russian-language religious books. Ukrainian books and records were burned: in 1718 the archives and library of the Monastery of the Caves were destroyed; in 1780 the library of the Mohyla Academy suffered the same fate. Not only written but oral language was targeted; in 1786, for example, it was decreed that religious masses should be conducted in the Russian, not Ukrainian, pronunciation of Old Church Slavonic (Markus and Senkus 1993, 46; Pachlovska 1998, 105–106; Taniuk 2003).

After the modern vernacular-based standard Ukrainian language had begun forming in publications during the early eighteenth century, especially in western Ukraine, tsarist decrees instituted harsher restrictions than before. The decrees of 1863, 1876, and 1881 prohibited not only publication or import of Ukrainian books but also most public uses of Ukrainian. In the 1863 edict banning public use of Ukrainian, the tsarist Russian minister Valuev declared that "there was not, is not, and can be no distinctive Little Russian language [as Ukrainian was then referred to by the Russian administration]" (Markus and Senkus 1993, 46). Speaking Ukrainian could be interpreted as opposition to the government. The use of Ukrainian in theater was banned, and even Ukrainian song lyrics had to be translated into other languages. To avoid singing in Russian, sometimes songs would be translated into French (Chykalenko 1955, 86). The decrees also prohibited education in Ukrainian in schools. Latin, which had been widely used in colleges and seminaries, was also obligatorily replaced by Russian, which served to isolate Ukraine from Western Europe (Pachlovska 1998, 104). Teachers and students suspected of being Ukrainophiles were expelled, teachers in Ukrainian regions were replaced by ethnic Russians, and books in Ukrainian or by Ukrainophiles were removed from school libraries (Dmytryshyn 1970; Markus and Senkus 1993; Savchenko 1970; Subtelny 1988, 282–283). In the early 1900s in tsarist Ukraine children in government schools were punished for speaking Ukrainian with one another, and people were sometimes dismissed from their jobs for speaking Ukrainian (Chykalenko 1955, 86, 343).

The western regions of Ukraine, under Austrian and Hungarian rule, also experienced foreign linguistic domination during the late eighteenth and nineteenth centuries, although not as restrictive as under tsarist Russia. These regions were administratively subdivided, and linguistic policies varied among the different areas. The exclusion of Ukrainian was most extreme in the southwestern Ukrainian region of Zakarpattia (Transcarpathia), where only Hungarian was legitimate for public use and Ukrainian was progressively excluded from schooling. In the western region of Galicia, the dominant language of the majority of the urban elite was Polish. The status of Ukrainian was lower, but it was still used in education and publications. In Bukovyna, German and Romanian were the official languages. Despite the presence of other dominant languages, the relatively liberal legislation in Galicia and Bukovyna allowed the Ukrainian press and political and educational systems to flourish (Bider 1997). A small but active Ukrainian intelligentsia, originating from the peasantry, fostered this development. This group consisted primarily of clergy, teachers, lawyers, and physicians from peasant backgrounds who had obtained schooling thanks to some support for Ukrainian education under Austrian and Polish rule. Ukrainians were a minority in the middle and upper classes—there was almost no Ukrainian-speaking aristocracy or wealthy bourgeoisie, since urban Ukrainians switched to the language of the ruling state to advance their careers or social positions (Dingley 1990, 174; Shevelov 1987, 10, 22, 216–217). Even in private conversations, speaking Ukrainian could be indicative of low status, but it could also be a symbol of solidarity once a friendship was established.

Not all the elite completely assimilated to the language and culture of the dominant states. Despite all the restrictive measures, during the nineteenth and early twentieth centuries vernacular Ukrainian was shaped into a standard language.[4] Writers, politicians, and linguists, many who grew up in villages and whose native language was a Ukrainian variety, worked to promote the language even though they often faced ridicule or the threat of exile or imprisonment. Periods of less oppressive political domination and short-lived Ukrainian independence in the aftermath of World War I were key in fostering the development of the language.

Standardization of the Ukrainian Language

The formation of the Ukrainian language was stifled by restrictions on education and publications and by its low social status, but writers, ethnographers, and philologists began working on developing it in earnest during the nineteenth century. Before then, an early record of the spoken language that developed into modern Ukrainian and the first document of Ukrainian folk poetry is a ballad that appears in the text of the 1540 Kralits'ka Bible, whose similarity to modern Ukrainian is striking (Pachlovska 1998, 98). The beginning of the Modern Ukrainian standard language is usually put at the publication of Kotliarevs'kyi's *Aeneid* (*Eneïda*) in 1798, which was the first literary work to be written wholly in a language based in the regional vernacular, with only an occasional insertion of other languages.[5] Kotliarevs'kyi's work also contains evidence of the syncretic Ukrainian-Russian bureaucratic language used at the time as well as a Ukrainian-Latin mixture, reflecting the complex linguistic influences of the period.

The first Ukrainian grammar was presented by Aleksei Pavlovskii to the Russian Academy of Sciences in 1805 and was published in 1818 (Rowenchuk 1992, 48). Initially the approaches to the codification of Ukrainian orthography, lexi-

---

4. For further discussions of literary and political influences on the development of the standard Ukrainian language, see Arel 1993; Comrie 1987; Pachlovska 1998; Pylyns'kyi 1976; Shevelov 1986, 1987, 1989, 1993; and Wexler 1974.

5. See Shevelov 1980, 1993, and Pachlovska 1998, 89ff., on the history of earlier forms of the Ukrainian language.

con, and grammar were divided between those based on historical Church Slavonic forms (usually closer to Russian, which was itself modeled on Church Slavonic) and those based on the spoken vernacular forms (closer to what became modern Ukrainian). These approaches correlated with different ideologies of identity—those prioritizing the written and historical dimensions versus those prioritizing ethnographic realities of the time.

There was more freedom to develop the Ukrainian language in the western Ukrainian regions than in the eastern regions within the Russian Empire. Although western Ukrainian tendencies during the past century are generally characterized as rejecting Russian influences, this was not always the case. During the nineteenth century many western Ukrainians were most concerned with differentiating their language from Polish and German because of their own experiences of linguistic subjugation, and thus strove to identify more closely with Russian. They formed the "Russophile" (also called "Moscophile") movement that existed in Galicia from the mid-1800s through 1915 (URE 1962, 391; Wendland 2001). Their agenda included resistance to the imposition of the Latin alphabet for Ukrainian, and they introduced a written language, called *jazyčije*, that was closer to the Russian standard in that it prioritized etymological over phonetic spelling. Jazyčije combined elements of Ukrainian and Russian vernaculars with Old Ukrainian, Old Church Slavonic, and Polish elements (URE 1964, 460).[6]

Ultimately codification based on Ukrainian vernaculars prevailed, but then there were disagreements over preferences for different regional vernaculars, with a major divide between the eastern and western regions. Between 1818 and 1909 more than thirty Ukrainian grammars appeared. Until 1905, when the tsarist restrictions on Ukrainian language use were removed, these were mostly published in western Ukraine and elsewhere in the Austro-Hungarian Empire (Pachlovska 1998, 107–115; Rowenchuk 1992, 47–48; Shevelov 1980).

Russian efforts to restrict the development of Ukrainian and other Slavic languages were partly owing to the recent formation of its own modern standard. A pioneering Russian dictionary appeared in the 1790s, an official grammar in 1802, and for much of the nineteenth century the Russian nobility preferred to speak French. The first great writer in the Russian vernacular, Aleksandr Pushkin, wrote in the 1830s, contemporaneously with Taras Shevchenko, who is considered the first great writer in Modern (vernacular-based) Ukrainian (Reid 1997, 77).

Even though Ukrainian language developments were restricted in the parts of Ukraine that were within the Russian Empire, in the mid-nineteenth century

---

6. In keeping with the prevalent view of western Ukraine as dominated by Ukrainian nationalism, Russophilism has been dismissed as a movement purely incited and funded by Russia, and there has been little historical analysis of it until Wendland's 2001 study (Himka 1999). For an example of *jazyčije*, see chapter 4.

general agreement began to emerge among Ukrainian elites throughout eastern and western regions regarding the Ukrainian standard. The core of this standard was to be the language used by writers of the central Kyiv-Poltava area, with incorporation of vernacular western Ukrainianisms in the interest of fostering pan-Ukrainian unity (Shevelov 1987, 18–19; Wexler 1974, 74). The poet and artist Taras Shevchenko (1814–1859), an emancipated serf, was the most influential force. To this day he is an icon of literary genius, and he is often invoked as a symbol of Ukrainian national spirit (Hoian 1991; Matvienko 1994). Shevchenko's literary works epitomize Romanticism in Ukraine. The widespread view that his language is an ideal form embodying national identity reveals the rootedness of the concept of modern Ukrainian in Romanticist ideology (Shevelov 1980, 155).

Although a norm of usage developed in the mid-nineteenth century, it was not fully codified or standardized. The Ukrainian textbooks that were published in the 1860s and 1870s had no official backing. Textbooks, newspapers, and literary works all reflected the specific regional backgrounds of their authors, with influences of local dialects and foreign languages. In 1893 a grammar by S. Smal'-Stoc'kyj and F. Gartner was authorized by the Austrian Ministry of Education and published in Lviv, but it was much disputed (Rowenchuk 1992, 49; Shevelov 1987, 18). The first attempt at language regulation by a Ukrainian organization was published in 1904 in Lviv by the Shevchenko Scientific Society (Shevelov 1987, 24).[7]

The beginning of the twentieth century was a time of active debate over the regulation of the Ukrainian language in all areas of Ukraine. In eastern Ukraine, when tsarist restrictions on language were eased in 1905, people became openly involved in issues of standardization, and Ukrainian language publications proliferated. In 1917 Ukrainians in Kyiv organized a government and declared an autonomous Ukrainian People's Republic within a federated Russian Republic, which led to war between Ukraine and Russia. In 1918 the Ukrainian government proclaimed full independence from Russia, which lasted, with a couple of changes in government, through 1920. During this brief period of independence the Ukrainian language flourished, its status increased, and its spheres of use

---

7. The Shevchenko Scientific Society, first named the Shevchenko Society, was founded in 1873 in Lviv with the aim of fostering the development of Ukrainian literature through its own press and publishing house. In 1893 the society, comprised of 137 members, was reorganized, modeled after Western European scientific institutions, to support the development of science and art in Ukrainian and to preserve and collect historical materials. The society was outlawed during World War I and again during the Soviet occupation. During the Soviet period it continued its activities through chapters in Europe, Canada, Australia, and the United States. In 1989 it was established once again in Ukraine. The Shevchenko Scientific Society continues to support scholarly activities in Ukrainian, including conferences and publications in a wide range of fields, including linguistics, literature, history, mathematics, natural sciences, and medicine (Kravtsiv and Kubijovyc 1993).

were expanded. Ukrainian was later suppressed again by the Polish and Soviet Russian occupying regimes, but developments in the brief period of independence fueled future Ukrainian linguistic and cultural activities (Pachlovska 1998, 115–117; Shevelov 1987, 67–85).

There was still much disagreement over the parameters for the development of Ukrainian, but there was a general purist tendency, reflecting the desire for an authentic "truly Ukrainian" language (Wexler 1974). People actively debated whether authenticity was to be found in eastern or western Ukrainian vernaculars, and whether words rooted in Church Slavonic, Polish, Russian, German, or other languages were better. In the definition of its standard language, the definition of a pan-Ukrainian identity was at stake.

In the 1920s, under Soviet power, initial restriction of Ukrainian was followed by a time of relative support for non-Russian cultures and languages. An official committee of linguists and literary scholars was established to deal with the standardization of the Ukrainian language. The work of this committee resulted in the *Ukraïns'kyi pravopys*, which outlined the basic rules of grammar and orthography. These standards were approved, with the participation of Galician Ukrainians, at the 1927 Kharkiv Orthographic Conference and formally instituted on January 1, 1929. While this represented a culmination of the process of Ukrainian standardization, Soviet language policies and ideologies of linguistic and cultural development would still have a transformative impact on the Ukrainian language, sometimes by brutal means. After independence in the 1990s, the 1929 codification continued to serve as the standard for language planners seeking to undo the concerted Russification of Ukrainian that took place during the Soviet period (Ponomariv 2004; Rowenchuk 1992).

Language Policies in the Early Soviet Period

With the establishment of Soviet rule in eastern and central Ukraine after the country's few years of independence following World War I, Russian regained its prior dominance. The conditions for Ukrainian language and culture at this time were dire. In 1918, during Ukraine's brief independence, there were 1,084 Ukrainian books and 239 Ukrainian newspapers published; under Soviet power in 1922 only 186 Ukrainian books and 53 newspapers were published (Dashkevych 1990, 56–57). Russian language symbolized communism and the revolution, whereas Ukrainian was portrayed as anticommunist, antirevolutionary, and nationalist. This symbolism was further elaborated by the urban/rural cultural geography in which the city embodied the progressive sphere of the proletariat while the village embodied backwardness and conservatism. In general, Russian was the language of the cities, and Ukrainian was the language of the villages (Pachlovska 1998, 116–117).

The Ukrainian writer and communist activist Volodymyr Vynnychenko

(1980) poignantly illustrated Russian Bolsheviks' discrimination against Ukrainian culture and identity in his diary entries from 1920. He felt torn between his desire to work toward the realization of socialist ideals in Ukraine and his recognition that the Russian Bolsheviks were intent on subjugating and exploiting Ukraine just as the Russian tsarist regime had:

> Oh, how differently they would greet and receive me, if I showed myself to be a "real" communist, that is, if I declared to them that I am not a Ukrainian, that I am ready to join them in doing all that they are doing with the Ukrainian nation. (438)

> I don't know what to do anymore. I see no way out, since there are only two ways out: either to renounce being a Ukrainian and then be a revolutionary; or to leave the revolution completely and then I can be a Ukrainian. I can do neither one nor the other, both options are fatally painful for me. But history does not permit the joining of the one with the other. (445)

Vynnychenko was deeply disillusioned, for if he were to act according to the desires of the Russian Communist Party, which clearly wanted to use him as a means of obtaining the support of Ukrainians, "every Ukrainian would come to the conclusion that it is enough to become a communist in order to become a traitor of national emancipation" (442). His disillusionment with the progress of the revolution in the hands of Lenin and the other Russian Communists was vivid and prophetic:

> Saddest of all is that in losing us, in losing Ukraine with their outdated views, they are losing themselves, and with themselves the revolution in the West. And I fear the time when the revolution, the very idea of communism will be discredited in the eyes of the masses. And the higher everyone—even the bourgeoisie—regards Lenin now, the lower he will fall, even in the eyes of the communists. And he will seem to everyone so small, so laughable, a stubborn fanatic, a lifeless maniac. (438)

The Russian Communists were initially unwilling to recognize the validity of aspirations for Ukrainian emancipation from Russian subjugation, but Ukrainian resistance ultimately led to a change in policy. Vynnychenko had argued for such a change earlier, but, as he wrote in 1920, the Russian Communists were not driven by the ideals they proclaimed: "It would not be due to fairness, or emotion, nor on the basis of principles, nor program, but only from necessity that they have to come closer to their own principles, program, and declarations of fairness" (Vynnychenko 1980, 443–444). The indigenization policies of the 1920s were just such a strategic move.

Ukrainianization

In order to placate Ukrainian resistance, Lenin decided that the Russian Communist Party needed to be patient with the Ukrainian language and culture and should "endeavor to convert Ukrainian into a weapon of communist enlighten-

ment" (Wexler 1974, 110). Lenin ultimately realized that the resentment and resistance of other nations in response to the forced imposition of Russian could
jeopardize the success of the revolution, because it replicated the mistakes of the
tsarist regime. Lenin's vision of a "single, proletarian, non-national world culture"
did entail a single world language, but he believed that nations would voluntar-
ily adopt a single language as this became economically beneficial and as they
evolved toward socialism. Although before the revolution Lenin had thought
that national differences were already beginning to die away, afterward he decided they would still continue to exist for a very long time even after the dicta-
torship of the proletariat had been established on a world scale (Goodman 1968,
720). Indeed, Soviet institutions themselves ensured that nationality remained
an important axis of social divisions, for it was reinforced in official practices
such as passport entries, censuses, and cultural performances (Goujon 2000, 88–
89; Motyl and Krawchenko 1997; Slezkine 1994; Verdery 1996, 83ff.).[8]

The sixth year after the October Revolution, 1923, saw the establishment of
policies of *korenizatsiia*—'indigenization' or 'nativization'—that supported the
development of the non-Russian languages—a strategic response to non-Russian
national movements (Dashkevych 1990; Martin 2001; Pachlovska 1998, 118;
Smith 1998). In Ukraine this took the form of *ukraïnizatsiia* 'Ukrainianization'.
This process was not just about language and culture but also had economic and
political ramifications. Economists showed that Ukraine had remained a colony
under Soviet Russia's control and that more capital was being taken from Ukraine
than even in tsarist times (Dashkevych 1990, 61).

Indeed, during Ukrainianization in the 1920s, great strides were made in the
development, standardization, and codification of the Ukrainian language. These
were accompanied by growth in the number of Ukrainian publications, theater
productions, and schools. Ukrainian schools did not exist in the regions within
the tsarist empire before the revolution, but, by 1929, 83.2 percent of all primary

---

8. The terms "ethnicity" and "nationality" were used largely synonymously in the post-Soviet regions, with "nationality" the more commonly used term denoting a politicized social
identity. Nationality meant membership in a "nation" as defined by cultural, linguistic, and
hereditary parameters, which was very different from "citizenship," which was membership
in a particular state, such as the USSR. All citizens of the USSR had an entry in their passports
designating their nationality, whether it was Tatar, Uzbek, Jewish, Ukrainian, Estonian, Russian, Gypsy, and so on. Some Soviet nationalities corresponded to political units, such as Soviet Republics, and some did not. This Soviet understanding of nationality meant that one
could speak of "the nations of our country" and "the strengthening of friendly international
ties between the peoples of our country" (Lomtev 1949, 131). This understanding of nationality is very different from common usage in the West, where "nation" and "state," and "citizenship" and "nationality," are basically interchangeable, and cultural identity is referred to
as ethnicity (Wanner 1998, 10–15). Here I follow the practice customary in the region under
study, treating "nationality" and "ethnicity" as largely synonymous.

school students (2.4 million children) were enrolled in Ukrainian schools, and by 1933 the proportion had grown to 88.5 percent (Liber 1992, 109). Many schools and organizations serving other national minorities in Ukraine were also established at this time. More Ukrainians gradually entered the Communist Party and related organizations, although leading positions were still predominantly held by Russians (Dashkevych 1990, 58, 61). The proportion of Ukrainians in the Communist Party of Ukraine rose from 23 percent in 1922 to 52 percent in 1927, to 60 percent in 1933, but those claiming Ukrainian as a native language never exceeded one-third of the party. As Liber argues, it was less divisive to enroll urban Russified Ukrainians than Ukrainian-speaking peasants, "far easier to fill quotas than to overcome the structural legacy of Russification" (Liber 1992, 100).

Throughout its duration (1925–1933) Ukrainianization was controversial and proceeded erratically. In some cities official paperwork remained completely in Russian, there were "relapses into Russification," and Ukrainians in the government were harassed and the language sometimes ridiculed (Chaban 1994, 12; Goodman 1968, 724; Shevelov 1987, 122). During this period, in 1931, a Russian linguist even put forth the theory, argued in Marxist terms, that Ukrainian is inherently a peasant language and Russian a proletarian one, and that therefore Ukrainian was slated for extinction (Smith 1998, 73). Not all languages were categorized in such class terms, but communist ideology held that eventually national languages would die out, even if this would not happen as quickly as first envisioned.

A play written in 1929 by Mykola Kulish, titled *Myna Mazajlo,* illustrates the conflicting forces with hilarity and bitterness, and provides a rich ethnographic glimpse into the sociolinguistic situation of early Soviet Ukraine.[9] In this play a man aspires to acquire Russian culturedness by changing his last name, Mazajlo ("Greaser"—which sounds typically Ukrainian and decidedly lower-class). His wife and daughter are like-minded, but his son, Mokij, is an ardent young Communist supporting Ukrainianization policies, who revels in everything Ukrainian, especially the language. An uncle from western Ukraine portrays a stereotypical Ukrainian nationalist, and an aunt from Kursk, Russia, represents a provincial but self-assured Russian chauvinist who would just as soon forget her Ukrainian roots. The original text is all in Ukrainian orthography, with the Russified aunt's language portraying Russian forms to varying degrees, as indicated below. (All play excerpts are from Kulish 1955.)

> *Mazajlo (the father):* I тобі, Мокію, раджу не вірити українізації. Сердцем
> передчуваю, що українізація—це спосіб робити з мене провінціяла,
> другосортного службовця і не давати мені ходу на вищі посади.

---

9. My sincere thanks to Lubomyr Hajda for recommending this play, a veritable treasure of sociolinguistic information.

[And to you Mokij, I recommend that you don't believe in Ukrainianization. I feel in my heart that Ukrainianization is a way to make me into a provincial, a second-rate civil servant and to bar my access to higher posts.] (169)

Aunt Motia: Не бачили, не читали? Харків—написано. Тільки що під'їхала до вокзалу, дивлюсь—отакими великими літерами: Харків. Дивлюсь—не Харьков, а Харків! Нащо, питаюсь, навіщо ви нам іспортілі город? [The last two words portray Russian forms, the rest is in standard Ukrainian.]

[Didn't you see, didn't you read? It is written—Kharkiv. I just arrived at the train station, I look—and in such huge letters: Kharkiv. I look—not Khar'kov [Russian spelling], but Kharkiv [Ukrainian spelling]! Why, I ask, why did you ruin the city for us?] (151)

Боже!.. По-моєму прілічнєє бить ізнасілованой, нєжєлі українізірованой. [This whole statement is Russian, portrayed in Ukrainian orthography.]

My God, in my opinion it would be more decent to be raped than to be Ukrainianized. (186)

Uncle Taras: Їхня українізація—це спосіб виявити всіх нас, українців, а тоді знищити разом, щоб і духу не було... Попереджаю!

Their Ukrainianization—it is a way to uncover all of us Ukrainians, and then to destroy us all together, so that there won't be a ghost of us left ... I am warning you! (169)

In the end Mazajlo does have his name officially changed to "Mazenin," which sounds decidedly Russian. He revels in the newspaper listing announcing this change, and the Russified Aunt Motia frames the newspaper page. However, when another character reads the framed announcement, what he finds on that one page reveals the complexity of the processes of Ukrainianization. As he reads through listings on the page to find the announcement, he comes across the following notices (intervening comments of other characters are omitted):

«Українізація [...] Адміністрація маріупільського заводу не пустила на завод комісії в справі українізації... [...] За останній час на багато збільшився попит на українську книжку поміж робітництвом на Харківських заводах... За систематичний зловмисний опір українізації... [...] Стривайте! Стривайте! Та невже?.. [...] За постановою комісії в справах українізації, що перевірила апарат Донвугілля, звільнено з посади за систематичний і зловмисний опір українізації службовця М. М. Мазайла-Мазеніна.»

"Ukrainianization. [...] The administration of the Mariupol factory refused to allow entry to the commission on Ukrainianization ... [...] Recently demand has greatly increased for Ukrainian books amongst the workers of Kharkiv factories ... In response to the systematic and ill-intentioned opposition to Ukrainianization ... [...] Wait! Wait! It couldn't be?.. [...] According to the commission on Ukrainianization, which inspected the administration of the Donvuhill'a coal factory, administrator M. M. Mazajlo-Mazenin has been relieved of his position due to his systematic and ill-intentioned opposition to Ukrainianization." (201–202)

Although Mazajlo-Mazenin lost his job, infighting among the pro-Ukrainian components of his family allowed him to achieve the Russification of his name, and his yearning for Russian culture and disdain for Ukrainian culture had not diminished. In the play the pro-Ukrainian communist youths remained optimistic, but, in real life, Uncle Taras's warning that "Ukrainianization—it is a way to uncover all of us Ukrainians, and then to destroy us all together"—was borne out. While Ukrainianization had achieved some successes, by 1928 the repression of the Ukrainian intelligentsia had begun. And in early 1933, four years after the play was written, Ukrainianization came to a complete halt with the onset of Stalinist terror and a politically engineered famine. The famine, instituted through brutally enforced and unrealistically high grain requisitions, was intended to break resistance to collectivization and decimate the peasantry, the base of support for Ukrainianization. Most of the new Ukrainian communist elite and intelligentsia were executed or deported to prison camps in northwestern Russia and Siberia, while millions of Ukrainian peasants perished in the artificial famine.[10]

Return to Policies of Russification

Stalin's theories of language and nationalities shifted during his lifetime. In 1925 he had stated,

> [I have] very little faith in this theory of a single all-embracing language. Experience, in any case, does not speak for, but against this theory. Up until now the socialist revolution has not diminished, but increased the number of languages, since it has aroused the broad masses of humanity, pushed them onto the political stage and awakened a new life in a whole series of new nationalities, which were formerly unknown or almost unknown. (Cited in Goodman 1968, 719)

---

10. The famine of 1933 was not a result of agricultural shortages but was politically instituted. The extremely high grain requisitions were intended to support industrialization and to break resistance to Sovietization. Food was rationed in urban and industrial areas and grain was exported outside the USSR in exchange for imported machinery. Meanwhile, in Ukraine and regions of the North Caucasus (also populated by many Ukrainians), an estimated six million peasants starved to death or were shot for noncompliance with grain requisitioning (Conquest 1986; Markus 1984). There are different interpretations regarding the extent to which the famine was targeted based on ethnicity or class or both. For a detailed analysis of the relationship between Ukrainianization and the grain requisition crisis, see Martin 2001, 301–307. See Mace and Heretz 1990 for a compilation of oral histories of the 1933 famine, in Ukrainian with English summaries.

Later, in 1929, Stalin no longer rejected the idea of a world language and found ways to dissociate himself from his earlier position. In the years that followed, his views and Soviet government policies shifted from the belief that the world language would be a new language incorporating features of existing national languages to the position that the world language would be Russian. The indigenization policies of the 1920s empowered the non-Russian regions, and this came to be seen as a threat to centralized control. The lack of adherence to standard literary norms in the Russian language that was used in the various regions further disrupted the construction of a unified linguistic marketplace throughout the USSR (as discussed in Smith 1998, chapter 1).

The shift toward policies of Russification and the belief in the inevitability of the emergence of Russian as a world language was also driven by a rivalry with English, which was becoming widespread around the world (Goodman 1968, 723–724; Lomtev 1949). To Soviet leaders the spread and influence of English was insidious, whereas the expansion of Russian influence was supposedly voluntary and "natural." Starting in the 1930s the dominant Soviet linguistic theory clearly exalted the Russian language and nation above others in the USSR:

> The great Russian language, which as a result of the victory of the Great October Socialist Revolution has received a new, socialist direction in its development, has become the source of enrichment and flowering for the national languages. The progressive meaning of the Russian language has grown immeasurably as a result of the liquidation of state privileges and the establishment of equality of all languages and the socialist cooperation of all nations.
>
> Comrade Stalin teaches that the Russian people "is the most prominent nation of all the nations that comprise the Soviet Union."
>
> The Russian language is great, rich, and mighty. It is the instrument of the most advanced culture in the world. From its inexhaustible treasures, the national languages of the USSR draw a life-giving elixir. It is the language that all of the peoples of the great Soviet Union learn with love, viewing it as the mighty tool of their cultural elevation and socialist reform. (Lomtev 1949, 136)

In the 1930s the "love" for Russian became more directly instituted through Soviet policies. Even though the official view was that "there is no doubt that the national languages will be disappearing due to their gradual dying out, and not due to abolition by a decree from above," the central Russian Soviet government became frustrated with the lack of any evidence of disappearance of national languages (Lomtev 1949, 139). To the contrary, the linguistic developments of the 1920s had strengthened the distinctiveness of the various national languages and thus threatened their subordination to Russian. In order to rein in the non-Russian regions, beginning in the 1930s Soviet officials began to enforce Russification on the structural level by means of the regulation of dictionaries and textbooks. Certain words, syntactic constructions, grammatical forms, and spelling standards were banned, while others patterned on Russian or directly transplanted from Russian were promoted (Shevelov 1987, 220). In Ukraine the use of Ukrainian terms that had alternate variants more similar to the corresponding Russian words was viewed as "sabotage" (Dingley 1990, 181; Pachlovska 1998, 119–121; Shevelov 1987, 221). Books were "literally arrested, just like people" (Fedyk 1991, 140). Thus, in addition to "classic" methods of linguistic domination, such as the imposition of the Russian language through education or career opportunities and exclusion of other languages from public use, the Soviet system interfered directly with the structures of other languages. This subjugation was unlike any under previous regimes—the rulers of imperial Russia had forbidden the use of the Ukrainian language and denied its existence, but they had not tried to redefine just what this language was.

The period from the late 1920s to the early 1930s brought an end to the (albeit superficial) support for indigenization, with purges of those who had worked on developing the national languages and the institutional representation of non-Russians. In Ukraine the liquidation was extreme in some spheres: 100 out of 102 members and candidate-members of Ukraine's Central Communist Party Committee were purged, most of them shot (Dashkevych 1990, 62). Two-thirds of those who participated in the language reforms of the 1920s were arrested and eventually shot or died as a result of Stalin's policies (Pachlovska 1998, 119; Rowenchuk 1992, 121). Those who were active in the indigenization movements in other republics suffered similar fates.

Developments in all the non-Russian languages were condemned as the work of "bourgeois nationalists," who were faulted for any development that differed from Russian. The "bourgeois nationalist" linguists supposedly had wanted to eliminate international terminology and "artificially bred provincial words and forms in order to interfere with the permeation of Russian words and forms into the native language" (Lomtev 1949, 135). The inclusion of word forms in the developing standards that shared similarities with languages other than Russian was also seen as disruptive by the central Russian officials:

> The bourgeois nationalists strove to orient themselves towards foreign languages, by all means possible reducing the significance of the Russian language. Belorusian and Ukrainian nationalists littered their native language with aristocratic elements from the Polish language; Moldovan nationalists aspired to drag into their language the courtly elements of the Romanian language; Latvian nationalists, in submission to the German nobility, aspired to germanicize their language. The bourgeois nationalists of our eastern republics littered their native languages with Arabo-Persian and Turkish elements. (Lomtev 1949, 135)

Although the plan was to diminish the differences between Russian and Ukrainian, in other cases linguistic differentiation was desirable. For example, the drive to bring literacy to Central Asian peoples had operated under a policy of "divide and conquer," artificially enlarging upon the differences between languages when codifying them. Where similar sets of synonyms had existed in most of the Central Asian languages, linguistic codification allocated one term to each language, and, with time, the other terms no longer became synonyms but instead "foreign words."[11] The Soviet rulers were afraid of allowing pan-Islamic or pan-Turkic ties to develop: "While non-Russian languages were codified by the score, their development was carefully channeled and their divergences inflated so that no new regional non-Russian language could evolve among them" (Goodman 1968, 725). Central Asian languages were differentiated in codification, but ultimately they were also to be brought closer to Russian, like the western Soviet languages (Smith 1988, 139). In the development of languages and their terminologies, whether Slavic or non-Slavic, words were to be borrowed from Russian rather than derived from local language forms.

Archival materials bear testimony to the direct attack on the forms and constructions of Ukrainian during the Stalin years (Wexler 1974, 157ff.). For example, treatises such as Khvylia's 1933 article, "To Destroy the Roots of Ukrainian Nationalism on the Linguistic Front," spearheaded the efforts of special language censorship brigades in 1933–35 (Kocherga and Kulyk 1994). These brigades took up the task of censoring terminological dictionaries, systematically excluding the existing Ukrainian terms in favor of Russified ones. Bulletins produced by these committees listed "corrections" to existing dictionaries. The titles and headings express the agenda of the compilers: "Against Nationalism in Mathematical Terminology" (Drinov and Sabaldyr 1934, 5–22), "To Uproot Nationalism in Construction Terminology" (Mustiatsa 1935), and "To Liquidate Nationalist Sabotage in Soviet Physical Terminology" (Kalynovych and Drinov 1935). Later, after the revisions had been instituted, these bulletins, as evidence of the censoring process, were either destroyed or held in "special reserves" (*specxrany*) in libraries, with no public access until recently Kocherga and Kulyk 1994).

The linguistic interventions included grammatical, morphological, and orthographic rules that were to make Ukrainian more similar to Russian and thus more "politically correct." Karavans'kyi (1994, 103–109) identifies 29 such changes in the language standards between 1928 and 1933, and Pachlovska (1998, 119) identifies 126 such changes instituted between 1933 and 1946. For example, the genitive case ending for feminine nouns with roots ending in two consonants was changed from "и" /y/ to "i" /i/. The Ukrainian letter "ґ" /g/ was eliminated, its place to be filled by the remaining letter "г" /h/; the phonetic distinction between /h/ and /g/ was thereby eliminated in othography to match the lack of this distinction in Russian which only has the letter "г" /g/. The transliteration of

---

11. Lubomyr Hajda, personal communication, 2002.

words with Greek roots was changed to match the transliteration applied in Russian: for example, the transliteration of Greek *theta* was changed from "т" /t/ to "ф" /f/, as in the words анатема (*anatema*) which became анафема (*anafema*) 'anathema', and мит (*myt*) which was changed to міф (*mif*) 'myth'. Other international words (words of foreign origin that already existed in Ukrainian) were modified to follow Russian forms more closely phonologically and morphologically: for example, Ukrainian геодет (*heodet*) became геодезист (*heodezyst*) to resemble Russian геодезист (*geodezist*) 'geodesist', and плястер (*pl'aster*) became пластир (*plastyr*) to be closer to Russian пластырь (*plastyr'*) 'plaster' (Wexler 1974, 162–163). Often the new forms, more similar to Russian, were linguistically less efficient than the originals: автомобілярня (*avtomobil'arn'a*) became завод автомобільний (*zavod avtomobil'nyj*) 'auto factory', терезярня (*terez'arn'a*) became мастерська вагова (*masters'ka vahova*) 'weighing shop' (Karavans'kyi 1994, 160).

In some cases the original Ukrainian form was based on a Greek or Latin root, as with the words for "arsenic," "vacation," and "cinnamon," while in other cases it was the Russified word that was closer to a Greek or Latin form, as with "suffix," "fruits," "dash," and "thesis" (Karavans'kyi 1994, 82–86) (see Table 3.1).

In addition to the modification of word forms to more resemble Russian, starting in the 1930s dictionaries were edited to prioritize or single out forms closer to Russian where earlier Ukrainian dictionaries had listed more than one variant or a range of synonyms. A comparison of two versions of the leading *Russian-Ukrainian Dictionary*, the 1924–33 edition, and the 1948 edition, shows this trend clearly, as in the example of the Russian term благополучие (*blagopalučie*) 'good fortune'. The Ukrainian equivalents provided in the 1924–33 edition are "добра доля, щастя, добробут, гаразд" (*dobra dol'a, ščast'a, dobrobut, harazd*)— all expressing different shadings of the meaning "good fortune." In the 1948 edition the Ukrainian equivalents with further Russian specifying terms (in italics) are "благополуччя, благополучність; (*счатье, удача*)—щастя" [*blahopolučč'a, blahopolučnist'; (ščastie, udača)—ščast'a*] (Masenko 2004, 38–41). New Ukrainian forms modeled directly on the Russian term were listed first, and three of the original Ukrainian terms were excluded altogether in the later dictionary.

In the 1930s and 1940s hundreds of minute as well as major changes were instituted in order to push Ukrainian closer to Russian so that it could be "enriched" by the "more cultured" language and thereby move forward on the road to socialism. Karavans'kyi (1994) views the linguistic manipulation as a personified violence, referring to the eliminated Ukrainian words as "pogrom victims," "words that were crippled, contorted, and suffered from discriminatory codification in dictionaries or elimination from use." In his personified portrayal of words he highlights the embodiment of identity in language, part of an ideol-

TABLE 3.1. **Examples of Russified linguistic forms imposed on Ukrainian standards during the 1930s (from Karavans'kyi 1994)**

Original Ukrainian	Imposed 1930s Form	Russian	English
арсен [arsen]	миш'як [myšjak]	мышьяк [myšjak]	arsenic
вакації [vakaciji]	канікули [kan'ikuly]	каникулы [kan'ikuly]	vacation
цинамон [cynamon]	кориця [koryc'a]	корица [kar'icə]	cinnamon
наросток [narostok]	суфікс [sufiks]	суффикс [suffiks]	suffix
овочі [ovoči]	фрукти [frukty]	фрукты [frukty]	fruits*
риска [ryska]	тире [tyre]	тире [t'ir'e]	dash
теза [teza]	тезис [tezys]	тезис [t'ezis]	thesis

*The original Ukrainian word for fruit, *ovoči*, is very close to the Russian word for vegetables, *ovošči*. Vegetables in Ukrainian were referred to as *jaryna* or *horodovyna*. In late Soviet-era Ukrainian practices, both terms for fruits and vegetables were modeled on Russian usages, with *ovoči* referring to vegetables and *frukty* to fruits.

ogy of language and nation as living beings, also reminiscent of Sophia's statement that language is like her body (see chapter 2).

By effacing the distinctness of the Ukrainian language and identity, and subsuming it to Russian, the central Soviet government endeavored to solidify its hegemony over the Ukrainian Republic. Indigenization came to be seen as an erroneous policy that needed to be remedied in order to return the various Soviet nations to the "correct" path of Russification, toward unity within one symbolic system.

Russification and Linguistic Engineering in the Late Soviet Period

The addition of western Ukrainian regions to the Ukrainian Soviet Republic after World War II brought a population whose language had not directly experienced Russian domination as had the eastern Soviet Ukrainian areas. In contrast to the severe repression and linguistic engineering in Soviet Eastern Ukraine between the world wars, in the non-Soviet western Ukrainian regions the Ukrainian language could be used more freely. The most striking development in language status occurred in the western Ukrainian region of Galicia, under Polish rule. The Polish language generally had more power and prestige, but Ukrainian political and educational institutions were allowed to exist, and there the Ukrainian language became widespread as a symbol of ethnic pride and defiance of colonizing regimes, with a relatively high symbolic value. It is significant that eastern

Ukraine was always integral in western Ukrainians' ideologies of national and ethnic identity. Following transfer to the USSR, western Ukrainian ethnolinguistic pride posed a new challenge to Soviet policies of Russification, which had to counter the linguistic influence of Polish and German as well as the more developed national aspirations of western Ukrainians.

Even after eastern and western Ukraine were united into a single Ukrainian Soviet Socialist Republic, the various regions of Ukraine continued to experience different influences. Immigration from other republics, especially Russia, was mostly directed toward urban and industrial regions, particularly the southeastern Donbas. Severe repressions, deportations, and efforts to eradicate national sentiment were focused on the newly Sovietized western region, although Ukrainian was still taught in schools and used officially at the local level. This region tended to be stereotyped by nonwestern Ukrainians as a hotbed of nationalist guerrillas who had arms buried near their houses or in the woods.[12] Open pride in the Ukrainian language that had developed in Galicia was quelled and hidden, although it later resurfaced with Ukraine's independence in the early 1990s.

In 1938 a policy had been instituted that required all Soviet pupils to study Russian starting in second grade (Dashkevych 1990, 63; Smith 1998, 159). Later, Khrushchev's school reforms of 1958–59 allowed parents to choose the primary language of instruction for their children, which facilitated the even greater dominance of prestigious Russian (Dingley 1990, 184). This policy, along with increased immigration of Russians to urban areas in Ukraine, paved the way for the Russification of schools in Ukraine. This was most pronounced in the southeastern regions, although the quality and availability of Ukrainian-language schooling decreased steadily throughout the country (Arel 1993, 143–202). It was widely accepted that having a Russian-language education increased the chances of entering higher education and getting a better job. Russian schools tended to have better-trained teachers, and entrance examinations were usually in Russian. Ukrainian was viewed as useless by many parents (especially non-Ukrainians), who often had their children exempted from having to study it. This was especially the case with recent Russian-speaking immigrants. In the later years of Soviet rule fewer and fewer Ukrainian-language schools operated in the cities, so even those parents who may have wanted to send their children to a Ukrainian school did not always have the choice (Arel 1993, 180, 193–195). "Soviet internationalism" had thus become not really international but rather Russian in character, as a Soviet anecdote critical of Soviet linguistic policies illustrates:[13]

---

12. During World War II nationalist partisan units formed the Ukrainian Insurgent Army (Ukraïns'ka Povstans'ka Armiia, or UPA), which fought both German and Soviet forces.

13. As related to me by Lubomyr Hajda, 2002.

What do you call someone in Ukraine who knows three languages?
A Zionist. [This would be a culturally aware Jew who knew Ukrainian, Russian, and Hebrew.]

What do you call someone in Ukraine who knows two languages?
A bourgeois nationalist. [Someone who found it necessary to know both Ukrainian and Russian.]

What do you call someone in Ukraine who knows one language?
An internationalist. [A monolingual Russian speaker.]

As time went on the status of the Russian language became cemented as the language of prestige, high culture, science, and power throughout the USSR. The non-Russian Soviet languages were viewed as backward and unsophisticated, or at best their place was restricted to literary and local folkloric venues. Relatively few resources were available for non-Russian publications or presentations. Higher-quality films and books were usually in Russian, and it was the language of the educated urban population, of authority, and of "high culture"— *kul'turnost'* 'culturedness' in general. In Ukrainian villages, speaking Russian was sometimes referred to as speaking "по городскому" (*po horodskomu*) 'city-talk', consistent with the pre-Soviet and early Soviet paradigms equating Russian with urbanity and Ukrainian with the rural sphere, paradigms that still held true for many people even after independence. According to a model of diglossia, Russian was the high language and republic languages, like Ukrainian, were low.

Negative or demeaning treatment of Ukrainian speakers was common during the late Soviet period. Some Kyivites told me that, in the 1970s and 1980s, if they spoke Ukrainian in the city they were asked why they speak the dog's tongue, or can't they say it "на человеческом языке" 'in human language' (see also Myzychenko 2002, Szporluk 1975, 203). Not everyone encountered such overt disdain. While Ukrainian was not considered prestigious, in many contexts it was accepted as normal and unremarkable. One could also find pockets of support for Ukrainian, such as in the Ministry of Foreign Affairs or on a particular university exam commission.[14] Positive views could also be openly expressed for Ukrainian as a necessary embodiment of Soviet acceptance of ethnic diversity. More direct aspirations of Ukrainians to maintain and legitimize Ukrainian language and culture and to fend off Russification were more controversial (e.g., see Taras's narrative in chapter 2).

The direct intervention in the structure of the Ukrainian language that was

---

14. See Borys Tarasyuk's narrative in chapter 2 regarding the situation in the Ministry of Foreign Affairs. Two interviewees in 1992 told me of their participation on university exam commissions that were supportive of students who spoke Ukrainian, particularly students from villages.

TABLE 3.2. **Examples of the Russification of Ukrainian archaeological terms in the 1980s**

Ukrainian 1970s Term	Russified 1980s Term	Standard Russian	English Gloss
скребачка [skrebačka]	скребок [skrebok]	скребок [skr'ebok]	scraper
платівка [plat'ivka]	пластина [plastyna]	пластина [plast'inǝ]	blade
вкладень [vkladen']	вкладиш [vkladyš]	вкладыш [fkladyš]	microblade
відлупок [vidlupok]	відщеп [vidščep]	отщеп [atš'š'ep]	flake

so intense under Stalin slowed but did not cease in the later Soviet years (Masenko 2004). Under Khrushchev in the late 1950s and early 1960s Ukrainian literature, research, and education enjoyed a temporary revival, only to be stifled again in the following decades. One of the most severe impediments to the development and functioning of the Ukrainian language in science was the conversion in the 1970s of almost all the scientific journals of the Academy of Sciences of the Ukrainian SSR into the Russian language (Strikha 1990, 160).

A Kyiv archaeologist recounted an example that further illustrates Soviet policies of linguistic intervention. The archaeology institute in Kyiv would occasionally receive lists of terminology that were no longer to be used, and replacement words that were more similar to the Russian translations. Table 3.2 shows Ukrainian terms used in the 1970s that were replaced by Russified terms in the 1980s.[15]

Another example comes from a language historian. In his submissions for publication in academic journals in the mid-1980s, his usages of the terms "чинник" (čynnyk) 'factor' and "царина" (caryna) 'sphere' consistently were replaced by editors with their Latin-based synonyms, "фактор" (factor) and "сфера" (sfera), which are identical to the corresponding Russian terms. With time this scholar said he learned to monitor himself to avoid using the more distinct Ukrainian terms.[16]

During the last few decades of Soviet rule, in both scientific terminology and everyday terms, Russification affected both morphology and grammatical patterning. Some examples provided by Karavans'kyi (1994, 86–92) are reproduced in Table 3.3.

The examples in Table 3.3 illustrate the continued efforts, begun with the linguistic reforms of the 1930s, to diminish the differences between Ukrainian and Russian forms. These efforts were one sided, since there was a concurrent policy of maintenance of Russian purity and, with it, the "high cultural level" of Russian.

The plan to efface ethnolinguistic boundaries was countered by institutional

---

15. Leonid Zalizniak, personal communication, 1995.
16. Yuri Shevchuk, personal communication, 2002.

TABLE 3.3. **Examples of common Russianisms in late Soviet Ukrainian usage (from Karavans'kyi 1994)**

Pre-Soviet Forms	Late Soviet Forms	Standard Russian	English Gloss
колишній	бувший	бывший	late, former
[kolyšn'ij]	[buvšyj]	[byvšij]	
прибутки	доходи	доходы	profits
[prybutky]	[doxody]	[daxody]	
відтак, відтоді	з тих пір	с тех пор	since then
[vidtak, vidtod'i]	[z tyx pir]	[s t'ex por]	
на адресу	за адресою	за адресом	at the address*
[na adresu]	[za adresoju]	[za adr'esom]	
а втім, а проте	тим не менше	тем не менее	nevertheless
[a vt'im, a prote]	[tym ne menše]	[t'em n'e m'en'eje]	

*The original Ukrainian form uses locative case, while the late Soviet and Russian forms use the genitive case.

practices and experiences of discrimination that helped maintain the awareness of the opposition between Ukrainian and Russian. Discriminatory treatment of Ukrainians in the army or in school, which starkly contradicted the official rhetoric of ethnic equality, incited some who were apathetic to start feeling pro-Ukrainian (as related to me in interviews, including in the case of Taras's brother mentioned in chapter 2). Many peasants as well as educated urbanites (who did have access to good Russian education) maintained Ukrainian and had their children learn it for reasons of sentiment or pride. It was their mother tongue, a symbol of their ethnic identity, and, according to them, it would have been wrong or unnatural to give it up. Thus the idea of a Ukrainian language, and linguistic practices that people identified as Ukrainian, were alive, and ready to be resuscitated, when the Soviet Empire fell and Ukraine embarked on the project of developing its independence.

Language Status and Independence

The issue of language status was central in the breakup of the Soviet Union. One of the first legislative moves of each republic toward independence was the declaration of its titular language (the language bearing the same name as the republic) as its official language. In October 1989 the Law on Languages made Ukrainian the official state language of the Ukrainian SSR. The Supreme Soviet of the USSR responded in April 1990 by passing a law declaring Russian the official language of the Soviet Union (Markus and Senkus 1993, 48). Until then, the official language of the USSR had not been overtly designated, even though the de facto dominant language of the Union was Russian and there were laws promoting its use. The 1990 Soviet law making Russian official quickly became irrelevant as, one by one, the republics declared their independence from the USSR.

Ukraine declared its independence in August 1991. After centuries of subjugation to other regimes, ethnic Ukrainians abruptly became the majority in their own nation, and their "peasant language" became a state language. The language law legislated the increased use of Ukrainian in official, educational, and public spheres, with "the goal of fostering the all-around development of the spiritual creative forces of the Ukrainian people, to guarantee its future as a sovereign nation-state" (Prosvita 1991, 3). The Ukrainian Constitution, ratified in 1996 after much debate on the language question, reaffirmed the status of Ukrainian as the sole state language. The law assured the freedom to use other languages, but the study of Ukrainian and its use in specific official contexts became mandatory.

During my fieldwork in Ukraine I could see significant changes toward more widespread Ukrainian usage.[17] People I interviewed in 1992 already felt that the national language was in the process of becoming more prestigious. Many testified that it was rare to hear Ukrainian in the city of Kyiv before the 1990s but that after perestroika things were decidedly different. Especially after the referendum of December 1991, in which the overwhelming majority of citizens voted for independence and chose a president, Ukrainian could be heard more often on the streets of Kyiv and on radio and television.

During the first decade of independence compliance with the language law was uneven and fraught with controversy. Newspaper articles lamented its slow application and criticized establishments that persisted in using Russian (e.g., Anon. Editorial 1, 1995; Bezhbovska 1995). After an initial surge in support for Ukrainian in 1991–92, there was a reversal back to more Russian usage in the cities in 1993 in reaction to worsening economic conditions. I was told of two unrelated instances that occurred in Kyiv in 1993, where people waiting in a line were harassed for speaking Ukrainian and blamed for the economic hardships.[18] In many contexts, especially urban ones, speaking Ukrainian was a marker of Ukrainian patriotism, and some people associated the downfall and instability of the economy with Ukraine's independence. In 1995 a mathematics professor at the Dnipropetrovsk State University told of the uneven progress of introducing Ukrainian instruction: although many classes had begun to be taught in Ukrainian and students were becoming used to instruction in this language, in 1995 many instructors in that eastern city were reverting back to Russian since there seemed to be less impetus to continue in Ukrainian.

---

17. My fieldwork in Ukraine consisted of nine months in 1991–92, twelve months in 1994–95, two weeks in 2000, and four months in 2002.

18. Assya Humesky and Oleksa Bilaniuk, personal communications, 1993.

Sign in the city of Dnipropetrovsk defaced to revert "Donetsk" from Ukrainian (Донецьк) back to the Russian spelling (Донецк) by removing the soft sign.

The tug of war between Ukrainian and Russian usage was evident in official signage (road signs, building names and lettering on official vehicles). Early on in Kyiv, rather than replacing whole signs, where possible only some letters were modified in order to change a word into Ukrainian from Russian as quickly and inexpensively as possible. This made visible the process through which Ukrainian became official, detracting from the normalizing force that institutionalization, such as the presence of the language on signs, can have for a language. The authority backing Ukrainian appeared as poor and superficial as the changes on the signage (these were eventually replaced with new signs). In the western Ukrainian city of Lviv, in contrast, the complete replacement of street signs occurred practically overnight, as one man told me in amazement (since most city works progressed very slowly). In 1992 in Lviv I found cab drivers confused about where to go, searching through lists of the old Soviet names of renamed streets. In eastern Ukraine, in particular, the transformation of signs did not go unchallenged by opponents of Ukrainianization. For example, in 1995 in the central-eastern city of Dnipropetrovsk, on a new sign indicating the road to Donetsk, the paint was scraped off down to metal to remove the soft sign letter (ь). In Ukrainian Donetsk is written "Донецьк" whereas in Russian it is "Донецк," without the soft sign.

The east was not unanimously pro-Russian or pro-Soviet, and graffiti also showed the presence of nationalist sentiment. In 1995, in a Dnipropetrovsk community of towering apartment buildings, the walls around a construction site bore many anti-Russian messages; for example, "Away with the fifth column, out of Ukraine! Suitcase—Train station—Great Russia!" In this statement "Great Russia" was written in Ukrainian orthography but depicted Russian pronunciation, "Велікая Расія," which resulted in a caricature of the Russian language. Another message read, "Away with the Muscovite occupiers of Georgia! And out of Ukraine!" These slogans may not have reflected majority opinions in eastern Ukrainian cities, but their presence and visibility reminded people that times were changing. Ten years earlier such graffiti would have been quickly effaced and the perpetrators severely punished.

There was much resistance to the emergent status of Ukrainian from Russians and Russian speakers who missed the advantage of being native speakers of the dominant language. The introduction of Ukrainian was particularly problematic in Crimea, the traditional vacation destination of the Russian-speaking Soviet elite. After the Ukrainian government bought the rights to the U.S. television series *Santa Barbara* in 1995, this show began to be aired with a Ukrainian-language voice-over translation. Until then, the show had been aired with a Russian translation. The switch to Ukrainian dubbing created an uproar among many Crimean residents who did not know Ukrainian and had no desire to learn it. The imposition of (lowly, rural) Ukrainian into the mouths of (wealthy, powerful) Americans was portrayed by the press as being particularly ridiculous. The decision to air the desirable Western program in Ukrainian was probably strategic, an effort to create more exposure and impetus for people to learn the language, and also reinforce the authority of the independent Ukrainian state. However, as a Russian newspaper article humorously argued, this decision was potentially more dangerous than cutting off electricity or not paying salaries (Frolov 1995). The Crimean Parliament ultimately decided to return to airing a Russian-language version, in the hope of "avoiding the kindling of anti-Ukrainian actions" (quoted in Frolov 1995).[19]

Some Russophones I spoke with explained that they had nothing against a slow increase in the use of Ukrainian since it had every right to exist as a state language, but others were frustrated that opportunities were being closed to them because they did not speak Ukrainian. Knowledge of Ukrainian became particularly necessary for people entering the job market in the media, in education, and in businesses that had dealings with the Ukrainian-speaking diaspora. Ukrainian

---

19. For a reply and criticism of Frolov's belittling stance toward Ukraine and its language, see Polevs'ka 1995. On the cultural politics of the *Santa Barbara* show in Russia, see Anon. Editorial 2, 1995.

handbooks geared to assist Russian speakers appeared on bookstands, and Ukrainian language courses were offered privately and in some workplaces.

In the first years of independence there was much leeway in the implementation of the language law in workplaces. Some schools that had become officially "Ukrainian" continued to (unofficially) provide most instruction in Russian because of the preferences and skills of the teachers. In western Ukraine, where use of Ukrainian otherwise became quickly widespread, I was told that, in a high school and medical school, there was tolerance for older faculty who could not speak Ukrainian well, although the newly hired faced more stringent expectations. Employment in general was no longer guaranteed as it had been in the Soviet system, and the expectation of Ukrainian-language knowledge was problematic for young people who grew up in the 1980s and had not invested in learning it. A good knowledge of Russian, which used to be sufficient, was no longer enough for some jobs.

Not only Russophones but some native speakers of Ukrainian also initially resisted change in the language regime. For example, in Kyiv in 1992, a Ukrainian linguist heard two young saleswomen speaking Ukrainian to each other, but when he addressed one of them in Ukrainian, she answered in Russian and seemed annoyed by his use of Ukrainian. His understanding of the incident was that she preferred not to use Ukrainian with him because she wanted to prove that she was "good enough" to speak Russian.[20] She resisted a change in language statuses that would devalue the Russian linguistic capital she had acquired, which differentiated her from the Ukrainian peasant population. Even a decade after independence, Russian retained the connotations of a prestigious city language for many people. As related by Borys Tarasyuk in 2001 (chapter 2), newcomers to Kyiv would still insist on trying to speak Russian, although not very well, despite encouragement to speak their native Ukrainian.

A belief expressed by cynical nationalists was that when Ukraine's independence seemed economically beneficial for its citizens, more people tended to be positive about the Ukrainian language; when new shortages and difficulties occurred, a more negative attitude toward independence, nationalism, and the Ukrainian language prevailed. According to this logic, the overwhelming support of Ukraine's inhabitants for the independence of the country in 1991, including approximately 50 percent of the ethnic Russians, stemmed from perceptions of the economic exploitation of their republic by the Soviet center. During the final Soviet years, less than a quarter of Ukraine's income remained in the republic. Through the centralized allocation of resources controlled from Moscow, Ukraine only received a fraction of the per capita investment that Russia did:

---

20. Bohdan M. Azhniuk, personal communication, 1992.

for example, per capita expenditure for the development of basic science research was 6.3 rubles in Ukraine and 25.5 rubles in Russia; per capita expenditure on culture was 3.8 rubles in Ukraine and 12.8 rubles in Russia; and the per capita investment in housing was 95 rubles in Ukraine and 145 rubles in Russia (Motyl and Krawchenko 1997, 245). Thus expectations were high for economic improvement once Ukraine's resources were no longer siphoned off, and disillusionment was acute when independence did not lead to immediate material improvements for the masses. In parallel, the initial fervor for embracing Ukrainian language and identity was often replaced by a lack of desire to expend effort to make symbolic (linguistic) changes in one's life. These attitudes are portrayed in a 1990 rock song by western Ukrainian singer Vika, titled "Shame" ("Han'ba"): "You gripe about the purity of the Ukrainian language, but it is all the same to me whether it's sausage [in Ukrainian] or sausage [in Russian], as long as it's available." Vika then goes on to decry this attitude (and others also deemed unworthy), yelling out, "For shame!" The song portrayed opponents of Ukrainianization and language purity as low-minded materialists. This criticism was not only relevant to the 1990s but also historically, since, during the past few centuries, the adoption of Russian by Ukrainians was driven in part by material benefits.

In contrast, those who opposed independence and Ukrainianization ridiculed the prioritization of symbolic matters over practical concerns. Regarding Ukraine's problems, a participant in a Dnipropetrovsk e-mail chat group wrote:

> All that is IMHO [in my humble opinion][21] the result of the construction not of the government but of the "independent state" ["нэзалэжнойи дэржавы" (Ukrainian pronunciation in Russian orthography)], we pay more attention not to economic problems, but to political ones, the transition to Ukrainian language is evidence of that, after all an official [чыновнык (Ukrainian term written in Russian)] who thinks not of *what* to say but of *how* to say it IMHO won't do much, and it is possible to bring up a large number of such examples. And one more thing, stop pondering the question— do Russians want war? and start considering—do Ukrainians want to eat? that in my mind is more important at the moment. (Samoylovich 1995; translated from standard Russian with exceptions noted)

While the electronic posting above belittled attention to form, its author used linguistic resources creatively to bolster his point. The use of the Ukrainian terms for "independent state" and "official," but spelled in Russian, portrayed them as abnormal and not equivalent to their Russian counterparts. The use of the Internet-style English expression "in my humble opinion" as an acronym,

---

21. The English acronym IMHO was used in the original. Abbreviations that have developed in English-language electronic communication constitute another form of symbolic capital, layering both the exclusivity of a knowledge of English and proficiency in electronic communication.

scrutable only to the initiated, also revealed that the author was just as concerned with "how to say things" as to get his message across. The form was part of his effort to portray himself as sophisticated so as to lend credence to his statement.

Transparency of form is only possible when it is habitual and "normal." Independence and the language law of Ukraine destabilized the preexisting linguistic norms, making people more aware of language. It was to the advantage of those who would rather maintain the Russian-dominant status quo to deflect this awareness of language, to maintain the "normalcy" and transparency of Russian dominance. And yet, as the statement above showed, the allure of the prestige of English "Internetese" was also disrupting the hegemony of Russian.

In my observations of everyday life I found that in codeswitching people negotiated their desires for solidarity and status, sometimes favoring Russian, sometimes Ukrainian. The tug of forces shaping linguistic values and language use was vividly illustrated in an interaction I observed in 1991 on the main road between Kyiv and Kharkiv, which passes through the countryside (Bilaniuk 1993). Peasants commonly sell produce along the side of the road, and urbanites often plan to shop along the way if they travel. My friends, a married couple, stopped and got out of the car to buy some red peppers displayed on a table outside the fence of a house by the road. An old woman came out of the house and first addressed the couple in a nonstandard mixed Russian-Ukrainian language. Then, when she heard them speaking in Ukrainian with me, she switched to Ukrainian, which was close to standard, and which she spoke with greater ease. When she asked if we were from Kyiv, we answered that we were, and she started telling us about her daughter who lives in Kyiv (still speaking Ukrainian). Then, in deciding whether to buy, the man and woman exchanged a few words with each other in Russian. Automatically the woman also reverted to her more Russian speech.

In choosing which "voice" to use in communicating with us, the pepper seller used cues to judge our identity, and thus our language attitudes. By using Russian more, her first impetus may have been to use the most widely accessible code or to proclaim her respectability and knowledge or to show willingness to identify with us, the city folk, to make a more comfortable setting for selling. When she heard us speak Ukrainian, she reverted to it, trying to identify with us further by telling of her daughter in Kyiv. Then the couple consulted with each other in Russian, in a way that showed it was the more usual language for them. Just as they had at first spoken Ukrainian to identify with her or make it easier for her, likewise she was determined to speak like them, the more prestigious Russian speakers from the city. In this interaction, competing ideologies and histories were enacted in the pepper seller's choice of language, as she strove to choose the most fitting way to speak.

A similar case that a friend related to me occurred at a market in Kyiv in 1992. Produce markets in the city are interfaces between urban and rural: the urban shoppers bargain with sellers commuting in from villages. The woman who was shopping asked a seller, in Russian, the price of his meat. "По сколько?" 'How much?' When he told her the price (meat had become notoriously expensive), she exclaimed, in Ukrainian, "Ой Господи!" 'Oh Lord!', which only differs from Russian phonetically. The seller answered in Ukrainian, that if it's [oj hospody] then he'll sell the meat to her for a lower price. The difference between Ukrainian [oj hospody] and Russian [oj gospəd'i] was enough to evoke Ukrainian solidarity, leading him to give her an economic advantage (even though it was still expensive for her). This move increased the symbolic value of Ukrainian by translating it into a material benefit, and reinforced its "covert prestige." Such ethnic solidarity was rarely made explicit, but it may not have been an unusual occurrence. As a few of my Russian-speaking interviewees told me in 1992, they only used Ukrainian at the market since they believed that speaking Ukrainian might make Ukrainian-speaking sellers more favorably disposed to them. Normally they would be embarrassed to try to speak Ukrainian, feeling that they speak it incorrectly or with an accent, but in the context of the "non–high culture" market, speaking nonstandard Ukrainian could bring symbolic and material benefits. On the one hand, this reinforced the rural connotations of Ukrainian, but, on the other, the power of Ukrainian could increase as more urbanites recognized the value of using it. The farmers' marketplace was thus literally an alternative linguist marketplace, where values of linguistic forms were different than elsewhere in society.

The choice between languages was not always materially driven but depended on a person's mood and linguistic skills and the context. While developments were not unilinear, from the time of independence more people gradually acquired and used Ukrainian, and more public contexts became appropriate for Ukrainian usage. Overall the status of Ukrainian rose. This general trend varied greatly in different regions and tended to be polarized by people's ethnic allegiance.

More than a decade after independence, in many regions Ukrainian still suffered the limitations of a minority language, low status and poor institutionalization, while the dominance of Russian persisted. Efforts to elevate Ukrainian were bolstered by the fact that, in the USSR, Ukraine had the largest Academy of Sciences outside Moscow. However, many administrators and teachers were unprepared to work in Ukrainian, and few resources were available to help them learn it. The transition was complicated by the stigmatization of the "imperfect" Russian influenced Ukrainian   an almost inevitable intermediate stage for Russophones. Purism prevailed in the semiotic turmoil, as people became much more aware of language use and negotiated the worth of different language forms.

Once the consistent policies of Russification were brought to light after independence, the question arose of whether the linguistic engineering of the Soviet era should be reversed. The forms institutionalized during the Soviet period had become habitual after prolonged exposure, and, for most people living in Ukraine, relearning the "non-Russified" forms would require conscious self-monitoring. Western Ukrainians were quicker to resuscitate pre-Soviet forms, but even in Western Ukraine the newer forms had become deeply rooted in everyday practices.

Some saw the proposed reverse engineering as a return to "true" Ukrainian forms, while others saw it as misguided, just like the Soviet interventions. At the root of these viewpoints were competing ideologies of language: those pushing for linguistic reforms believed that there was an authentic essence that could be excavated and revived from history, whereas those preferring the status quo argued for the need to support the language that was currently alive. These opposing viewpoints did not correspond to a simple choice between two sets of linguistic rules. There existed many layers of contemporary and historical forms of Ukrainian and Russian, replete with regional variations, mixtures, and jargons. On the basis of beliefs that had been instilled through their upbringing and life experiences, people worked hard to construct this diverse mass of practices into opposed poles.

The post-Soviet struggles over symbolic (historical, linguistic, cultural) values echoed the struggles that took place at the inception of Soviet power. Early Soviet debates in the 1920s and 1930s centered around the role of language as a tool of social engineering and central political control according to various interpretations of Marx's "scientific" theory of historical social development (Smith 1998). After independence in the 1990s the need for correction of linguistic problems (historical injustices, impurities) was again a key issue, but with debates focused on language in theories of national historical legitimacy. In both periods of social turbulence—namely, the inception and the demise of the Soviet system— definitions of linguistic and historical values, which were key to the legitimation of social and political power, were contested.

In the case of Ukrainian after independence, what needed correction was an array of historical shortcomings: the lack of political unity of a Ukrainian state during long historical periods, domination by neighboring states and their languages, suppression of the use of Ukrainian, and concerted manipulation of Ukrainian standards to make them closer to Russian. At issue was not just the struggle of Ukrainian versus Russian (or other languages) but linguistic purity and the maintenance of boundaries between languages (as chapter 4 explores in greater depth). All these historical factors contributed to an ideological shortcoming: a sense of doubt and insecurity regarding the legitimacy of independent Ukraine and the Ukrainian language. The latter was the greatest obstacle to establishing the hegemony of Ukrainian, which required a commonsense belief in the high value of this language. Through correction of the language (both its forms and spheres of use), many Ukrainian activists sought to establish the symbolic value of Ukrainian and dissociate it from low connotations. But historical events could be interpreted in various ways, with different implications for the hierarchy of symbolic values. Had Ukrainianization been a period of "natural" or "artificial" linguistic development? Was Russification a violent desecration of Ukrainian, or was it the beneficial coming together of kindred peoples? How exactly were Ukrainian and Russian to continue their coexistence in the newly independent Ukraine? A decade after independence these questions were still debated. Their answers were not limited to language policy but were also tied to ideologies of social differentiation.

4 Surzhyk

A History of Linguistic Transgressions

*But in truth, I was also afraid of the man in the field. I had
never talked to people like that, poor farming people, and similar to most people from Odessa, I speak a fusion of Russian and
Ukrainian, and they spoke only Ukrainian, and while Russian
and Ukrainian sound so similar, people who speak only Ukrainian sometimes hate people who speak a fusion of Russian and
Ukrainian, because people who speak a fusion of Russian and
Ukrainian come from the cities and think they are superior to
people who speak only Ukrainian, who often come from the
fields. We think that because we are superior, but that is for
another story.*

—JONATHAN SAFRAN FOER, *EVERYTHING
IS ILLUMINATED*

Sighting Surzhyk

Cultural politics constructs a clear boundary between Ukrainian and Russian,
but, in practice, there are many forms of talk that mix features of these two related
languages.[1] The transgression of the conceptual divide between categories of language stirs anxieties that are quelled by labeling linguistic hybrids as despicable,

---

1. Jonathan Safran Foer's best-selling novel *Everything Is Illuminated,* from which the epigraph to this chapter is taken, tells of a young Jewish man from the United States who has
come to Ukraine to look for connections to his family's past and is guided by a young Ukrainian translator from Odesa. The epigraph is in the voice of the translator, whose accounts are
written in a version of English transgressing standards, described as a "sublimely butchered
English" on the book jacket. The translator's English could itself be called a surzhyk.

absurd, unworthy of notice, or laughable. Anxieties over linguistic impurities mirror anxieties over other forms of pollution: as Mary Douglas (1966, 39) argued, "Any given system of classification must give rise to anomalies, and any given culture must confront events which seem to defy its assumptions. [...] A rule of avoiding anomalous things affirms and strengthens the definitions to which they do not conform." Language that is perceived as mixed is often referred to as "not language at all." Through such criticisms the transgressions are disarmed and the categories defended. But the phenomenon of mixed languages in Ukraine has been persistent, meriting its own label: surzhyk. Surzhyk conceptually unites various kinds of language mixing, serving as the antithesis to the concept of linguistic purity. Purity and surzhyk thus define each other. Surzhyk started as an informal term and now figures prominently in public discourse, a key player in the post-independence struggle over language values.[2]

The term "surzhyk" originally meant a mixture of wheat and rye flour, which was considered lower grade than pure wheat flour (Podvesko 1962). The term has also carried other etymological connotations. Hrinchenko's (1909) dictionary defined the term as "1) mixed grains or flour made thereof; 2) a person of mixed race: 'This is *surzhyk:* the father was a gypsy, the mother a girl from our village.'" The second definition brings up the concept of miscegenation and the undesirability of racial mixing, a connotation that was resuscitated in at least one post-independence author's discussion of the evils of linguistic surzhyk (Stavyts'ka 2001, 20). I did not encounter the term used in this way anywhere else during my fieldwork. The 1978 eleven volume dictionary of Ukrainian limited its definition to language, defining "surzhyk" as "elements of two or more languages, united artificially, not following the norms of literary language, impure language" (*Slovnyk* 1978, 854).

In the post-Soviet period "surzhyk" has been predominantly used to mean a mixture of languages, retraining the connotation that a mixture is degraded when compared to something pure. An analogous phenomenon exists in Belarus: *trasianka*, originally meaning a mixture of hay and straw, now refers to mixtures of the Belarusian and Russian languages (Woolhiser 2001). The single label in each case creates a unit of "impure language" in opposition to standard "ideal" language. I also heard the term "surzhyk" used metaphorically to express disapproval for nonlinguistic mixtures: for example, mirrored facades built onto old-style buildings, common in post-Soviet Kyiv, were referred to as an "architectural surzhyk" because these additions destroyed the integrity of the traditional style.[3]

There has been little linguistic work to determine the actual parameters of

---

2. See Bilaniuk 1997b, 12–18; 2004, for further discussions of this chapter's topic.
3. Ol'ha Kocherga, personal communication, 2000.

Majdan Nezalezhnosti 'Independence Square' in the center of Kyiv: the remodeling of the square resulted in a cacophonous blend of styles that some call an "architectural surzhyk." Photographed in 2002, with the author's five-year-old daughter, Laska, flanked by friends in the forefront.

surzhyk, such as its geographic regularity or variability.[4] Any perceived mixing of different languages may merit the label, and perceptions vary depending on individuals' linguistic backgrounds. The term can refer to a high degree of code-switching by bilinguals or to a linguistic code in which the elements of the two languages are inextricably fused. Thus the definition of "surzhyk" as a whole remains primarily ideological, although we can list the influences and forms that fall under this umbrella term, as I do later in this chapter.

I first encountered the term "surzhyk" in Ukraine in 1991. I was soon intrigued by the frequency of its invocation and its place at the crux of language attitudes. Independence had brought with it a heightened concern for correctness and authenticity, and surzhyk, the embodiment of impurity and baseness, became a central trope in Ukrainian discourse. The deployment of the label "surzhyk" in evaluating language was key in processes of correction and in struggles over social status.

---

4. Flier (2000, 2002) analyzes structural rules underlying language mixing based on samples of surzhyk used in literary works and in the taped speech of politicians. There have been no linguistic field studies to date of surzhyk in Ukraine.

When I told people, in the early 1990s, that I was interested in studying the phenomenon of surzhyk, they were usually surprised. Some found it funny—typical of the bizarre practices of foreigners. Others found it threatening; by taking surzhyk seriously as a researcher I was somehow legitimizing it, irresponsibly expending effort on it when such effort could more constructively be directed toward supporting the development of standard language skills, particularly in Ukrainian where these skills were seen to be most lacking. Some even thought that I wanted to promote surzhyk, and thereby continue to undermine Ukrainian as was done during Soviet times.[5] Surzhyk was viewed as threatening because it was the antithesis of correctness in Ukrainian and, by extension, of Ukrainianness. While the statuses of Ukrainian, Russian, and surzhyk were in flux, the emergence of discourse defining surzhyk as low and unacceptable was key in dissociating Ukrainian from low status and moving it to a position of prestige.

The problematic nature of surzhyk is rooted in a history of inequality of interethnic and interlinguistic relations. Whereas the previous chapter examined the history of Ukrainian as an idealized category, in tension with other idealized categories such as Russian and Polish, this chapter takes another look at history, focusing on the blurred boundaries of linguistic categories. The communicative processes through which surzhyk was defined, as forms of talk were construed as being "pure/correct" or "impure," reveal the forces of heteroglossia at play in language. An examination of the areas in which the division between "Ukrainian" and "Russian" was blurred reveals the processes defining meanings, language units, and identities, and their symbolic power.

The History of Purism and Mixed Languages in Ukraine

Issues of linguistic purity and language mixing have long been concerns in Ukraine, and they have regained importance in the political turmoil of nation building after the fall of the USSR (Wexler 1974). Language mixing can be discerned in written works predating the development of the vernacular-based Modern Ukrainian standard, as exemplified in the literary and philosophical works of Hryhorii Skovoroda (1722–1794). Skovoroda's language is characterized as traditional "bookish language" (книжня мова) that was in use until the end of the eighteenth century, a mixture of Old Church Slavonic, and Ukrainian and Russian vernaculars. Skovoroda also added his own word coinages, mixing Russian

---

5. The latter reaction is reminiscent of attitudes in the United States to the proposed legislation regarding African American English/Ebonics in California in the late 1990s, where many assumed that the nonstandard language would be taught in place of standard English, thereby holding back African Americans, or that it could be a means of promoting a separatist black nationalist ideology (Holmes 1996; Pullum 1997).

and Ukrainian morphemes and also borrowing from Latin and Greek.[6] The specifics of Skovoroda's language mixing varied during his lifetime and also depended on the genre he was writing in (Derkach 1972; Shynkaruk and Ivanio 1973). The poet Taras Shevchenko later characterized Skovoroda's language as a *vinegret*—a finely chopped mixed salad—and believed that Skovoroda's success was limited because he did not use the vernacular language of his people (Ostrianyn, Popov, and Tabachnykov 1961).

Prior to its incorporation into the Russian Empire, the Ukrainian cultural elite of the seventeenth century was generally competent in four or five languages, and this plurilingualism was key in shaping the emerging modern Ukrainian literary language (Pachlovska 1998, 103). In addition to the languages of neighboring regimes, Latin was widely used in academia. Latin was taught at the Mohyla Academy in Kyiv, and students were even expected to use it with one another outside the school. Children of villagers also had exposure to Latin and Greek in their schooling (Pachlovska 1998, 102). The writer Ivan Kotliarevs'kyi (1769–1838) portrayed the influence of Latin in a comical Ukrainian-Latin surzhyk mixture in passages of his *Eneïda* (*Aeneid*):

> *Transliteration from Ukrainian:*
> "Eneus noster magnus panus, i slavnyj trojanorum kn'az', Šmyhav po morju, jak cyhanus, Adte o reks! Pryslav nunk nas"; "Peccatum robyš, frater mylyj . . ."
> *English translation (with Latin elements untranslated):*
> "Eneus noster magnus lordus, and glorious Trojanorum prince, you have zig-zagged the seas like a gypsyus, adte o rex, he has nunc sent us"; "You are committing a peccatum, dear frater . . ."[7]

Aside from his humorous portrayal of Latin-Ukrainian, Kotliarevs'kyi's *Eneïda* is considered the first literary work to be written in Ukrainian vernacular, marking the beginning of the development of the Modern Ukrainian literary language. Elsewhere Kotliarevs'kyi also portrayed characters using the mixed Russian-Ukrainian administrative language of the late eighteenth and early nineteenth centuries. Examples are the characters Voznyj and Fyntyk in the play *Natalka Poltavka*, who speak the bureaucratic surzhyk of provincial administrators of the time, whereas the other characters speak the pure, "virginal," "natural" Ukrainian vernacular (Strikha 1997, 136, Pachlovska 1998, 508). The surzhyk of the bureaucrats is a result of their mixing their native Ukrainian with Russian, the language behind their authority. The villagers, as represented in this play,

---

6. At the time philosophy was taught only in Latin at the Kyiv-Mohyla Academy, and Skovoroda knew this language well, along with Ancient Greek.

7. These selections are highlighted by Pachlovska (1998, 507); I take direction from her Italian translation in my English translation.

may have recognized the authority of the administrators but they did not try to imitate their language, their own village standards prevailing instead. Their contact with Russian as a language of power was still too limited.

The "natural, pure" Ukrainian of Kotliarevs'kyi's Natalka, maintained in Ukrainian villages, was disrupted by the end of the nineteenth century by the advent of modernity (Strikha 1997, 136). The development of industries such as sugar refineries, the train system, and obligatory military service all greatly increased villagers' contacts with Russian-speaking administrators, industrialists, police, and army officers. Thus the relative linguistic purity of Ukrainian in most villages no longer existed by around 1900, since village life came into regular contact with the Russian-dominated state.[8]

Increased contact with the tsarist state led villagers to try to speak Russian and, owing to their incomplete knowledge of Russian, to mix languages. The motivation for this varied. Russian was the language of the officials in power, including tsarist administrators and military commanders. The accommodation of Ukrainian speakers to Russian would facilitate their ability to communicate and would also curry favor with their superiors according to the logic of linguistic accommodation, in which modifying one's language to be closer to the language of one's addressee signals positive intentions (Giles, Bourhis, and Taylor 1977). Russian also gave access to upward social mobility through access to jobs in the state system.

With the increased presence of the Russophone tsarist regime, the status of Ukrainian became correspondingly low, iconic of uneducated villagers. Peasants "were often ashamed of speaking Ukrainian and, in conversations with persons of the upper classes, inserted as many Russian words as they could" (Shevelov 1989, 9). According to the memoirs of a prominent Ukrainian civic leader of that time, in the late 1800s village boys who came to study in the city were ashamed of their native Ukrainian language and tried to conceal their knowledge of it, hoping to get rid of the stigma of *mužyctvo*—of being "village hicks"—as quickly as possible (Chykalenko 1955, 86–87).

The impetus for Ukrainians to use Russian existed not only in the city and when among Russians but also became a factor in interactions among Ukrainian peasants. In choosing among linguistic forms with one another, villagers faced an

---

8. Industrialization and greater interaction with the Russian tsarist state increased Russian Ukrainian linguistic influences, but the purity of language in villages is relative since purity is always a social construct. In this case the use of the term "purity" refers to the condition of little exposure to another language system backed by greater state power. There would always have been some social and generational linguistic variation within villages, and exposure to the linguistic differences of neighboring villages and travelers. I distinguish this kind of linguistic variation from the colonizing linguistic influence of a state.

internal struggle between the state-backed symbolic power of Russian and the value of Ukrainian as a language of in-group solidarity.[9] The negative value of Russian as an imposed outsider's language was counterbalanced by the negative connotations of Ukrainian as a backward village language.

The great poet Taras Shevchenko (1814–1861) was not immune himself to pressures that led him to mix languages. The correspondence between Shevchenko and his brother, Mykola, in 1839–40 illustrates these forces at play. In his short letter of November 15, 1839, from St. Petersburg to Mykola in Ukraine, Taras reiterated three times his plea for his brother to write back to him in their own Ukrainian language and not "*po-moskovs'ky*"—in the Muscovite, Russian language. Taras wrote that he yearned to hear a "dear, native word"—*ridne slovo*—from his brother. Taras's requests indicated that Mykola had not written in Ukrainian previously, and nor had he complied again despite his brother's fervent pleas. In the next letter of March 2, 1840, Taras scolded his brother:

Я твого письма не второпаю, чортзна по-якому ти його скомпонував, ні по-нашому, ні по-московському—ні се ні те, а я ще тебе просив, щоб ти писав по-своєму, щоб я хоч з твоїм письмом побалакав на чужій стороні язиком людським.

Ja tvoho pys'ma ne vtoropaju, čortzna po-jakomu ty joho skomponuvav, ni po-našomu, ni po-moskovs'komu—ni se ni te, a ja šče tebe prosyv, ščob ty pysav po-svojemu, ščob ja xoč z tvojim pys'mom pobalakav na čužij storoni jazykom l'uds'kym.

I can't understand it, the devil knows what language you composed it in, neither in our language, nor in Muscovite language—neither this nor that, and I had even beseeched you, that you write in your own language, so that at least through your letter I could have a chat in a human language in this foreign land.

Despite Shevchenko's desire for Ukrainian, he included quite a few Russianisms in his own letters to his brother, so that a reader today could even label some passages as surzhyk. But because the Ukrainian language was not yet standardized, it is not really appropriate to call this language surzhyk. Nevertheless, given that the language Shevchenko used in his literary works was used as a basis for defining the standard and still today is considered exemplary Ukrainian, the different quality of the language in his letters to his brother is notable, and, moreover, also differs from the language of his letters to other people. In the excerpt above, the terms for "letter" (*pys'mo*) and "language [genitive case]" (*jazykom*) are Russianisms. The following passages from his November 15, 1839, letter provide more examples. I have italicized nonstandard forms that would be seen as

---

9. On the positive pressures for speakers to use local nonstandard varieties, see Trudgill 1974 and Woolard 1985.

Russian-influenced according to the contemporary Ukrainian standard, although some of these could be interpreted as dialectisms that happen to be similar to Russian:

Твого лиха я не *возьму* на себе, а свого тобі не *оддам*. Так що ж з тих *писем?* Папір *збавлять* та й годі. Воно, бач, і так і не так, а все таки *лучше*, коли *получиш*, прочитаєш хоч одно слово рідне. [. . .] Ще *письмо, которе найдеш* у моєму *письмі* *запечатане, оддай* Івану Степановичу Димовському і поклонись йому *од* мене.

Tvoho lykha ja ne *voz'mu* na sebe, a svoho tobi ne *oddam*. Tak ščo ž tyx *pysem?* Papir *zbavl'at'* ta j hodi. Vono, bach, i tak i ne tak, a vse taky *lučše*, koly *polučyš*, pročytaješ xoč odno slovo ridne. [. . .] Šče *pys'mo, kotore najdeš* u mojemu *pys'mi zapečatane, oddaj* Ivanu Stepanovyču Dymovs'komu i poklonys' jomu *od* mene.

I will not *take* your misfortune upon myself, and I will not *give* you mine. So what of those *letters?* Enough *wasting* paper. It is, you see, neither this nor that, but it is after all *better* when you *receive* and read at least one native word. [. . .] Also the *letter that* you *find* *sealed* inside my *letter, pass on* to Ivan Stepanovyč Dymovs'kyj and bow to him *from* me. (Shevchenko 1964, 10)

Such mixed language is not common in Taras Shevchenko's writing, but it is evidence that at least occasionally something drew Taras to stray from the "purer" Ukrainian that was the hallmark of most of his oeuvre. We cannot know whether Taras purposely chose to use language that included more Russianisms when writing to his brother nor to what extent the language mixing was inadvertent. Given Mykola's desire to try to write in Russian, Taras's mixing may have been linguistic accommodation, reflecting a desire to be closer to his brother by using similar language, using Russified forms that his brother likely used as well.[10] Mykola was not unusual in his desire to write to his brother in Russian. Taras had recently gained his freedom from serfdom and was living in the Russian cultural center of St. Petersburg. The associations of Russian with urban high culture, as opposed to lowly rural Ukrainian culture, were clear. Thus even between close kin we see the play of forces that led Ukrainians to mix languages.[11]

A literary work that offers us evidence of the social politics of mixed language is Staryts'kyi's 1883 play, "За двома зайцями" 'After two hares', in which a rich Ukrainian peasant family tries to present itself as more cultured and pres-

10. For a more detailed discussion of factors motivating linguistic accommodation, see Giles et al. 1977 and Winford 2003, 119–124.

11. The dynamics between Taras Shevchenko and his brother, Mykola, are reminiscent of the situation described by Mr. Borys Tarasyuk in chapter 2. Despite Mr. Tarasyuk's insistence that he preferred Ukrainian, his relative from the village kept attempting to use Russian, even though he knew it poorly.

Statue of the surzhyk-speaking characters Pronia and Holokhvostov from Staryts'kyi's 1883 play "За двома зайцями" 'After two hares,' erected in the late 1990s in downtown Kyiv.

tigious by using Russian words, resulting in a mixed nonstandard language. Staryts'kyi reworked a story originally written by Nechui-Levyts'kyi in 1875, adding the critical element of surzhyk to the text. This play remains an icon of surzhyk in Ukrainian popular culture to this day. A bronze statue of the two main surzhyk-speaking characters, Pronia and Holokhvostov, was erected in the late 1990s in central Kyiv right next to the Andriïvs'ka Church. Historically this location was a marginal zone, on the edge of "upper" central Kyiv, just above the physically and culturally "lower" Podil.[12] An updated version of the play was produced

---

12. My thanks to Marko Pavlyshyn for pointing this out.

in Kyiv in 2002, further testifying to its contemporary resonance. In the updated 2002 version the story line was the same as in the 1883 original, but the costumes, set, and some of the language were redesigned to portray post-Soviet urban peasants and nouveau riche "New Ukrainians," complete with glittery imported T-shirts, cell phones, and flashy suits.

The key character in the story of *After Two Hares* is the surzhyk-speaking son of a recently urbanized peasant, a nouveau riche who has lost almost all the money he inherited from his father. He tries to display the symbolic goods of prestige (dressing in fancy clothes and speaking mixed Russian-Ukrainian, with some French words thrown in), but his attempt at prestige ultimately fails miserably. Many people initially fall for his act: one character says admiringly of the surzhyk-speaking pseudo-gentleman, "He speaks such learned words that you can't even understand a thing" (Staryts'kyi 1945, 11). The tensions between the values of Ukrainian and Russian are brought forth in the name of the male protagonist: Holoxvostov, which means "naked tail" in Ukrainian.[13] The young man insists that he is "Holoxvastov" or "Halaxvastov," thus attempting to mask the embarrassingly lowly meaning of his name with Russian phonology (a misplaced *akanie* according to which unstressed [o] is pronounced /a/). But, in the end, he is revealed for the poor two-timing poser that he is. He wins neither of the two girls he sought to marry: neither the poor beautiful Ukrainian-speaking village girl nor the rich unattractive surzhyk-speaking city girl (whose parents are urbanized peasants). The play clearly portrays surzhyk negatively and treats the desire to be something you are not as misguided.

Social pressures for Ukrainians to use Russian led to language mixing, but variations in language that blur linguistic boundaries also existed as a result of incomplete standardization and competing norms before the standard was established. Even after Taras Shevchenko's literary works appeared as a paradigm for a vernacular-based literary Ukrainian, western Ukrainians continued to use dialectical westernisms. Also, in the second half of the nineteenth century in western Ukraine the Russophile movement developed the *jazyčije* language to foster closeness with eastern Slavic languages in the context of Austro-Hungarian domination. Jazyčije was a mixture of local vernacular Ukrainian, Russian, Old Ukrainian, Old Church Slavonic, and Polish elements (URE 1964, 460).[14] One

---

13. Such humorous surnames were not unusual in Ukraine, originating in Cossack naming traditions. Many people with more embarrassing surnames like "Durak" (idiot) have changed them by now, but some, such as "Netudykhata" (home is not that way) have retained them.

14. The Russophile (also called "Moscophile") movement and the *jazyčije* language could be celebrated as additional evidence of the desire for unity among Ukrainians and Russians, but the entries for these terms in the *Ukrainian Soviet Encyclopedia* of 1962 (vol. 9) and 1964 (vol. 16) downplay this interpretation. These entries reveal the strength of Ukrainian purist ideology during the relative easing of restrictions on non-Russian cultural developments during the 1960s. The entries describe the Moscophile movement negatively as attempting to prop-

well-known writer who used this language in his early works and letters to Russophile editors was Ivan Franko. His letter of July 3, 1875, to Vasyl' Davydjak, who worked on the journal *Druh,* illustrates the linguistic syncretism of jazyčije. In the letter Franko argued that his Galician usages should be legitimate and not edited out (Shchurat 1956, 48; orthography of original retained, some key Russianisms are italicized out of the many non-standard elements, and translation into contemporary standard Ukrainian is provided for comparison):

Franko's writing: А тепер *еще* дещо *о* украïньск*их* форм*ах*, котрі міні закидуєте. Не знаю, які там у Вас в Львові *мнінія взглядом* руского *язика.* Міні здаєся, що форми граматичні, чи то украïньскі, чи то галицкі, то вспільне добро цілого руского народа, вспільний скарб книжного *язика. Различіє* їх в тім, що коли украïньске *нарічіє* любить на кінци форми скорочувати, наше задержує їх в повнішім, звучнішім виді.

[A teper *ješčo* deščo *o* ukrajin'sk*yx* form*ax*, kotri mini zakydujete. Ne znaju, jaki tam u vas v L'vovi *mninija vzhl'adom* ruskoho *jazyka.* Mini zdajes'a, ščo formy hramatyčni, čy to ukrajin'ski, čy to halycki, to vspil'ne dobro ciloho ruskoho naroda, vspil'nyj skarb knyžnoho *jazyka. Razlyčije* jix v tim, ščo koly ukrajin'ske *naričije* l'ubyt' na kintsy formy skoročuvaty, naše zaderžuje jix v povnišim, zvučnišim, vydi.]

Standard Ukrainian: А тепер *ще* дещо *про* украïнські форм*и*, котрі мені закидуєте. Не знаю, які там у Вас в Львові *думки щодо* руської *мови.* Мені здається, що форми граматичні, чи то украïнські, чи то галицькі, то спільне добро цілого руського народу, спільний скарб книжньоï *мови. Різниця* їх в тім, що коли украïнське *мовлення* любить на кінці форми скорочувати, наше задержує їх в повнішім, звучнішім виді.

[A teper *šče* deščo *pro* ukrajins'k*i* form*y*, kotri meni zakydujete. Ne znaju, jaki tam u vas v L'vovi *dumky ščodo* rus'koji *movy.* Meni zdajet's'a, ščo formy hramatyčni, čy to ukrajins'ki, čy to halyc'ki, to spil'ne dobro ciloho rus'koho narodu, spil'nyj skarb knyžn'oji *movy. Riznyc'a* jix v tim, ščo koly ukrajins'ke *movlenn'a* l'ubyt' na kinci formy skoročuvaty, naše zaderžuje jix v povnišim, zvučnišim, vydi.]

English: And now *still* something *about*[15] the Ukrainian forms that you impose on me. I don't know what your *opinions* are in Lviv *regarding* the ruskyj[16] *language.* It seems to

---

agate imperialist tsarist ideology, and *jazyčije* as the "artificial" and "haphazard" mixing, and "crippling," of language.

15. The original jazyčije and standard Ukrainian use a different preposition meaning "about," which requires different case endings on "Ukrainian forms," as indicated by italics in the original and transliterated texts.

16. I leave *ruskyj* untranslated, because it is not clear whether Franko meant Ruthenian, pan-east-Slavic, or some other definition. This passage implies that central-eastern Ukrainian as well as Galician (western) Ukrainian both fall into this category.

me that the forms are grammatical, whether they be Ukrainian or Galician, that is the common wealth of the whole ruskyj people, the common treasure of the book *language.* The *difference* is in the fact that where the Ukrainian *speech* likes to shorten forms at the end of words, ours [western Ukrainian Galician] retains them in their fuller, enunciated form.

Franko later abandoned the jazyčije language and embraced the vernacular-based Ukrainian that was becoming standard, although, true to the argument he made in the excerpted letter above, he retained many features of his western dialect in his writing.

During the late nineteenth and early twentieth centuries scholars developed a general consensus about what is standard Ukrainian. This was codified in dictionaries and grammars, but their distribution and institutionalization was limited and some aspects were disputed. This resulted in variation in the language of publications and other public uses of language. Kyiv editors accused the newspapers in Lviv of mixing the words and structures of other languages into Ukrainian; meanwhile, the Lviv editors criticized Kyiv papers for using peasant language rather than more refined literary forms (Shevelov 1989, 40, citing Chykalenko archives). Through these criticisms of each other, regional publishers vied for control over the definition of the authoritative, legitimate language. Meanwhile, the uneven language of Ukrainian publications, full of Russian and Polish calques, provided material for jokes deriding the Ukrainian language (Shevelov 1989, 78, 85).

In addition to looking toward literature for evidence of the historical sociology of language use, it is useful to consider the literary functions of different varieties of language, surzhyk in particular. In Staryts'kyi's (1883) *After Two Hares* surzhyk was clearly used as a reflection of the falsity and shallowness of the characters who spoke it. The use of surzhyk also made the moral and social shortcomings of the characters humorous. In the 1930s writer Ostap Vyshnia (1889–1956) also used surzhyk as a vehicle for humor and social satire. Other writers like Khvyliovyi (1893–1933) and Vynnychenko (1880–1951) used surzhyk to achieve realism. However, most authors adhered to standard Ukrainian: their writing was an effort to protect the threatened existence of this language, and the "degraded" mixed surzhyk was to be avoided as the unfortunate evidence of the reality of the threat from Russian (Strikha 1997, 139).[17]

A later, well-known example of surzhyk used in performance, still frequently mentioned in Ukraine today, is Tarapun'ka, of the Štepsel' and Tarapun'ka pair, a "Laurel and Hardy"–type pair of comedians who performed in the 1950s, 1960s, and 1970s. In their skits tall Tarapun'ka played a devious surzhyk-speaking vil-

---

17. Disagreements over the advisability and implications of the use of surzhyk in literature and performance persisted after the fall of Soviet power, as is discussed further in chapter 5.

lage hick, in contrast to the short Štepsel', a Russian-speaking urban Ukrainian Jew whose expressions were more simple and direct. While Tarapun'ka was the "lower-cultured" of the two, he nevertheless sometimes got the upper hand in wit.[18]

Outside the works of Ukrainian writers, a stereotype emerged in Soviet-era popular culture of the *xoxol*-Ukrainian, an uncultured oaf.[19] Russian writers and cinematographers who often knew little Ukrainian language or culture used stereotypical markers of Ukrainianness (linguistic and other kinds) to symbolize cultural lowness, producing their own surzhyk in the process. In many Soviet movies the Ukrainian was a slow, dim-witted, rural simpleton, much like the figure of the Southerner in old American movies. Alternatively the Ukrainian character was the enemy of the working class. Ukrainianness and surzhyk (as a marker of Ukrainian for a Russian-speaking audience) were depicted as laughable, low, or politically dangerous (Strikha 1997, 140).

Soviet academic works also treated Ukrainian as less valuable than Russian. The Russian language, like the Russian people, was "first among equals." Accordingly "bilingualism" became a catchphrase for Russification. In 1992, disturbed by my assertion that I was interested in bilingualism, linguists in Lviv showed me a succession of published studies which revealed that, through time, Soviet linguistic publications on bilingualism became ever more clearly geared to promote good knowledge of the Russian language, and deviations from standard Russian were only identified in order to be fixed. In contrast, deviations from standard Ukrainian that brought it closer to Russian were not officially problematic, in that they were in line with the ultimate Soviet prognosis that national languages would eventually be dispensed with. Ideally the languages were to die out without institutional intervention. However, as the Lviv linguists demonstrated, policies of bilingualism were a mask for systematic intervention designed to promote standard Russian and efface the distinctiveness of other languages.

An exception to the overall trend of academic works promoting Russian above other languages is exemplified in Chizhikova's 1968 ethnographic study of villages in northeastern Ukraine. This study stands out in its even-handed documentation of mixtures of linguistic and cultural practices, and how these were influenced by the complex histories of settlement by different ethnic groups. Because of settlement patterns, the northeast border between Ukraine and Russia generally shows a sharper break between dialects than do the northern or western borders of Ukraine.[20] According to Chizhikova, villages in the northeastern

---

18. My thanks to Volodymyr Dibrova for detailed information on Tarapun'ka and Štepsel'.

19. *Xoxol* (plural *xoxly*) is a term for an ethnic Ukrainian person that is usually (but not always) derogatory. Etymologically it refers to the lock of hair that Cossacks left on top of their otherwise shaved heads.

20. Michael Flier, personal communication, 2002.

TABLE 4.1. **Examples of Ukrainianisms in the Russian language of villages of northeastern Ukraine in the 1960s (as documented by Chizhikova 1968).**

Local Form	Standard Russian	Standard Ukrainian	English Gloss
kvjetki	cv'ety	kvity	flowers
hodyna	č'as	hodyna	hour
sn'idat'	zaftrəkət'	sn'idaty	to eat breakfast
n'ed'el'a	vəskr'is'en'ijə	ned'il'a	Sunday

area differed in their ethnic composition and the time that they were settled by different groups, with more interethnic marriages and more language mixing in villages where Ukrainians and Russians had coexisted longer.

In villages with a compact ethnic Russian population, the Russian language had Ukrainian features. For example, on the phonetic level, *r* was hard in word final position and before the front vowels, *e, i,* as in the words *pryhór, trý, hrapký,* whereas in standard Russian the *r* would have been palatalized. On the grammatical level, the Russian verbal suffixes *-yva-, -iva-, -ieva-* were replaced by the Ukrainian forms *-uva-, -iuva-* as in *hariuvály, tancuvály, puv'azuvály;* Ukrainian prepositions *povz* and *ponad* were used *povz sxod solnca, ponad šlaxom.* On the lexical level, Russians used Ukrainian forms in otherwise mostly Russian speech, as in the examples in Table 4.1 (Chizhikova 1968, 25):

Meanwhile, the Ukrainian language in predominantly ethnic Ukrainian villages had Russian features: for example, on the phonetic level, there was *akanie*—the pronunciation of unstressed *o* as *a*—as in *vadá* for standard Ukrainian *vodá* 'water,' *xavát'* for *xováty* 'to hide'; the replacement of /e/ by /o/ when in stressed position before hard consonants (as in *ov'os* for *oves* 'oats' and *m'od* for *med* 'honey'); on the grammatical level, the Ukrainian noun suffix *-em* was replaced by Russian *-om* as in *kalod'ižom* 'water-well' (instrumental case) and *bahačom* 'wealthy man' (instrumental case), and in morphology, neuter-gender nouns could take the Russian diminutive form *-onok,* as in *tel'ónok* 'little calf' and *jahn'onok* 'little lamb.' The many Russian and Ukrainian lexical borrowings meant that both Russian and Ukrainian-based mixtures shared a growing set of vocabulary, and sometimes both Russian and Ukrainian variants were used by the same people (Chizhikova 1968, 25, 28).

In Chizhikova's study the ethnic and linguistic mixing also expressed itself in how people identified themselves. Many people had difficulty naming their identity, and others said that it is not important to them whether they are called Ukrainian or Russian. Still others chose the ethnonym *xoxol,* sometimes used as a derogatory term for Ukrainians by Russians, as noted earlier, but here embraced by the Ukrainian population.[21] Yet another declared identity was that of *pere-verten'*, which can translate as "convert" or "turncoat" but seems to have been used to justify ambiguity without negative connotations: "We are not Russians and not Ukrainians, we are *perevertni*" (Chizhikova 1968, 24). Chizhikova praised the processes she depicted as positive evidence of ethnic rapprochement made possible by the Soviet system, and did not single out either Ukrainian or Russian influence as being better. By showing how ethnolinguistic categories were blurred, her study also departed from the essentialist, atomizing ideology of ethnoses that came to prevail in Soviet ethnology (Slezkine 1994).

Hybrid Ukrainian-Russian ethnolinguistic forms continued to developed during the later Soviet period. Villagers who moved to cities often could speak little or no Russian but could usually understand it from exposure to language on television and radio. Russian-medium schools were absent in villages except in Crimea and some areas of eastern Ukraine, and in rural areas the teaching of Russian as a second language was often of low quality (Arel 1993, 170). Newly urbanized villagers would "Russify" their language, using Ukrainian with whatever Russian words or constructions they knew, just as villagers did in tsarist times. This Russification of Ukrainian, that is, the development of a syncretic Russo-Ukrainian language, also took place in villages near large cities since peasants traveled regularly into the cities to sell their produce. Relatively stable syncretic languages were also able to develop in suburban residential complexes, where most urbanized peasants lived. Their children generally studied in Russian-medium schools, with Ukrainian language only taught as a subject, as Ukrainian-medium schools became ever scarcer in urban areas in the 1970s and 1980s. These children were often bilingual (in Russified Ukrainian and Russian) if they continued to maintain ties with home. The "mixed" languages, which came to be labeled surzhyk, were stigmatized since they reflected the efforts of people of low socioeconomic status to gain higher status, and since they violated the ideally clear borders between Ukrainian and Russian.

Ideologies of Purity and Mixing after Independence

With independence in the 1990s the elevation of Ukrainian to a higher status was accompanied by the resurgence of an ideology of linguistic purism. In part this was a reflection of the desire to define a distinct Ukrainian identity separate from the Soviet identity that was intertwined with Russian language. But, more im-

---

21. *Xoxol* was also used positively by Yurij, as related in chapter 2. Usually it is considered a derogatory term for Ukrainians. Literally it refers to the tuft of hair on an otherwise shaven head that was worn by Ukrainian Cossacks.

portant, purism proved to be a means of dissociating Ukrainian from the negative connotations it had accrued in relation to Russian. After all, for most of the Soviet period Ukrainian had been widely treated as less valuable and backward, and many people found it difficult to accept its new official status as a state language. By focusing on an ideal, pure form of Ukrainian as the language meriting prestige, the negative connotations could be relegated to "impure," "imperfect" forms of the language. Thus, while during imperial and Soviet times diglossia was constituted by Russian as the high language and Ukrainian as the low language, after independence *pure* Ukrainian and Russian vied for the position of high language, and surzhyk (in its various manifestations) took on the role of low language.

Differences in regional dialects continued to account for some of the linguistic variation throughout the Soviet period and after independence, primarily among rural inhabitants (or urbanites who learned their Ukrainian language during childhood summers in the village). The dialect continuum that predated and crossed national borders continued to exist to some extent, but many local usages were displaced by standard language schooling, media, and contact with administrators (political boundaries determined which standard language was instituted). Strong local linguistic traditions and limitations in standard language schooling (e.g., teachers who spoke the local dialect even in classes) served to maintain some regional differences despite nonstandard forms being marked as uneducated and nonprestigious outside the village context. Regions closer to borders with other countries had pronunciation, lexicon, and syntactic forms similar to other standard languages, namely, Polish, Russian, Belarusian, Romanian, Hungarian, and Slovakian. Likewise, on the other side of the border outside Ukraine, spoken languages shared features with standard Ukrainian. Even if a linguist could determine that the supposedly foreign borrowings were indeed longtime local characteristics, many listeners would take this to be language mixing. For most people who were not dialectologists, an unfamiliar dialect form simply sounded incorrect. In my fieldwork I encountered several such cases in which dialectisms were interpreted as impurity of language and labeled surzhyk.

This did not necessarily mean that border-area languages were always characterized by marked syncretism or mixing. A Ukrainian linguist told me how in the early 1990s when traveling by train he complemented a fellow passenger on her beautiful, pure Ukrainian language, and she replied that she was speaking Belarusian.[22] In the judgment of the linguist her native language was very close to standard Ukrainian (and similar to some dialects of northern/central Ukraine), but she considered herself Belarusian, and her home village was within the borders of Belarus. The political definition of her home region was the basis for her

---

22. Bohdan Azhniuk, personal communication, 1994.

affiliation with a linguistic label, consistent with an ideology of direct correspondence between language, place, and identity.

The nationalist ideology positing organic unity of language, culture, land, and people located the wellspring of ethnolinguistic authenticity in villages. However, the low economic and social position of peasants gave them little authority in the greater social market beyond the village. Regional variations and "local color" tended to devalue "village language" as nonstandard and therefore not prestigious. A woman in the western Ukrainian city of Ivano-Frankivs'k once told me that "the villages saved the [Ukrainian] language," and a minute later she spoke of the "awful village language." I was stunned by the close coexistence of such contradictory views in her thinking: the romanticized ideal of the village versus the village as lacking culture. Her statements illustrated the tension between sources of authenticity and sources of authority. The belief that the "organic," "authentic" material of the village must be refined to reach its true potential resolved this contradiction. In this view the ideal Ukrainian language was based on "authentic" vernacular sources but was then refined by great poets and writers, and knowledge of it required formal education that was not accessible to everyone. This ideology reinforced the ties between the acquisition of linguistic capital and economic and social positions (Bourdieu 1991, 64).

Some people directly attributed the low status of Ukrainian to the state's lack of care, complaining that during the past few decades the Ukrainian language was "neglected" and "unkempt." For example, in the southeastern city of Zaporizhia, a retired male electrician in his sixties explained his belief that linguistic value required institutional refinement and correction (Russian and Russian-influenced forms in his otherwise Ukrainian speech are indicated in italics):

Jakščo cv'ax ležyt' joho ne to, to vin poržavije. Tak i vse *šo*, vse žytt'a my šlifuvaly vse, poliruvaly i tak dal'še rosijs'ku movu. Bulo v hazet'i, po radijo, po telebachenn'u, *ruskyj jazyk samyj luščyj*. Urok *ruskəvo jazyka*—za ukrajins'ku movu ničoho. Tak jak ty budeš znat' *joho xarašo*, jak pro *joho* n'ide ne čuješ. N'ide. N'i po radijo, n'i po *t'el'evidenn'u*, v hazet'i, n'ide. A hazetu viz'meš, daže *vot* našu Zaporiz'ku Pravdu viz'meš tam i dyvyšs'a—aha. Rosi- urok rosijs'koji movy. Telebačenn'a—aha. A za ukrajins'ku, koly tam ukrajins'ke "Slovo pro slovo," koly ne koly, des'. A to ž joho nemaje. Oce s my peredplačujemo Molod' Ukrajiny tak tam *jest'* rubryka bude jak—ja zabuv mmm. *Xaroša*. Jak pravyl'no i slova kaza*t'* i dal'še jak tam *d'iktory* hovorjat'.

If a nail lays there and you don't [do anything to it], it will rust. And so [it] always [was] that, all our life we always refined, polished, and so on, the Russian language. It was in the newspaper, on the radio, on television, *the Russian language is the best*. A lesson *in Russian language*—but nothing about Ukrainian. So how are you going to *know it well*, when you don't hear about *it* anywhere. Nowhere. Neither on the radio, nor on *television,* in the newspaper, nowhere. But you take a newspaper, even *look here* our *Za-poriz'ka pravda* [*Zaporizhian truth*] you take it and look there—aha. Russi- A lesson in Russian language. Television—aha. But about Ukrainian, rarely is there the Ukrainian "A word about a word," once in a while, somewhere. But mostly it's not there. We now subscribe to *Molod' Ukraïny* [*Youth of Ukraine*] and there, there *is* a column called—I've forgotten mmm. *A good one.* How *to say* words correctly and then, how *newscasters* speak.[23]

In my fieldwork the dominant belief was that institutional intervention is necessary to establish and maintain linguistic purity and value. However, I also encountered views that considered language mixing to be "natural," a result of life circumstances (Bilaniuk 1997b). For example, in 1992 a retired nurse in her seventies (born in a village but then living in the city of Zaporizhia) told me that people in villages speak Ukrainian, but when they come to work in cities they start using more Russian. When I asked how she felt about mixed language, she said (Russian and Russian-influenced forms in her speech are indicated in italics; the rest is Ukrainian):

Ta normal'no. *Uslovja* j de ty žyvjoš. *Pon'al'i? Jesl'i* vy ot *postojannyj* žytel' sela, znaješ tak uže pryvykaješ, taka i mova. A ot jak teper l'udy j tudy j s'udy j *eto* . . .

It's normal. *Conditions* and where you *live. Understood? If* you are a *permanent* inhabitant of a village, you know you get used to that, and such is your language. And now that people are going here and there, and *so* . . . [24]

Based on the rest of my conversation with her, her implication was that, by spending time in both villages and cities, people are mixing Ukrainian (the rural language) and Russian (the urban language).

As surveyed so far, there is a wide range of forces that led people to mix languages: settlement patterns leading to interethnic and linguistic contact, interactions with representatives of a dominating regime, the desire to include features of a higher-status language in one's own native speech, incomplete institutionalization of standards, institutionalized language mixing (according to the Soviet policy of the flowing together of peoples and the ultimate disappear-

---

23. This man spoke mostly standard Ukrainian with occasional Russian forms and some codeswitching. He switched to Russian when referring to the "Russian language lesson," and he used Russian forms for "well/good," one instance of "television" (the other two were in Ukrainian), "is," "[look] here" and "spokesperson." He also referred to "language" with a masculine pronoun in Ukrainian: "language" is a masculine noun in Russian, feminine in Ukrainian. Two infinitival verb endings were /-t'/ instead of standard Ukrainian /-ty/.

24. This woman spoke primarily Ukrainian, with many Russian influences on pronunciation, word choice, morphology, and syntax. Another sample of her speech is analyzed in detail later in this chapter.

ance of languages other than Russian), and the purposeful use of mixed language for humor. Also, once mixed languages became established in a community, using them signaled local solidarity. Thus, despite the stigma of using impure language, surzhyk persisted in many forms.

A Typology of Surzhyk and Forces Leading to Language Mixing

Recently scholars have argued that linguistic mixing, hybridity, and ambiguity should not be viewed as marginal but rather at the center of struggles through which languages and identities are defined (Argentier 2001; Hill and Hill 1984; Jaffe 1999; Parkin 1994; Woolard 1988, 1998b). In the case of surzhyk, the labeling of what is not "good language" has been key in defining what is good and thus socially valued, Ukrainian or Russian. To disentangle the diverse array of linguistic phenomena that has been referred to as surzhyk, here I systematize the different historical, social, and ideological factors that have shaped the emergence of different surzhyks. I present a taxonomy of the different phenomena that fall under the label "surzhyk" as it is used by nonspecialists.

Linguists have used "language mixing" and "codeswitching" to refer to a wide range of practices that involves "the alternate use of two or more languages in the same utterance or conversation" (Grosjean 1982, 145; Winford 2003, 102). Whereas earlier analyses of codeswitching had based their explanations on underlying discrete codes that could be clearly separated, recent studies argue that language choices are often more fluid and hazy than the hard-edged alternations implied by the concept of codeswitching (Gardner-Chloros 1995; Milroy and Muysken 1995). This is certainly the case with most manifestations of surzhyk: it is often difficult to define the boundaries between the languages that are being mixed. Further, the very term "codeswitching" has been problematized in the argument that the "code" in a given community can itself be a mixture of languages (Alvarez-Cáccamo 1998; Franceschini 1998). Thus a speaker can switch from a mixed-language code to a nonmixed code.

Mixed languages can be distinguished from pidgins and creoles, since the former were not formed through processes of pidginization and creolization, that is, they did not develop as a result of complete mutual incomprehension or pass through a phase of simplified grammar.[25] Mixed languages can involve closely

---

25. Pidginization is the result of contact between people who have no linguistic basis for mutual comprehension. A pidgin is a common language characterized by simplified grammar, incorporating elements from the contact languages. Linguists have shown that there are universal regularities in the formation of pidgins, reflecting general structural features of human language capabilities. When a pidgin language is learned as a native language by children in a community, their innate language instinct leads them to elaborate the grammar into

related languages (as with Ukrainian-Russian surzhyk) or unrelated languages, when these have coexisted in a community of bilingual speakers. People who mix languages are not necessarily fully bilingual, and they may even learn a mixed language without much exposure at all to another "unmixed" language.

Mixed language is a widespread phenomenon. It includes, for example: *trasianka*, Belorusian-Russian mixing in Belarus (Woolhiser 2001); "mountaineer-Russian speech" in the North Caucasus (Smith 1998, 56); *Spanglish*, Spanish-English mixing in the United States; *Mexicano* (Aztec/Nahuatl)-Spanish mixing in Mexico (Hill and Hill 1984); *joual*, nonstandard Quebec French with English admixture (Handler 1988, 162–169); *Italoschwyz*, Italian-Swiss-German mixing in Switzerland (Franceschini 1998); *bahasa gadho-gadho* (literally, "language salad"), mixed bilingual Javanese-Indonesian usage (Errington 1998, 98–116); and *Sheng* and *Engsh*, two different mixtures of English, Swahili, and other African languages in urban Kenya (Abdulaziz and Osinde 1997). Not all cases of mixing and codeswitching have a special label, like Lingala-French and Swahili-French language mixing and codeswitching among Zairans (Meeuwis and Blommaert 1998).[26] Multilingualism is more the rule than the exception, and where there is more than one language, there will very likely be some form of mixing; or, if not, then a lot of energy (which may be more or less overt) has been put into preventing or stigmatizing that mixing.

While it is sometimes difficult to separate the diverse types of language interaction that have been variously referred to as mixing, codeswitching, borrowing, and interference, Auer (1999) has proposed a useful typology to systematize these phenomena by viewing them as points on a continuum. On this continuum Auer distinguishes the prototypical phenomena that he labels "codeswitching" (CS) and "fused lects" (FL) as the extreme poles, and "language mixing" (LM) as the halfway point between them. Auer defines "codeswitching" as the "pragmatic" pole of language contact, in which "the contrast between one code and the other (for instance, one language and another) is meaningful, and can be interpreted as indexing (contextualizing) either some aspects of the situation (discourse-related switching) or some feature of the codeswitching speaker (participant-related switching)" (1999, 310). In codeswitching, the speaker is free to use different codes as a creative conversational device. This use of the term "codeswitching" is consistent with a view of the contributing languages as discrete and separable. In language mixing, the language alternation is not func-

---

a complex system on a par with the grammar of other "regular" languages. This fully grammatical language is called a "creole" language, developed through the process of creolization, which can occur in one or more generations (Winford 2003, 268–358).

26. For additional examples and analyses of mixed languages, see Winford 2003, 168–175, and the articles in Auer 1998 and Heller 1998.

tional, there is no preference for using one language at a time, and the mixing of languages itself is a group style (or we could say it is the "code"). Finally, in fused lects the mixing is obligatory, regularized, and constrained grammatically.[27] Whereas the transition from codeswitching to language mixing involves pragmatic factors (there is social significance in how the codes are mixed), the transition from language mixing to fused lects is grammatical (the mixed language becomes increasingly regularized and the grammar is sedimented, creating a fused lect).

The Ukrainian-Russian surzhyk mix includes phenomena at various points on Auer's continuum, from fused lects to codeswitches. Only infrequent and clearly demarcated codeswitches, such as where the borrowing of a word or phrase from the other language has a clearly comic, ironic, solidarity-forming, or other effect, will avoid being labeled surzhyk by purists. But if someone codeswitches too frequently, that also could be called surzhyk by an avid purist, for this behavior can give the impression that one lacks knowledge of the vocabulary in the original language. The social dynamics through which the label "surzhyk" is deployed are examined in the next chapter.

Since independence, the term "surzhyk" has been used by different people to refer to disparate phenomena. Those with some knowledge of dialectology may define "surzhyk" as the incorrect mixing of forms that belong to different linguistic systems, as distinct from dialects. People without knowledge of dialect varieties may evaluate dialect speech as surzhyk simply because it is not what they know as the standard. Still others may evaluate their own close-to-standard speech as surzhyk because of insecurity in their linguistic knowledge.

Having an accent—that is, speaking one language with the phonology of another—is often labeled surzhyk because of stereotypes: someone for whom Ukrainian is not a first (or early) language is frequently presumed not to know Ukrainian very well. Given the strong linkages between linguistic and ethnic allegiance, accent serves as a shibboleth for the underlying "true" identity of a speaker. For example, accent is singled out as the problem in the criticism of politicians by a twenty-five-year old businessman in Kyiv whom I interviewed in 1991 (Russian and Russian-influenced forms are italicized, the rest is Ukrainian; "(...)" indicates a pause):

> Možna pobačyty v televizori jak sesiju Verxovnoho (...) *Sovjetu* tam jakos' *na* rosijs'koju hovorjat' z takym akcentom ukrajins'kym znaješ (...) čy ukrajins'koju z rosijs'kym akcentom (...) suržyk, suržyk i tam je.

---

27. As pointed out by an anonymous reviewer, since all languages have integrated forms from other languages at some point, all languages could be referred to as fused lects at some level, but in Auer's sense, as used here, the focus is on the fusion of elements of two or more labeled and socially recognized language forms into a third form.

One can see on television in the sessions of the High (...) Council [Parliament] there somehow [they] speak Russian with a Ukrainian accent you know (...) or Ukrainian with a Russian accent (...) surzhyk, surzhyk is there, too.[28]

An example of the importance of accent is also highlighted in the play *Myna Mazajlo* by Mykola Kulish, written in 1929 (also discussed in the previous chapter). Mazajlo, the Ukrainian man who wants to Russify his name, hires a teacher, Baronova-Kozino, to instruct him in proper Russian pronunciation. As they begin their lessons the pronunciation of *h* and *g* arises as a focal issue (Kulish 1955, 141–142):

Baronova-Kozino: Oh, my God! But in Russian language there is almost no "h" sound, there is "g." The "h" sound occurs only in the word "God" [*boh*], and even that is pronounced . . .

Mazajlo: I know! That very "heh" is forever my misfortune. It is a condemnation, some kind of Mark of Cain, by which people will see me for what I am, even once I am speaking not only pure Russian but the heavenly language of angels.

Baronova-Kozino: Do not be upset, my dear! Do not give in to despair!

Mazajlo: Oh, how can I not get upset when for ages that very "heh" has burned me and ruined my career . . . I will tell you . . . When I was still young . . . the governor's daughter fell in love with me from afar. She pleaded, she begged: introduce me to him, introduce me. They said, he is not a noble, just some kind of registrar . . . Introduce me to him, introduce me! They summoned me there—she looked upon me as if I were Apollo. When she heard from my lips my "heh" . . . "heh"—she turned away, she grimaced.

Baronova-Kozino: I understand her.

Mazajlo: And me?

Baronova-Kozino: And now I understand you.

Mazajlo: Oh, how I have myself tried in conversation to say . . . "xe."

Baronova-Kozino: "Geh?"

Mazajlo: I couldn't and I can't . . . I doubt that even you can teach me . . .

Baronova-Kozino: Oh, my God. Now this is my only source of income—geh . . . It is just from that one "geh" that I now make my living. Try, my darling. Now say it one more time: over the meadows. Over the meadows [*Nad lugami, Nad lugami*].

Meanwhile, Mazajlo's pro-Ukrainian son, Mokij, is trying to teach his new Russophone girlfriend proper Ukrainian pronunciation, and they are having the opposite problem. She is incapable of pronouncing *h*; instead she always says *g*:

---

28. This man was primarily speaking Ukrainian, but it is not his habitual language and during the interview he used Russian forms occasionally and self-corrected a few times. In this statement he paused before using the Russian term *soviet* for "council" (in Ukrainian the term is *rada*, and would have required a feminine instead of masculine ending on the preceding adjective). Also, he began the expression "speak Russian" with the preposition *na* (as required in standard Russian) but then he used the instrumental case ending (as required in standard Ukrainian, but then it should be without the preposition).

Mokij: Now Ulia, where is there a "go," when in the book it is written "ho"? In the Ukrainian language it is altogether rare to find the "g" sound, only in words such as "lump, blackbird, shepherd's staff" [*gul'a, gava, gerlyga*], otherwise we say "h" everywhere.

In the play both sides find approximations in trying to learn correct pronunciation, with Mazajlo saying *x* for *g* (to avoid saying *h*) and Ulia saying *x* for *h* (to avoid saying *g*). But for both the exercise appears futile, unlike the success achieved by Professor Higgins in transforming Eliza through linguistic instruction in Shaw's *Pygmalion/My Fair Lady*. The parallel with Shaw's story was reinforced in the 1998 dubbing of the movie *My Fair Lady* for the Ukrainian television audience, and in the 2002 production of the play *Pygmalion* by a major Kyiv theater: in both cases surzhyk was used in place of Cockney (Levbarh 1998; Smirnova 1998). But there are problems in the parallel: in Ukraine it is not just the case of a vernacular low language versus a high language; surzhyk is also at the crossroads of the struggle between two literary languages, Ukrainian and Russian. A truer parallel would involve Scots or Welsh versus King's English, and some mixture thereof.

The term "surzhyk" is currently used rather broadly, and it is useful to survey the forms and historical influences that can fall under this label. I propose a typology of forces leading to the formation of surzhyk that corresponds to five prototypical categories.[29] This typology is based primarily on historical and demographic conditions, and also includes consideration of pragmatics, directionality of language influence, and Auer's (1999) categories of language interaction. An ideology of purism and correctness underpins all the definitions.

I distinguish five major categories of surhzyk: (1) urbanized-peasant surzhyk; (2) village-dialect surzhyk; (3) Sovietized Ukrainian surzhyk; (4) urban bilinguals' surzhyk (habitual language mixing by bilinguals); and (5) post-independence surzhyk. These categories and the parameters that define them are summarized in Table 4.2.

Category 1: Urbanized-Peasant Surzhyk

Urbanized-peasant surzhyk is the archetypical surzhyk. It could also be called "upwardly mobile–class surzhyk." Its origins have been explained above: it came about with industrialization and urbanization as Ukrainian-speaking peasants increasingly came into contact with Russian-speaking administrators, and moved to cities where they tried to speak the more prestigious and powerful language—Russian. These urbanizing peasants did not have adequate schooling in Russian, and most of their interactions were with others like themselves at work or in their suburban communities. In these conditions the archetypical surzhyk languages developed. The social value of speaking Ukrainian "purely"—that is

---

29. An earlier version of this typology appears in Bilaniuk 2004.

TABLE 4.2. **Defining features of five surzhyk prototypes (from Bilaniuk 2004)**

| Type of surzhyk | Historical/Demographic Context | | | Direction of Influence | Auer's Continuum CS→LM→FL |
	Specific Description	Rural-Urban Context	Era		
Urbanized-Peasant	Working-class urbanized Ukrainian peasants	rural→ urban	19th c. to present	Rus. onto Ukr. base	LM/FL
Village-Dialect	Ukr. villagers in contact with Rus. administrators and media	rural	19th c. to present	Rus. onto Ukr. base	LM/FL
Sovietized-Ukrainian	Codified Ukrainian w/planned Russian influence	urban (institutional)	1930s to present	Rus. onto Ukr. base	planned FL
Urban Bilinguals'	Urban bilinguals w/either native lang.	urban	Soviet and post-Soviet	both directions	CS/LM
Post-Independence	Russophone urbanites newly using Ukr. in public	urban	post-Soviet	both directions	CS/LM

without Russian elements—was largely limited to the urban intelligentsia. For urbanized peasants, speaking surzhyk was more prestigious than just speaking Ukrainian, which connoted provincialism or, more dangerously, nationalism. With these origins it is not surprising that this surzhyk is stigmatized. It connotes a peasant background, lack of education, lack of esteem for one's native language, and a low socioeconomic status.

According to the definition of this prototype, we would not expect language alternation for pragmatic reasons but rather for the purpose of using as many Russian elements as possible, resulting in Auer's terms, in "language mixing." With time, in many cases, the Ukrainian-Russian mixture became regularized and grammaticalized as recent arrivals from villages adapted to the evolving norms of the previously urbanized peasants, creating "fused lects." Children of these families likely were taught standard Ukrainian and Russian at school, but their first language would be the mixture spoken in their community. Whether the children developed and maintained proficiency in a standard language or in their native surzhyk in later life or in both depended on their professions and spheres of interaction, and the costs and benefits of particular language choices in these contexts.

The degree to which urbanized-peasant surzhyk differs structurally in different cities remains to be studied. This surzhyk includes not only standard Ukrainian and Russian forms but also elements of regional village dialects. In my own experience I have encountered lexical differences in the surzhyk spoken by urbanized peasants from different regions. Thus, even within this one category of surzhyk, significant structural variation may emerge in different contexts but based on similar conditions and the same socio-historic forces.

Below is an analysis of a brief transcribed speech sample of an urbanized-peasant fused lect. It is an excerpt from a taped interview with a Ukrainian woman in her seventies, who lived and worked as a nurse for more than twenty years in the central/southeastern city of Zaporizhia but who grew up in a nearby village (she was also quoted above). The transcriptions reflect pronunciation, not orthography.[30] The woman's words are indicated by WOM, and the standard Ukrainian and Russian forms are indicated by UKR and RUS. The abbreviation GLS gives a word-by-word gloss in English, and ENG provides the English translation. The woman is answering my question about which language she uses with members of her family.

WOM:	Brat	moj	mnohə	rabo:ta	u	horod'e.
UKR:	Brat	mij	bahato	prac'uje	v	mist'i.
RUS:	Brat	moj	mnogə	rabotaet	v	gorəd'i.
GLS:	Brother	my	much	works	in	city.
ENG:	My brother works a lot in the city.					

WOM:	Vin	ostajo:c'a	tam.
UKR:	Vin	zistajec'a	tam.
RUS:	On	astajocə	tam.
GLS:	He	remains	there.
ENG:	He stays there.		

WOM:	Prɪjiža	dodomu—	to	vže
UKR:	Prɪjiždžaje	dodomu—	to	vže
RUS:	Prɨježaet	damoj—	tagda	uže
GLS:	Comes (by vehicle)		to home—	then	already
ENG:	When he comes home—then already			

---

30. In this transcription I distinguish the Ukrainian "и" and Russian "ы" vowels that are customarily both transcribed as "y." Here I use the International Phonetic Alphabet, with /ɪ/ representing the Ukrainian high close front centralized unrounded vowel (и), and /ɨ/ for the Russian high close central unrounded vowel (ы).

WOM:	vin	po-rus'kı	načına.
UKR:	vin	po-rosijs'kı	počınaje.
RUS:	on	pa-ruski	nəčinajət.
GLS:	he	in Russian	begins.
ENG:	he begins [speaking] in Russian.		

I then asked about people from villages who generally live and work in the cities.

WOM:	A	doma	prıjižajut'
UKR:	A	dodomu	prıjiždžajut'
RUS:	A	damoj	priiž'ajut
GLS:	But	to home	come
ENG:	But when they come home		

WOM:	vonı	vsida	rozhavarjut'	po-ukrajins'kı,	da.
UKR:	vonı	vse	rozmovl'ajut'	po-ukrajin's'kı,	tak.
RUS:	ani	fsigda	rəzgavarivajut	pa-ukrainski,	da.
GLS:	they	always	speak	Ukrainian,	yes.
ENG:	they always speak Ukrainian, yes.				

WOM:	A	u	horod'i	vže	načınajut'	nu.
UKR:	A	v	mist'i	vže	počınajut'	nu.
RUS:	A	v	gorəd'i	uže	nəčinajut	nu.
GLS:	But	in	city	already	begin	well.
ENG:	But in the city, they already begin [speaking Russian], well.					

WOM:	V	horod'i	jak	tə	až	nevdobno	bulo
UKR:	V	mist'i	jakos'	to	až	nezručno	bulo
RUS:	V	gorəd'i	kak	tə	uš	n'iudobnə	bılo
GLS:	In	city	how	that	so	awkward	was
ENG:	In the city, it was somehow awkward						

WOM:	jak	ran'še	bulo	počut'	ukrajinc'i,	da.
UKR:	jak	raniše	bulo	počutı	ukrajinc'iv,	tak.
RUS:	kak	ran'še	bılo	uslišit'	ukraincəf,	da.
GLS:	how	earlier	was	to hear	Ukrainians,	yes.
ENG:	when one would hear Ukrainians back then.					

WOM:	A ha ha,	staralıs'a,	da.
UKR:	A ha ha,	staralıs'a,	tak.
RUS:	A ha ha,	staralis',	da.
GLS:	unh huh,	[they] tried	yes
ENG:	Yes, they tried [to speak Russian] there, yes.		

At this point I asked why they tried to speak Russian, and she explained:

WOM:	Nu,	vıdno	šo	s	sela	čolovik.
UKR:	Nu,	vıdno	ščo	z	sela	čolovik.
RUS:	Nu,	vidnə	što	s	sila	čelav'ek.
GLS:	Well,	visible	that	from	village	person.
ENG:	Well, it was obvious that the person was a villager/peasant.					

My interviewee chuckles after saying this. Perhaps it made her uncomfortable to state so plainly that the Ukrainian language was associated with the peasantry and was out of place in urban settings. As she explained further, young people did not face the embarrassment of not knowing Russian, since they had acquired Russian proficiency in city schools.

WOM:	A	molod'ož	vse	včılas'
UKR:	A	molod'	vse	včılas'a
RUS:	A	məlad'oš	fsigda	učilas'
GLS:	But	young people	always	studied
ENG:	But the young people always studied			

WOM:	v	horod'i	bol'šınstvo.
UKR:	v	mist'i	bil'šist'.
RUS:	v	gorəd'i	bəl'šinstvo.
GLS:	in	city	most.
ENG:	in the city, mostly.		

WOM:	Vs'o	ž	na	ruš'ke	perexodıla.
UKR:	Vse	ž	na	rosijš'ke	perexodıla.
RUS:	Fs'o	ž	na	ruskij	pirixod'ila.
GLS:	All	—	on	Russian	going over.
ENG:	They all [the young people] switched over to Russian.				

WOM:	A	svoju	onı	ne	zabıvalı.
UKR:	A	svoju	vonı	ne	zabuvalı.
RUS:	A	svoj	an'i	n'i	zəbıval'i.
GLS:	But	own	they	not	forget.
ENG:	But they did not forget their own [language].				

WOM:	Dodomu	prıjižalı,	vse	ravno	doma
UKR:	Dodomu	prıjiždžalı,	vse	rivno	vdoma
RUS:	Damoj	prijižal'i,	fs'o	ravno	doma
GLS:	To home	[they] came	all	even	at home
ENG:	When they came home, all the same at home				

WOM:	z	bat'kom,	z	materju	rozhovaɪɪl'i	pa-svojemu.
UKR:	z	bat'kom,	z	matirju	rozmovljalɪ	po-svojemu.
RUS:	s	accom,	s	mat'ir'u	rəzgəvar'ivəl'i	pa-svoimu.
GLS:	with	father,	with	mother	spoke	their own way.
ENG:	they spoke in their own language with their father and mother.					

Category 2: Village-Dialect Surzhyk

Village dialects that appear to contain features of both Ukrainian and Russian constitute the second category in this typology. This category differs from the first mainly in the locus and social dynamics of its development. Rather than the linguistic creations of peasants who permanently moved to cities, village-dialect *surzhyk* developed in villages. This type of surzhyk may have had features of both Ukrainian and Russian because of its position on the dialect continuum prior to standardization, and in this state this type would be a mixture only in retrospect, by comparison with the standards established later. The base languages would then be altered through contact with administrators, visitors, or through temporary visits of the villagers to cities. This contact would result in language mixing, which we would expect at later stages to achieve obligatory grammaticalization, creating fused lects. The most common situation in which this type of surzhyk developed would be through Russian influence onto a Ukrainian base, but the opposite also occurred. Chizhikova's (1968) study provides examples of such dialect mixtures with both Russian and Ukrainian base languages, as discussed above. Surzhyk of this type is most common in the northeastern and eastern areas of Ukraine, but I have also encountered Russian words as key elements in Western Ukrainian dialects, and the origins of these remain to be researched. Even a few such elements in otherwise standard Ukrainian will often lead a listener to judge the language as "impure," and hence as surzhyk.

Category 3: Sovietized-Ukrainian Surzhyk

Sovietized-Ukrainian surzhyk is the focus of purists who wish to resuscitate pre-Soviet standards. Although some Russian influences in the codification of Ukrainian predate the Soviet period, the processes of the Soviet era are by far the most significant, hence the label that I have chosen for this type of language mixing. This is an institutionally created fused lect, a result of the decades of direct Soviet manipulation and the influence of the widespread use of Russian. As a rule, forms closer to or identical to Russian were promoted in dictionaries, grammar books, and advisories to editors and publishers (see the discussion and examples in chapter 3). Also, since many bureaucratic and professional practices were in Russian during the Soviet period, specialized terminology in Ukrainian that was hastily put into use after independence also bears the influence of Soviet Russian.

After independence there was much debate over the need to correct the Soviet-era institutionalized standard. At conferences there were often heated discussions among groups of linguists from different regions of the country, as well as scholars in different fields who had taken on the task of developing specialized terminological standards in their field. The process was complicated by competing sources of legitimation and funding for dictionaries: from the Ukrainian government, which in 1994 authorized a committee of linguists, literary scholars, and writers (Natsional'na Pravopysna Komisija) as the ultimate arbiter, and also from sources in the diaspora, who were especially keen to "de-Russify" (Ponomariv 2004).

A very critical view of post-Soviet Ukrainian was evident in a few of my interviews in 1992 with interviewees stating that nobody speaks pure Ukrainian. Some academics likewise saw the language situation as extremely problematic. For example, Radchuk (2002, 3) contended that the majority of the population of Ukraine speaks surzhyk, and the few that speak correctly are made to feel like oddities and foreigners, a diaspora in their own country. Another scholar, Karavans'kyi, was keen on remedying what he called the "legalization of surzhyk." He proposed his own "typology of surzhyks" based on the historical period that Russianisms were introduced and institutionalized, some formations predating the Soviet era (Karavans'kyi 2000). By using the term "surzhyk" to refer to various codifications of language, Karavans'kyi was trying to dislodge the complacency he saw in the general acceptance of institutionalized forms as they were. He believed that "today's opponents of surzhyk don't even have any idea, that in fighting surzhyk, they are themselves using a damaged Ukrainian language" (Karavans'kyi 2000, 8). In this vein of extreme criticality, a letter to an editor in a newspaper commended an article criticizing surzhyk but then went on to criticize the language of that article as also having surzhyk elements (Makitra 2000).

It also makes sense to include in this category nonstandard linguistic practices that became extremely widespread but were not formally codified. A popular example is the form for specifying time: to say "five o'clock," people commonly say *pjat' hodyn* 'five hours', whereas in standard Ukrainian one should say *pjata hodyna* 'the fifth hour'. Other examples abound in publicized speeches, internal memos of government officials, and advertisements. These transgressions are targeted in many anti-surzhyk books, articles, and brochures (e.g., Hanitkevych 1995; Hnatkevych 2000; Serbens'ka 1994). The prevalence of these nonstandard Russified forms in institutions and the media makes them fit in the Sovietized-Ukrainian category; however, the degree of institutionalization of these practices varies and they are not codified as standard, so they can also fit in the next category, urban bilinguals' surzhyk. How one might choose to classify a given mixed linguistic practice would depend on the degree of one's purist ideology, and on the extent of its codification and institutionalization.

Cover of the 1994 book, edited by Oleksandra Serbens'ka, titled *Anti-Surzhyk,* aimed at correcting linguistic transgressions.

Category 4: Urban Bilinguals' Surzhyk

The fourth category is what I call the surzhyk of urban bilinguals. This type ranges from codeswitching to language mixing on Auer's continuum, and is generally not regularized or grammaticalized. This category may also be called "habitual language mixing by bilinguals."

This is the most diffuse category. It entails unstructured mixing, usually by people who more or less know both languages (but borrow terms from the other language out of habit) and sometimes switch for stylistic effect, sometimes for no apparent reason at all. In home or work environments where two languages co-exist, some people have the habit of *partial* adaptation to the language of their interlocutors.

This type of mixing results from various forces. Either language can be the base language that is influenced by the other, or the two languages can be mixed in equilibrium. While a major force on urban bilinguals was toward the "improvement" of their Russian through standard schooling and media, there was also a factor of local solidarity. This was the attitude that celebrated being different from Russia and thus supported the development of uniquely Ukrainian-Russian linguistic practices (in this case, using Ukrainianisms in Russian).[31] However, changing language statuses during the first decade of independence destabilized this process as surzhyk became more openly stigmatized and disputed. Nevertheless, the force of solidarity entailed the avoidance of the stigma of being "too pure." For this reason people adhered to Russified forms in Ukrainian that were the status quo rather than using forms they knew to be correct Ukrainian but that would stand out. This habitual mixing could also be a result of incomplete language training (but to a lesser degree than was the case for categories 1 and 2) and could include having an "accent" as a result of learning the other language late, or having incomplete knowledge of the grammar and lexicon of the other language. Both pragmatics and language skill come into play.

Habitual code-switching and mixing reflect a "fashion for intertextuality" (Azhniuk 2001, 54). These linguistic practices allow people to avoid having to choose between Ukrainian or Russian and permit them to use the full range of language resources in their bilingual environment. An example illustrating this category comes from a letter to the editor of the youth music magazine *Moloko* (Natalka 2002, 64). The degree of Ukrainian-Russian bilingualism in this magazine has varied over the several years of its existence. The example presented here reveals yet another layer of mixing that emerges in written language. The text is reproduced as it appeared in print in the original. In the transcription the Ukrainian text is indicated by underlining, Russian text is in italics, and words whose written forms are identical in Russian and Ukrainian are in roman type.[32] A hybrid form that renders Ukrainian pronunciation using a markedly Russian letter is shown in bold. An English gloss is also provided.

---

31. This attitude was exemplified by Yurij in his narrative in chapter 2.

32. The word "людей" is identical in print in both languages, but its pronunciation differs slightly: it is *l'udej* in Ukrainian and *l'ud'ej* in Russian. In the case of the words "и," "информаций," and "музику," the orthography is markedly that of one of the languages, but the pronunciation is very close in both languages.

Но в нашей родине стільки людей які люблять та слухають
No v *našej rod'in'e* st'il'ky l'udej jaki l'ubl'at' ta sluxajut'
But in *our homeland* there are so many people who like and listen to

важку серёзну музыку и так мало информаций про це направление
važku **serjoznu** muzyku *i* tak malo *informacij* pro ce *napravl'enije*
heavy **serious** music *and* so little *information* about this *direction*

Category 5: Post-Independence Surzhyk

The fifth category, post-independence surzhyk, emerged most recently and falls on the codeswitching through language mixing end of Auer's continuum. It entails mixing by Russophone adults who are not used to speaking Ukrainian (especially in official contexts) and are trying to do so because of the new status of Ukrainian as a state language, drawing on the Ukrainian they learned in their childhood in summer village visits or at school or are now just learning. When lacking a Ukrainian term, these speakers borrow words from Russian and use Russian phonology, which adds to the perception of impurity. This surzhyk has been referred to as "reverse surzhyk" (Krouglov 2002), but it does not necessarily correspond to a Ukrainianized Russian base language, since the speakers in this category, although primarily Russophone, often had acquired some Ukrainian in their childhood or through schooling.

While post-independence surzhyk is different from previous surzhyks in that it is usually spoken by those in higher socioeconomic groups, it is similar to other surzhyks in that it sounds "impure." After independence, linguistic correctness became a focus for contesting social legitimacy, and the label "surzhyk" was used to discredit people in high political or socioeconomic positions. Politicians were a favorite target of such criticism, as the next chapter shows in more detail. Here a quote from former president Kuchma serves as an example of this category of surzhyk. It appeared in a list of laughable quotes in a news magazine, in which his Russianisms were retained, making his quote even more ironic (Kuchma 2001, 24; in the transcription the Ukrainian text is underlined, Russian is italicized, words whose written forms are identical in Russian and Ukrainian are in roman type, and a nonstandard condensed Russian form is in bold lettering):[33]

Так ми щас виконуємо завєт Леніна: віддаємо землю
Tak my **ščas** vykonujemo *zav'et* Lenina: viddajemo zeml'u
So we **now** are carrying out *the bidding* of Lenin: we are returning the land

---

33. The word "землю" is identical in print in both languages, but its pronunciation differs slightly: it is *zeml'u* in Ukrainian and *z'eml'u* in Russian.

селянам і хто сьогодні проти цього?

sel'anam i xto s'ohodni proty c'oho?

to the peasants and who today is against that?

The five categories proposed above are prototypes; more categories are possible, and they may be blended in individual practices. Former president Kuchma provides a good example. The Ukrainian language that he heard when he was growing up in a village in the north-central Chernihiv oblast of Ukraine in the 1940s and 1950s was not standard Ukrainian but rather was a local dialect that shares many features with what are now standard Russian, Belorusian, and Ukrainian. On top of that base language he also had more recent Russian and standard Ukrainian influences through his education and professional demands. As a whole, his language includes the complex layering of different influences leading to mixed language, as well as correcting away from it.

Many other combinations of categories are possible, such as the surzhyk of urban Ukrainophones whose Russian knowledge is limited, or anglicized surzhyk. It is also useful to distinguish regularity versus transience—"native" versus "transitional" surzhyk. A significant social and linguistic division exists between those who speak a fused-lect surzhyk as a native language and are not fluent in any other language variety, and those who mix languages because of incomplete, nonnative knowledge of a language that they are attempting to speak.[34] These two different types are often lumped together in people's general negative evaluation of surzhyk/impurity. Also, the division between bilinguals and monolingual surzhyk speakers is blurred in the existence of category 4, the habitual language mixing by bilinguals.

In all cases, the attitude of the listener and the listener's judgment of the speaker's skill and intent are key in whether the language will be labeled "surzhyk." The concept of surzhyk in its current broad usage, meaning impure language in general, cannot be pinned down in linguistic terms, but, as analyzed above, various types of surzhyk can be distinguished based on the social, historical, and ideological conditions in which they emerged. The structural linguistic features that may be discerned as mixing are examined below.

A Linguistic Overview of Nonstandard Ukrainian-Russian Language Forms

While the term "surzhyk," as used in Ukraine, cannot be defined around a single set of linguistic forms, it is useful to examine the various linguistic features that

---

34. Mokrenko (2001), an opera singer who in his article admits to being a "native" speaker of surzhyk himself, argues for such a distinction. He labels his categories "aboriginal surzhyk" and "stadial/temporary surzhyk."

are often considered "mixed" and thus may mark a language as surzhyk. Not everyone would include all these features in their definition of surzhyk, but the point of this analysis is to categorize all the possible deviations from the standard. There are still no field studies of the geographic and social variation or unity of surzhyk, but in a study of surzhyk used in literary works Flier finds that "even the quite preliminary typology of interaction at the levels of lexicon, syntax, morphology, and phonology [...] shows that the process of russification within Surzhyk is by no means random or illogical, but is governed by specific hierarchies and implicatures" (Flier 2000, 129).

Here, in analyzing the various nonstandard forms, I use the standard languages as reference points. The standard Ukrainian features that I discuss are widely agreed upon unless regional differences of opinion are specified. Not all the phenomena can be put into clear-cut categories, but I have attempted to systematize them according to regularity and linguistic level.

I. Nonstandard Forms on the Phonetic and Phonological Levels

1. Many Ukrainians speak language varieties that mix the phonetic features of one standard language while speaking primarily the other. For example, the Ukrainian "и" and Russian "ы" vowels that are customarily both transcribed as "y" are not identical. The Ukrainian "и" is a high-mid front unrounded vowel (represented by /ı/ in the International Phonetic Alphabet), whereas the Russian "ы" is a high close central unrounded vowel (represented by /ɨ/). In the transcriptions that follow I use the customary "y," unless I need to stress a difference. Note that the high close front unrounded vowel /i/ is pronounced the same in both languages, although its orthographic representation is "i" in Ukrainian and "и" in Russian.

> Phonetic and orthographic differences in vowel transcribed as "y":
> Standard Ukrainian: и [ı] high-mid front unrounded vowel
> Standard Russian: ы [ɨ] high close central unrounded vowel
>
> Vowel transcribed as "i" (orthographic but not phonetic difference):
> Standard Ukrainian: i [i] high close front unrounded vowel
> Standard Russian: и [i] high close front unrounded vowel

A more complicated situation exists in the case of "г" in Cyrillic, which was highlighted in the excerpt from the play *Myna Mazajlo* above. "Г" is generally pronounced [g] (a voiced velar stop) in Russian and [h] (a voiceless glottal fricative) in Ukrainian. Ukrainian has just a few (historically more recent) lexemes with /g/. Whereas standard Ukrainian preserves the phonemic difference between /h/ and /g/, it is characteristic usage in Ukraine to pronounce [h] in all cases.[35] There is a

---

35. The unconscious equation of /h/ and /g/, both produced as [h], reportedly caused some

small set of minimal pairs, the most cited example being *graty* 'grates, prison bars' and *hraty* 'to play', which are easily distinguished contextually. The pervasive use of [h] is also typical of spoken Russian in Ukraine, even among people who do not speak Ukrainian. For example, many people say *hod* instead of standard Russian *got* ['year', *rik* in Ukrainian], or *horod* instead of *gorət*[36] ['city', *misto* in Ukrainian]. Such pronunciation is marked because the voiceless glottal fricative [h] is absent in contemporary standard Russian (CSR), except in rare cases such as the interjections *aha* and *hop*.[37] Speakers of standard Russian who do pronounce [g] also extend their pronunciation habits to other languages, tending to pronounce "Harvard" as [garvərd] and "hello" as [xel:o] (this also characterizes others who learned English through Russian).

The Russian /g/ and Ukrainian /h/ are indicated by the same letter, "г." According to the Ukrainian orthography of 1928, the voiced velar stop /g/ is indicated by the separate letter "ґ" (which differs from the previous letter only in that the hook at the end of the horizontal top bar turns up, not down). This Ukrainian letter was banned in the 1930s but has since been reinstated in the 1990s. The elimination of this letter, which is absent from Russian, made the two languages slightly more similar orthographically, but pronunciation has remained divergent.

2. Phonological rules of one language may be applied to the other: For example, the Russian phonological rule *akanie*, in which the unstressed /o/ is pronounced as [a] or [ə], may be heard in the Ukrainian speech of people whose native language is Russian. Thus standard Ukrainian *rozmovljaty* 'to converse' (*rəzgəvarivət'* in Russian) becomes [rəzmavljaty].

Sometimes forms are used that are incorrect according to the rules of either language: for example, the word "what" is що [ščo] in contemporary standard Ukrainian (CSU), and что [što] in standard Russian. Widespread nonstandard forms in Ukraine are [š':o], or [š'č'o], both reflecting the influence of Russian phonology in the softened sibilants. Yet another form is [č'to], reflecting a literal reading of the way the Russian word is spelled. The social significance of the phonological variation in this word is evidenced by the slang term *štokaty*, used by some to mean "speaking Russian," that is, using the standard Russian *što*.

3. The phonological features of local dialects may be used in speech, marking it as nonstandard. For example, in villages in Volyn' (a northwestern region),

---

embarrassment during Vice President Gore's visit to Kyiv in July 1998. His Ukrainian-English translator addressed him as Mr. [Hor], which, for her, amounted to "speaking with an accent" but for him carried potential offense. I do not know whether this pronunciation was used with Mr. Gore himself, but Mr. [Hor] would be normal and unmarked in Ukrainian discourse, and thus would have caused some amusement for those who do know English.

36. In this section which examines nonstandard language forms, the transliteration of Russian words represents their pronunciation, not their orthography.

37. According to the pronunciation rules in S. I. Ozhegov's *Slovar' Russkogo Iazyka* (1986, 13).

and also near Kolomyia (a southwestern town), I frequently heard people pronouncing CSU /ja/ as [je], and /ča/ as [č'e]. Thus people said [jebluko] instead of standard Ukrainian [jabluko] 'apple', [pjet'] instead of [pjat'] 'five', and [d'ivč'eta] instead of [d'ivčata] 'girls'.

Sometimes people from one region had stereotypes about the pronunciation of people from another. For example, one Kyivite expressed his dislike of the *čokannja* of Western Ukrainians, referring to their harder (less palatalized) pronunciation of sibilants. A woman from the eastern Luhansk oblast stated that Western Ukrainian speech has a drawl or is "drawn out"—"з затяжкой," unlike the normal Ukrainian of her area.

II. Morphology

1. The gender of nouns with the same referent may be different in the two languages, leading to incorrect suffixes on adjectives and verbs. For example, the Russian word for "language"—*jazyk*—is masculine, whereas the Ukrainian term *mova* is feminine. Several times I heard people speaking about language in Ukrainian but using descriptive adjectives with masculine endings. Often when it came to actually saying the word "language," people would catch their mistakes themselves. The gender distinction is obligatory in both languages, so use of an inappropriately gendered adjective always results in some awkwardness.

2. Some of the declensions and plural endings are different in the two languages. A common incorrect usage regards the plural for masculine nouns ending in a consonant. I frequently heard the Russian ending "a" used in otherwise standard Ukrainian, such as [profesora] when it should be [profesory] 'professors'.

III. Lexicon

1. Words from one language may be used in the other, either consistently or sporadically. This is often the case when the Ukrainian and Russian words do not resemble each other at all and when someone less accustomed to speaking a given language cannot remember a lexical item. Also, certain terms may be considered the accepted norm in a speech community, and the use of the standard term would stand out. Usually the borrowed word will be pronounced according to the phonology of the language the individual is trying to speak. Table 4.3 shows examples of a common occurrence I observed, an individual's use of Russian words while otherwise speaking standard Ukrainian.

Sometimes people alternated between variants in a conversation, depending on how closely they were monitoring themselves, which depended on their judgment of the context. If they were not used to speaking standard Ukrainian, they might remember the correct Ukrainian form after having used a Russian substitute; or they might return to using the more familiar Russian term when speak-

TABLE 4.3. **Examples of common lexical Russianisms in surzhyk**

Surzhyk Form	Standard Russian	Standard Ukrainian	English Gloss
stolovaja	*stalovəjə*	*jidal'n'a*	cafeteria
klubn'ika	*klubn'ika*	*polunyc'a*	strawberry
ostanovka	*astanofkə*	*zupynka*	[bus] stop

ing quickly and not being as conscious of avoiding Russianisms. Some Russian words, such as the examples in Table 4.3, are used in Ukrainian speech so regularly in some regions or social groups that they could become legitimized as borrowings acceptable in standard Ukrainian at some point were it not for the purist efforts of language planners.

2. Words specific to local dialects are used in otherwise standard speech. For example, "potato" is *kartopl'a* in standard Ukrainian usage.[38] Nonstandard variants that are also used include *bul'ba, ripa, kartofl'a, barabol'a, mandyburka, buryška,* and *krumpli,* depending on the dialect and the influence of other languages in that region. The standard Russian diminutive variant *kartoška* is also used when speaking Ukrainian.

Sometimes there may be disagreement as to whether a form is standard. For example, Podvesko (1962) lists both *hovoryty* and *balakaty* as legitimate glosses for "to talk," but a few of my informants argued that the latter is not standard.[39] Only one woman, from eastern Ukraine, used *balakaty* regularly in her speech, which was, as a whole, very different from either Ukrainian or Russian standards.

IV. Syntax

1. Syntactic forms of one language may be used in the other. A frequent Russianism in Ukrainian is the use of the locative Russian form instead of the instrumental Ukrainian form when saying, for example, "The book is written in English."

Surzhyk form:	*Knyha napysana*	*na*	*anhlijskij movi*
English gloss:	book written	on	English language [locative case]
Standard Ukrainian:	*Knyha napysana*		*anhlijskoju movoju*
English gloss:	book written		English language [instrumental case]
Standard Russian:	*Kniga napisana*	*na*	*anglijskom jazyk'e*
English gloss:	book written	on	English language [locative case]

---

38. According to Buriachok et al. 1999.

39. Balla (1996) does not include *balakaty* as a gloss for "talk" at all, but Busel (2001) defines *balakaty* as equivalent to *rozmovliaty* 'to converse,' without marking it as nonstandard.

2. Local dialects also have features that deviate from the standard on the syntactic level. In speech some people may interpret these nonstandard features as being surzhyk. For example, a construction typical of western Ukrainian dialects is the separation of the reflexive particle -*s'a* from the verb. *Ja s'a pomylyla* 'I made a mistake' instead of CSU *Ja pomylylas'a.* This reflexive construction was the focus of debate in the standardization and codification efforts of the early 1900s (Chykalenko 1955, 412).

V. Semantics

Ukrainian and Russian words that are identical or similar can have different meanings, which can lead to a mixing of standards. For example, the word *čas*, pronounced almost the same in both standard languages, is often used in mostly Ukrainian speech for its Russian meaning, "hour," instead of its Ukrainian meaning, "time." Ukrainian *ned'il'a*, similar to the Russian term *n'id'el'ə*, is often used for its Russian meaning, "week," instead of its Ukrainian meaning, "Sunday." In some cases Ukrainian terms have lost possible meanings that differed from the Russian meanings. For example, although dictionaries list "comfortable" for the word *vyhidno*, people in Kyiv now use the word exclusively to mean "profitable" or "advantageous," which is the only meaning of the similar Russian term *vygədnə*.

Surzhyk: Abstract and Concrete

Enumeration of features and concrete examples of surzhyk risk making it seem definable, that is, containable in finite lists of phonological and grammatical rules, "a language" like "Ukrainian" or "Russian." As a whole, the term "surzhyk" refers to anti-language, or mixed and marginal language, eluding a single structural definition. While it would indeed be possible to codify a surzhyk, or several types of surzhyk, these would always only be partial sedimentations of this linguistic phenomenon. Formal linguistic analyses of various surzhyks could, nevertheless, provide insights into the structural constraints operating on processes of language mixing.

Do legitimate languages differ that much from surzhyks? In fact, any named language is much more than its codifications and the institutions that propagate it. It exists in all the practices of speakers who identify with that labeled language and corresponding identity. By saying that they are speaking a particular language, people stake a claim on that language and play a role in defining its correct forms and their social value. Standard languages, by definition, are determined by sets of rules and their status may be legislated by institutions, but, whenever people use them, their status and correctness are negotiated between people. Particular spoken and written instantiations of standard languages will reflect the conditions of their acquisition and the experiences of their users. The linguistic differences between users may be large or small, depending on the extent and efficacy of homogenizing forces such as schooling and people correcting one another.

This analysis disentangles the diverse ways that the surzhyk label has been used, providing a systematic way to study this language that is not a legitimate language, that came into existence from people maneuvering between languages. Surzhyk is a label that has been used in struggles over language status to discredit the value and legitimacy of speakers, a dynamic that is explored in the next chapter. Surzhyk in its various manifestations has been targeted by people who see the correction of linguistic shortcomings as a means of remedying historical injustices, whether these be institutionalized Soviet inequality and ethnolinguistic manipulation or shame over Ukrainian language and identity. Surzhyk connotes an identity that should not be (because it is an illegitimate category), but, being named, it also helps to define what should be, that which is *not* surzhyk. As cultural politics shift with Ukraine's independence and the newly elevated role of the Ukrainian language, the practiced definitions of both standard languages and surzhyks shift as well.

CHAPTER 5 Correction, Criticism, and the Struggle over Status

*Language (discourse) explodes, fragments, diverges: there is a
division of languages, for which no simple science of communication can account; society, with its socio-economic and neurotic
structures, intervenes, constructing language like a battle-
ground.*

— ROLAND BARTHES, *THE RUSTLE OF LANGUAGE*

Language Criticism and Social Authority

The gradual ascent in status of the Ukrainian language after independence in 1991 was hindered by a deep sense of insecurity regarding its legitimacy, since for so long it had been seen as a second-rate peasant language. The potential change in status led to more stringent views of just what "good Ukrainian" is. An ideology of the rareness and exclusivity of true, pure Ukrainian emerged, which helped to elevate its symbolic value and dissociate it from the low connotations of its supposedly impure, unrefined incarnations. This ideology fostered a general critical linguistic stance, particularly toward the quality of Ukrainian but also toward that of the Russian language.

The judgment of the correctness and legitimacy of language was a way to accord or negate people's status. Mixing Russian and Ukrainian was seen as the counterpoint to correctness, and labeling language as *surzhyk* was a way for people to discredit those they deemed unworthy. Different visions of Ukrainian authenticity clashed, and the negotiation of linguistic values and meanings, which is always present to some degree, became much more vivid. This process was facilitated by the poor institutionalization of Ukrainian in the early years of independence. In addition to the opinions I elicited in interviews, I also found many examples of the negotiation of language values in my observations and in publications. People from all walks of life engaged in language criticism, since the potential changes in language status affected everyone's social positioning. People sometimes ceded claims to social authority by expressing insecurity in their language and denying its legitimacy, whereas others defended the value of their language, and thus their identity and status. The most frequent objects of public language criticism were individuals who presumed to have social prestige and authority (particularly politicians, educators, and television announcers).

The degree of awareness and confidence in language usage varied. Some people were insecure about their language usage, while others were simply assertive of their belief in the necessity of language purity, notwithstanding their own transgressions. Expressed language ideologies did not necessarily correlate with people's actual uses of language. It was not unusual for people in my taped interview sessions to mix languages blatantly (in my opinion) in the very act of telling me that they thought such mixing was terrible.[1] Others told me that their Ukrainian language is not very good, even though, as far as I could discern, it did not deviate from the standard.

In interviews I frequently encountered the belief that truly "pure," "correct," and "valuable" language is something exclusive and difficult to achieve. As a female technician in her thirties from a village in central Ukraine explained: "Because it is very difficult to wield Ukrainian purely, and it is rare for anyone to wield it like that." In another interview, when a Kyivan male scientist in his late fifties stated that it is bad to mix languages, someone else in the room said, "We all mix." My interviewee replied, "No, not all. Mykola Lysyč doesn't mix. That one—what's his, Oleksandr ... Fedorovyč ... Lubčenko didn't mix, didn't mix." His assertion that he knew two people, one of them a poet, who spoke pure Ukrainian underscored its rarity and exclusivity. This ideology echoed what one Ukrainian writer told me: "Only writers speak pure Ukrainian."

The stance that pure Ukrainian is rare and exclusive made it a more valuable commodity on the linguistic marketplace, but when the language was seen to be so elusive that nobody could wield it, this undermined the language altogether. In this vein, a few people I interviewed denied that "true" Ukrainian existed at all. They were not presenting a philosophical challenge to the reality of "ideal" language, since they saw Russian and English as existing in legitimate forms. In challenging the legitimacy of Ukrainian in particular, they questioned the existence of a "real" Ukrainian identity. By criticizing the language quality of Ukrainian speakers, critics not only sought to disempower individuals but also to discredit the legitimacy of Ukrainian as a whole.

---

1. See Romaine 1989, 112, for a similar case involving a Panjabi/English speaker mixing languages in the act of saying that mixing is a bad thing.

The importance of purity and correctness, and the widespread vehement disapproval for mixing languages, discouraged people, who felt they were not perfectly fluent, from trying to speak Ukrainian, especially in contexts where either language would be acceptable. Thus purism was working against language revival, which has been the case in Corsica and elsewhere in the world (Jaffe 1999, 274; Jernudd and Shapiro 1989). I often heard that it is preferable to speak whichever language one knows best, rather than to mix the languages.

Advertisements and signs sometimes used nonstandard mixed language because the sign painters lacked knowledge of the standard language, which prompted discussions regarding the quality of Ukrainian reminiscent of similar debates during the Ukrainianization period of the 1920s.[2] Signs that were misspelled or strangely worded were cause for comment in the press. For example, a particular source of amusement and disdain for the author of a Russian-language Dnipropetrovsk newspaper column were the various translations of a Russian movie title (Chihirinskaia 1995):

> Посмешнее исковеркать русское название—ну, чем не украинское, например, «ФІГЛІ-МІГЛІ СТАРОГО ШКАПА»? Это, если вспомните, был такой фильм—«ШАШНИ СТАРОГО КОЗЛА». Каким образом «козел» стал «шкапом» а не «цапом», как ему положено, Бог ведает. Конечно, слово «шашни» перевести еше труднее, но «шльондри» (так было написано на афише другого кинотеатра)—это все-таки «шлюхи», а не «шашни». «ФІГЛІ-МІГЛІ» рисовалщиков афиш произвели на меня куда болшее впечатленее, нежели сам фильм.» [...] «Господа, ну если вам лень лезть в словарь—не переводите! Никто вас не посадит!»

> To mutilate a Russian title more humorously, well, why not the Ukrainian, for example, "FIDDLE-DADDLES OF AN OLD SHKAP." There was, if you remember, such a film, "INTRIGUES OF AN OLD GOAT." By what manner a "goat" [*kəz'ol* in Rus.] became a "shkap" [nonsense word], and not a "goat" [*cap* in Ukr.], as it should, God knows. Of course, the word "intrigues" [*šašn'i* in Rus.] is even harder to translate, but "SLUTS" [*šl'ondry* in Ukr.] (so it was written on the poster of another movie theater) those are after all "sluts" [*šl'uxy* in Rus.], and not "intrigues." The "FIDDLE-DADDLES" of the sign painters' posters made much more of an impression on me than the film itself. [...] Ladies and gentlemen, well, if you are too lazy to peer into a dictionary, then don't translate! Nobody will send you to jail!

The author went on to chastise the makers of signs for their "cheap snobbism" and carelessness in assuming that Ukrainian was easy and required no schooling.

---

2. The issue of language quality of public signage is illustrated in Kulish's play *Myna Mazajlo*. In the play Mokij, the pro-Ukrainianization son, expresses concern over the purity versus artificiality of the Ukrainian language of film theater announcements (Kulish 1955, 117).

While the latter statement supported the idea of a refined legitimate Ukrainian language, the ridiculing of the poster reinforced the stigma against using Ukrainian incorrectly, ultimately arguing that it is better not to try to use it at all.

Vehement criticisms of impurity in language were the dominant trend in academic and popular publications, which depicted surzhyk as bad manners, lack of education, cognitive degradation, a moral and ethical evil, a perversion of the laws of nature, a crisis of civilization, a bastard, a genetic admixture, spiritual plebeianism, absence of aesthetics, linguistic evidence of being colonized, and a *sovkova mova*—embodiment of Soviet oppression and degraded culture (Dashkevych 1990, 63; Dziuba 1990; Karavans'kyi 1994; Karpenko 1990; Okara 2001; Shumylov 2000; Stavyts'ka 2001; Verkhovodov 2000, 159). A 1994 book entitled *Anti-Surzhyk* referred to surzhyk as "crippled language" (*skaličena mova*), a harmful parasite on legitimate language that "dulls people" and "primitivizes thought," an ailment that needed to be cured. (Serbens'ka 1994, 6–7). Syncretic Ukrainian/Russian language varieties were treated as indicative of cognitive and verbal deprivation, as was the case with African American English in the 1960s and *joual* in Quebec in the 1970s and 1980s (Handler 1988, 162–169; Labov 1972a). As expressed by Stavyts'ka (2001, 11), "*Surzhyk* is first of all a simplified cognitive paradigm, and thus a marker of spiritual-intellectual poverty. . . . *Surzhyk* is bad taste in lifestyle, in behavioral models, in interaction, in worldview." In the eyes of academics, surzhyk embodied lowness in language, and, to become elevated, Ukrainian had to be dissociated from this impurity.

Some of my interviewees voiced similar views. A Russian woman scientist in her forties who moved from Russia to Ukraine when she was very young described her reaction upon hearing a child speaking surzhyk:

> It pained me, that children do not know their own native literary [standard] language. Their whole life they will speak an awkward, rough language. And if they speak the language awkwardly, that means they think in those categories. Do you understand, therein is the horror. They will be underdeveloped. They will be able to read neither Ukrainian nor Russian books. Even if they read, they won't understand.

Another Kyivan scientist, a fifty-year-old man of mixed Ukrainian-Russian parentage, summed up his views thus, "It's an uncultured situation, when a person mixes, that's it. It means this is a person of little culture."

Before independence, surzhyk was mostly seen as the language spoken by lower-class people with little education. Independence led to a new situation, namely, urban Russian speakers in positions of power speaking what sounded like surzhyk. As a result of the language law, certain government officials were supposed to speak Ukrainian at work, and those who did not know Ukrainian well tended to mix Ukrainian and Russian features. Both policy and politeness at times required that one make an effort to speak Ukrainian, but, whenever possible, people avoided speaking a language they were not fluent in, as they did not want to be looked down upon and ridiculed for speaking surzhyk. Habits of pronunciation, which are particularly hard to change since one is not usually conscious of them, were also a focus of criticism, making "true Ukrainian" difficult to achieve indeed.

Politicians were frequently at the center of linguistic criticism in my interviews and observations, and in publications. Early on, many of those who filled positions in the newly independent government were former Soviet politicians, so their allegiance to Ukrainian independence was particularly suspect. Some publications that were intended to correct the errors of surzhyk specified as their target the poor language of politicians (e.g., Hnatkevych 2000). As pointed out by a Ukrainian female technician in her thirties from a village in central Ukraine regarding the use of surzhyk: "It is unpleasant, these words, even our leaders and even this Kravchuk [the first president of independent Ukraine] and all these activists, all the same they use these words, although they should not use them." A forty-year-old female Russian scientist who lived in Ukraine most of her life included Soviet and Russian politicians in her criticism:

> Take a look at how our whole government speaks: it is unseemly, as much the Russians as the Ukrainians. Gorbachev speaks with an accent—his language is not literary [standard]. What Yeltsin allows himself—there it's the incorrect grammatical case, his ending is wrong, there it's something else, or his word stress is incorrect. It's unseemly. If the leaders don't speak [correctly] then the people won't either.

Former president Leonid Kuchma, the second president of Ukraine, was originally elected in 1994 in part for his promise to make Russian a second official language of Ukraine. This was a selling point among Russophones, who were dissatisfied with the increased presence of Ukrainian at the expense of Russian and the plan to further increase the institutional use of Ukrainian in coming years. Kuchma's Ukrainian language skills were not as good as those of his predecessor, Kravchuk, but once Kuchma was elected (and subsequently reelected to a second term in 1999), he never did make Russian official and proceeded to increase and improve his use of Ukrainian. Despite improvements, his Ukrainian language continued to be peppered with Russianisms (in pronunciation, syntax, and lexicon). These linguistic imperfections were cause for criticism from the very beginning of his presidency. This criticism intensified in response to events that were seen to reflect his inadequacy and corrupt nature as a politician. In 2000 a former presidential security guard publicized tapes that he had allegedly made surreptitiously of President Kuchma speaking with other politicians in his office, tapes on which Kuchma can be heard expressing his desire to be rid of Heorhii Gongadze, a journalist who was critical of the government; later, Gongadze was found beheaded. The tapes were scandalous not only because of their content but also because they revealed that, in private meetings, Kuchma mostly spoke an ex-pletive-ridden mixture of Ukrainian and Russian. His imperfect Ukrainian was not just the public face of someone who was Russophone in private, as one may have expected from a stereotypical Soviet politico turned national leader. Instead, the tapes revealed the shocking fact that his private language was a non-standard one that could easily be labeled surzhyk. The frequent expletives were taken as part of the nonstandard language, further evidence that with linguistic impurity come other degradations. Kuchma's linguistic deficiency was sometimes cited as evidence of his moral and ethical shortcomings (Leonovych 2001,2). Meanwhile, that he was adhering to the law by speaking Ukrainian in his public role was ridiculed as a cover-up of his corrupt activities (Rakhmanin 2002).

Despite the controversies, President Kuchma stayed in power and made his own claims to Ukrainian legitimacy in a 513-page book whose title, *Ukraine Is Not Russia*, clearly states the author's intention: to educate Russians about Ukraine and the attitudes of Ukrainians. The book was released in Moscow at the Six-teenth International Book Fair in September 2003. As one journalist reported, Kuchma deflected language criticisms: "'I don't hide that the book was written in Russian,' Kuchma said to assembled book fans. 'I still can't write freely in Ukrai-nian. I can speak fluently, but not in the kind of Ukrainian that our writers curse me in'" (Nicholson 2003). Although Kuchma acknowledged his shortcomings, by saying that he "still can't write freely in Ukrainian" he made these limitations seem temporary, something he had been working on, part of the corrective self-trans-formation that many people were making in the transition to Ukrainian inde-pendence. Meanwhile, he demoted the negative evaluations of writers to "curses."

Criticism was most often directed toward Ukrainian, but it was the quality of Russian that was targeted in the critique of the pro-Western politician Viktor Yushchenko, who opposed exclusively close ties with Russia. The criticism of his Russian language in an article on a pro-Russian news website, "ukraine.ru," which was against his political stances, appeared to be an effort to undermine his au-thority (Semenova 2002). At the time Yushchenko, who was a former prime min-ister of Ukraine and leader of the "Our Ukraine" party block, was campaigning in Crimea for parliamentary office. Yushchenko was already seen as a frontrunner for the upcoming (fall 2004) presidential elections.[3] In the article, criticism of lan-guage served as a vehicle for the criticism of politics. The journalist reported that, in response to a "restrained grumbling" (*sdieržannyj ropot*) in the auditorium after

---

3. Viktor Yushchenko ultimately won the controversial 2004 presidential elections after hundreds of thousands of people took to the streets in what has come to be known as the Or-ange Revolution. Demonstrators protested the widespread election fraud that initially gave the run-off election win to his opponent, Viktor Yanukovych, who had been publicly backed by incumbent president Kuchma and Russian president Putin.

Yushchenko's first words, which were in Ukrainian, Yushchenko asked which language the students preferred. When the reply was "in Russian," Yushchenko continued in Russian. According to the journalist: "In the boring account that followed, on the effective work of Yushchenko's cabinet when he was premier, students caught Ukrainianisms and tittered. Viktor Andreevich stressed the first syllable in the word *sformirovat'* 'to form' and the second in the word *ukrainskij* 'Ukrainian' (1–2). In standard Russian, the stress should fall on the last syllable of *sformirovát'* and on the penultimate in *ukrajínskij*. Yushchenko's pronunciation of *ukrájinsk'ij*, while commonly used in Russian speech in Ukraine, is considered old-fashioned and substandard by those who know the current standard language well. It is notable that incorrect word stress was brought forth as a shortcoming worthy of laughter and comment. The journalist also reported that students near her said that Yushchenko's speech sounded indistinct and mumbled (*kosnojazyčnyj*). Her report of Yushchenko's linguistic imperfections contributed to her assessment of his inadequacy as a politician and orator. She again brought up the issue of linguistic refinement when she reported that a professor from Donetsk spoke Russian much better than Yushchenko did (3). That minute linguistic details figured in the discussion illustrates how assessments of language correctness are used to judge social and political legitimacy.

Politicians have been a popular target but anyone could become an object of criticism, and I was not immune. My background played a significant role: I am a native speaker of Ukrainian, born and raised in the United States. After two years in Ukraine I had lost much of the accent typical of the Western diaspora and "pulled my language up to the standard," as one linguist put it. As mentioned above, there were mixed feelings about the Ukrainian diaspora. Members of the diaspora who came to Ukraine were usually economically privileged compared to average Ukrainian citizens. Quite a few members of the diaspora had become involved in Ukrainian institutions, particularly in nongovernmental organizations, businesses, and academia. While their contributions were appreciated by some, others resented the outsiders with their pretenses about how things should be done in Ukraine. Members of the diaspora had been critical of language in Ukraine and were able to exert some influence on the establishment of official terminologies by providing private funding for publications such as dictionaries.

Sometimes when I used an unusual but Ukrainian-sounding word, people would comment admiringly at how very Ukrainian I was. This was most often the case with villagers, who tended to be less secure about their own language, especially in eastern Ukraine. One woman remarked that I was "even more Ukrainian" than they. This reaction is reminiscent of the situation described by Trosset in Wales, who found that Welsh language learners functioned as "linguistic consciousness-raisers," making native speakers more critically aware of their own language use (Trosset 1986, 174–181).

At other times my language seemed to be valued highly because of its exoticism and association with foreign prestige. People who were reluctant to acknowledge the value of local varieties of Ukrainian seemed more willing to accept diasporic language as legitimate. This appeared to be the case with a Russophone history professor whom I met in Dnipropetrovsk. He criticized another historian who had just presented a conference paper in Ukrainian, saying that she spoke surzhyk, not real Ukrainian. As far as I could judge her delivery was in standard Ukrainian, with perhaps a slight eastern Ukrainian accent (most notably a more rounded pronunciation of /a/), but without any evidence of Russian language influence. The man expressing criticism spoke only Russian, stating that he was embarrassed to try to speak Ukrainian because he did not know it well. Still, his lack of knowledge of the language did not prevent him from devaluing the other historian's Ukrainian with the pejorative label surzhyk while complimenting me on speaking "true Ukrainian." By locating the legitimate language outside Ukraine, in the diaspora, he seemed to disempower local Ukrainian speakers. He could value my somewhat exotic, far from local Ukrainian, but he was habituated to consider the variety of Ukrainian around him as low.

Although most people found my command of Ukrainian commendable, I also sometimes met with criticism, even after I had eliminated most typical diasporisms from my speech. In Kyiv, at the Institute of Linguistics, a visitor to the institute admired that I spoke Ukrainian but was critical and said that I did not have it quite right. She could not point out anything wrong in particular when I asked her to, but she sensed differences that she could not articulate. This showed that subtle variations in intonation and pronunciation could be the bases for establishing (or denying) linguistic legitimacy. The woman's reluctance to accord correctness and authority to the language of someone from the diaspora reaffirmed local control over symbolic resources.

As illustrated in the examples above, control over the evaluation of language was part of the exercise of social power. Language differences were used to mark social and interactional boundaries, and also served as markers of moral qualities. By denying linguistic correctness, people sought to deny speakers social legitimacy and authority. In seeking social affirmation, many people sought to "correct" their own language use to fulfill new roles (as presidents, professors, or citizens of an independent country). This correction sometimes entailed learning a new language, or monitoring and "fixing" a language they already claimed to know. Between criticisms and corrections, the social and political transition from Soviet regime to Ukrainian independence was taking form.

Disputed Standards and Disputed Authenticity

The challenge of avoiding surzhyk was compounded by disagreement over what exactly distinguished surzhyk from pure language. This was partly a result of the very broad use of the term "surzhyk," discussed in chapter 4. Although a Ukrainian standard was established for the most part, disputes over specific terms and constructions lent an air of uncertainty to the language as a whole. Institutional structures that normally support and impose a specific Ukrainian standard were in disarray: training for teachers and others who needed language instruction was insufficient, and teaching materials were lacking. Since the official use of Ukrainian in many spheres of public life was relatively new, many people did not know the language well or were not confident of their language knowledge. Even those who had always spoken Ukrainian at home had to learn new technologies at work (Rich 1992).

Linguists and scientists were busy producing dictionaries, and disagreement emerged regarding the determination of "correct" forms. In 1994 the Ukrainian Cabinet of Ministers authorized a committee of linguists to set the standard, the National Committee of Linguistic Standards (*Natsional'na Pravopysna Komisija*). The Committee's approval was required for government-funded publications of dictionaries. This did not bar publications funded by other sources, however, and so published reference materials were not always congruent. The authority and actions of the Committee were debated and challenged by linguists from all regions of Ukraine, who differed in their evaluations of regional practices and their attitudes toward the revival of pre-Soviet norms.[4]

There was much debate over the Ukrainian *pravopys*—the codified standard that includes morphological and syntactic specifications. After the codification of Ukrainian in 1929, the *pravopys* was revised during the Soviet period in 1933, 1946, and 1960 (Kocherga and Kulyk 2002). Revisions established in 1990 and 1993 were unsatisfactory to many people, because they changed little of the pre-existing Russified standard and included contradictory formations (Ponomariv 2001). The membership of the National Committee of Linguistic Standards, originally established in 1994, changed as different groups in the government and the Academy of Sciences sought control over the standard language. A reform-minded committee, seeking to reverse Russifying Soviet tendencies, proposed a significant revision in 1999 that led to intense public debate (Ponomariv 2004). Many feared that the new revision would shake people's often already weak grasp of Ukrainian rules and alienate them from the language they knew. Others felt that the de-Russification of the standard was bending to the will of the Western diaspora, who tended to oppose Russian influence because they found it alien. The majority of the diaspora had fled western Ukraine during World War II and therefore had not experienced life under Russian-language dominance. Their involvement in Ukrainian affairs was sometimes resented as the meddling of out-

---

4. Official decisions about correct language use were debated by scholars from all over Ukraine at a conference held in Lviv on March 2, 1995, titled Ukrainian Language as a Factor in the Formation of the National Consciousness of Youth.

siders. The proposed revision was tabled until later—a move that favored the Russified status quo (Kocherga and Kulyk 2002).

In 2002, the Cabinet reconstituted the National Committee of Linguistic Standards with members who generally opposed changing Soviet-era standards. In 2003 this Committee proposed a revision that actually reversed a few of the de-Russifying changes established by the 1993 standards. This proposal fueled further controversy among linguists (Ponomariv 2004).

Since it was known that linguists disagree, people felt less constrained by a definitive single authority and freer to develop their own opinions. As one linguist complained, "In contrast to other countries where linguists discuss changes in the orthographic and grammatical rules, in our country the whole population got involved in this issue" (Ponomariv 2004, 16). I found a variety of reasons used to justify linguistic opinions in interviews, newspaper articles, radio commentaries, and participant observation.[5] Frequently people were moved by their attachment to linguistic forms that they had used their whole life, which seemed correct and natural as opposed to the other forms being suggested in the frenzy of language standardization. Some explained that they just had a gut reaction that a certain word was alien, whereas another word felt right and native to them. In my interviews and in the press, people evoked the works of Shevchenko or some other great poet or writer as epitomizing the linguistic ideal, or professed the Herderian ideology that each nation naturally has a language that embodies the soul of its people (e.g., Hoian 1991; Pan'ko 1991). Politics also played a role: many viewed independence as the opportunity for de-Russification, asserting that only the forms most different from Russian were correct (regardless of whether they were similar to terms in other languages). People with this attitude tended to hypercorrection, where they discarded longtime legitimate Ukrainian words if there were alternate variants more different from Russian. On the other end of the spectrum were those who were comfortable with the similarity of their Ukrainian words to Russian, and discounted other variants as being Polish, German, or of other origin—a hypercorrection of another sort. I witnessed the latter stance most often with natives of Kyiv and Dnipropetrovsk reacting to visitors or television spokespeople from western Ukraine.

In claiming correctness, people were striving to claim power for their words and validity for who they were. This was the case with the interviewee I called Halyna, introduced in chapter 1. I interviewed Halyna in December 1991, when she was in a Kyiv hospital. She was a recently retired factory worker in her fifties, who had grown up in a village in the Luhansk region in eastern Ukraine. She claimed legitimacy for her language and her identity as "simply Ukrainian," even

5. The Sunday morning "Slovo" programs on national radio channel 1 in 1994–95 were particularly rich with information on this topic.

though this contradicted her admittedly very mixed Ukrainian-Russian language. Her assertions were facilitated by the disputability of standards in the early years of independence.

Halyna was particularly outspoken in criticizing other varieties of Ukrainian, even those that were institutionally validated (such as in the media), despite her own relatively low social status and limited education. Halyna had completed three years of primary school and had worked as an unspecialized worker—*prostaja rabocha*. Others whom I interviewed who had little education tended to be less assertive in defense of their language quality or conceded that it was not good. As illustrated by Halyna's case, institutional validation through schooling or professional position supported confidence in one's symbolic capital. Its presence or absence did not predetermine attitudes.

At the beginning of our interview Halyna identified her (and her husband's and parents') native language and ethnicity as Ukrainian, but she referred to the language that she, her parents, and her husband spoke as "neither Russian nor Ukrainian, but this way and that, a joint language." I would have also categorized it as such: features of both languages were interwoven on all linguistic levels, with some unique regional specifics. Although Halyna had first stated that her spoken language was mixed, in answering my question about which school she went to she said that her language was "simply Ukrainian, and that's all," and she did this in her mixed language (italicized text highlights Russified surzhyk forms):

To *šo* sami, v nas taka škola bulá. *Da* my, v svojim seli bulá svoja škola. *Prepodavaly ukrájins'kyj jazyk i prepodavaly rus'kyj jazyk*, a *imenno* vse ž bulo to *na ukrájins'kom* u nas. *Mat'ematika* ne taka jak na u Kyjevi, *šo* tut s akcentom, nu *ukrájins'kyj jazyk*, prosto *ukrájins'kyj jazyk i vs'o, ponimaješ* ty? Tut že z akcentom, z prot'ažkoju, z takym-to *vymovl'en'ijem*, a u nas n'e, prosto *ukrájins'kyj jazyk i vs'o*, jak udoma, tak ona i knyžky taki my *jzuchaly,* u nas c'oho "š'o, naš'o c'oho," v nas ce kaže, z prot'ažkoju *slov* cyx nemaje, prosto *ukrájins'kyj jazyk i vs'o*.

That's *what* we ourselves, that was the school we had. *Yes* we, in our village we had our own school. *They taught Ukrainian language and they taught Russian language,* and *namely* everything was *in Ukrainian. Mathematics* not like it is in Kyiv, *that* here it's *with* an accent, but *Ukrainian language,* simply *Ukrainian language, and that's all,* do you *understand?* Here it's with an accent, with a drawl, with such a *pronunciation,* and in our area no, simply *Ukrainian language, that's all,* like at home, such were the books that we *studied,* we didn't have this "what, what for" [her rendition of an incorrect pronunciation of these words], we don't have these *words* with a drawl, simply *Ukrainian language, and that's all.*

Whereas in earlier statements Halyna admitted that her language is a "joint" nonstandard, in her assertion that her language is "simply Ukrainian," she rejected the stigma of impurity that would devalue her language and identity. Then, in response to my question on her preferred language of television shows, she replied that Russian is more intelligible to her:

> Nu *bezslovno rus'ki.* A tomu *šo* ja *ukrájins'kyj jazyk im'enno čistyj* ja joho ne *pon'imaju.* A *rus'kyj* ja vsi slova *pon'imaju,* te *šo* vony peredajut' po televizoru. Ot i *vs'o.* Bo buvaje take, *šo* pytaju, a *šo* ce take? [laughs] I *čož* my tak. *Jesli* vony b mohly *peredat'* taku jak taku nače jak *im'enno* my jiji sami *jzučyly* z samoho *d'etstva,* to my b *pon'imaly,* a *jesli* vony peredajut', ot *prym'erno* ot Kyjiv, tam ot *Vinn'ica,* ta *druhoje,* tam s *prot'ažen'ijem* slova idut', i tam uže joho, ne *pon'imajem, šo* ce take. Tak *šo* my *bol'še na rus'komu.*

> Well *definitely Russian.* And because *namely pure Ukrainian language* I don't *understand* it. But [in] *Russian* I understand all the words *that* they broadcast on television. And that's *all.* Because sometimes it can happen *that* I ask, *what* is this? [laughs] And why do we do it like that. *If* they could *broadcast* it such as *namely* we *learned* it from *childhood,* then we would *understand,* but *if* they broadcast, *for example* Kyiv, *Vinnytsia* there, and *others,* there go the words with the *drawl,* and there we don't *understand* what this is. So we [watch] *more in Russian.*

From my experience speaking with Halyna and observing her interaction with others who addressed her in both Ukrainian and Russian, I later concluded that she was monolingual in her syncretic language, which sometimes included more than one variant of a given term. In response to my questions regarding the language she used in various contexts, Halyna stated that she does not change her language, but also that she answered Russian speakers in Russian and Ukrainian speakers in Ukrainian. Although this was contradictory on one level, in her perception her language "worked" in conversations with both Ukrainian and Russian speakers without her consciously switching codes. At one point she summed up her language use everywhere as being mixed, but also linked her adherence to one language variety to the solidity of her national identity:

> Nu ja ž hovorju *šo vid'e* i ne chysto *ukrájins'kyj* i ne chysto *rus'kyj.* Ja svoju naciju ne min'aju, jak umiju tak i *mohu* po *rus'kom* balakat', i možu po-*ukrájins'ky.*

> Well I am telling you *that everywhere* [I speak] neither pure *Ukrainian* nor pure *Russian.* I don't change my nation, the way I know how [to speak], that's the way I *can* speak in Russian and I can [speak] in *Ukrainian.*

Halyna implied that switching languages is tantamount to changing one's nation or nationality, claiming that her identity does not waver. At the same time she explained that her language is not pure, and that she used it to speak in Russian and in Ukrainian, thereby claiming that her language functions to communicate with speakers of both languages. In the quote above there are two variants of the verb *can,* the Russified form *mohú* and the standard Ukrainian *móžu,* showing that even if she did not see herself as switching between languages, she sometimes did choose between variants that are closer to one language or the other.[6] This was subsumed in the mixed nature of her language, which she presented as a strength, and she fended off the degrading connotations of mixing by her assertions that she stays true to her one native language and nation. Halyna exemplified a traditional surzhyk speaker—an urbanized peasant, but, in keeping with the dominant discourses that denigrated surzhyk, she avoided this pejorative label.

The negative connotations of surzhyk were prevalent in the media and in public discourse in Kyiv, but in my interviews many people expressed more neutral and, in a few cases, even positive views. In interviews from 1991–92 I quantified these views and found that the proportions of neutral and negative opinions varied greatly depending on the interviewee's background and on the context of the interview. In a scientific institute in Kyiv, out of thirty-five people about a quarter were neutral or accepting of language mixing, and three-quarters expressed negative attitudes. Among fifteen people temporarily gathered in a Kyiv hospital, eight were negative, six were neutral, and one (Halyna) can be said to be positive about language mixing, although she did avoid the surzhyk label. In a third sample of eight people in a suburban high-rise in a southeastern Ukrainian city, all but one had neutral or accepting views of mixed language. In some cases those who expressed neutral views still believed that standard Ukrainian should become more widespread in the future (Bilaniuk 1997b).

I met only a couple of people who went so far as to argue that surzhyk should be recognized as a legitimate language. These were two scholars from eastern Ukraine visiting in the United States who identified surzhyk as their native language. After viewing a video segment in which a comedian used standard language in spoofing traditional Ukrainian theater in one skit and then used surzhyk in another, both men felt that the "standard" speech was alien and artificial and that the surzhyk was natural and native to them. These two scholars were frustrated that I did not provide a clear "objective" linguistic definition of surzhyk rather than an ideological one. A concrete "scientific" definition—stating the precise linguistic structures that constitute surzhyk and defining the boundaries where it is spoken—would provide the first steps toward codification and a foundation for legitimating surzhyk as a language in its own right. I did not encounter anyone else who made this argument seriously, but the idea was brought up as a joke in an eastern Ukrainian newspaper, with the suggestion that surzhyk be legitimized "since probably more people speak it than Galician [a western Ukrainian language]" (Kulyk 2001, 12).[7]

---

6. The standard Russian form of the verb "(I) can" is *magú*.

7. Kulyk is citing Dmitrij Kornilov from the January 18, 2001, edition of the newspaper *Donetskyi kriazh*.

More common were statements in defense of surzhyk that rejected its treatment as an abomination while continuing to recognize it as something unfortunate that needed to be corrected to pure Ukrainian (Bilaniuk 1997b). In 1995, in an editorial discussing common mistakes in Ukrainian, a provincial Dnipropetrovsk oblast newspaper portrayed surzhyk as preferable to Russian (Stepanenko et al. 1995):

> But, dear friends, do not be ashamed to speak "surzhyk," because not having gone through the experience of our native "surzhyk," you will never learn to speak Ukrainian correctly. It is better to speak "surzhyk," gradually clearing it of mistakes, than to "jabber" [*tsven'katy*], as Shevchenko put it, demonstratively only in Russian, completely shunning the native language of one's land—Ukraine.

The editorial concluded with an admission that the newspaper sometimes published linguistic mistakes because of haste and oversight, and that it would be grateful for letters pointing out these mistakes. This linguistic humility reflected the low social status of this newspaper and its target readership in contrast to the confidence in language quality that correlated with the assertion of higher status. The newspaper's role as an adviser in cultural correction went beyond language: the editorial on surzhyk was sandwiched between a feature on how to tie a necktie and a self-quiz for women to assess their youthfulness.

At a conference on language issues in Lviv in 1995, Oleksandra Serbens'ka, a professor of journalism and the author of *Anti-Surzhyk* (a popular book published in 1994 pointing out frequent linguistic transgressions in Ukrainian), spoke of surzhyk as a halfway point between Russian and Ukrainian, and thus a good stepping stone for relearning correct Ukrainian. This was a change from the categorically negative stance toward surzhyk presented in her book. I also found the view of surzhyk as a necessary transitional stage in Ukrainian educational establishments in Lviv, where directors expected older instructors who were not fluent in Ukrainian to do their best to teach in Ukrainian. Although the resulting mixed quality of their language was regarded as unfortunate, it was seen as preferable to speaking Russian exclusively, since speaking Ukrainian (albeit with difficulty) set the example that Ukrainian is necessary, not optional. The preference for imperfect Ukrainian over fluent Russian contradicted the attitude that I found more common in public and in the media, namely, that people should speak the language they know best rather than speak poorly.

Six years later, in 2001, a similar discourse was presented in the Ukraine-wide newspaper *Ukraïns'ka hazeta*, in an article by the renowned Ukrainian opera singer Anatolii Mokrenko. Mokrenko confessed that his own native language upbringing was "far from ideal," in the northeastern Slobidska Ukraine region where the local Ukrainian language has plenty of Russianisms. He decried the extreme attitudes of purism in which not only the language is disdained but also its speakers, as if they chose to speak surzhyk on purpose for the joy of "crippling" the language. In conclusion, he wrote:

> Of course, one cannot love surzhyk, but it must be understood as trampled human dignity. It is our own, of the black earth, even though it is weak. Because it is not isolated, it is a part of the people with their age-old Fate. You cannot simply throw it away, its roots are deep. Such is our Ukraine. So far. Later it will be better. And LATER will come when we do not allow anyone to shame our language, neither foreigners nor our own people. With a fierce "correct" "better than thou" attitude [*chystopl'ujstvo*], disdain for our, after all, "native" surzhyk we alienate our own people from their native language, because in this we alienate them into the hands of a foreign state, where, for example, one is not judged for using "impure" Russian language.

The newspaper editors felt it necessary to comment on this article, stating that they agreed with many of Mokrenko's points, but then they launched into a tirade detailing the linguistic transgressions of political and cultural figures, listing their grammatical errors in detail. The editors argued that surzhyk is inadmissible among educated cultural figures. The nit-picking purism of their commentary tended to perpetuate the very trend that Mokrenko decried. Could the purity expected of the elite realistically be separated from the forces shaping language values among everyone else?

Surzhyk generally was seen as a degraded Ukrainian and not as Russian language. However, in the struggle over legitimacy, some Ukrainians retaliated against the frequent claims that pure Ukrainian is nonexistent or rare by criticizing the Russian language of their compatriots, including politicians. They argued that Russophones in Ukraine are deluded if they think that they really speak pure Russian, because in Moscow their accent would mark them as provincial outsiders (Okara 2001). This argument logically equated the legitimacy of Ukrainian and Russian, but, in practice, critiques of Ukrainian were more damaging because of the newness of its role as a language of prestige. In contrast, people were habituated to the higher status of Russian, even when it was rendered imperfectly.

One of my Russophone interviewees, a scientist in his late forties from eastern Ukraine, acknowledged having a marked Ukrainian accent in his Russian, but he did not experience this as damaging. On the contrary, he even put a positive spin on it by identifying Ukrainian-accented Russian as his native language. When I asked whether he himself mixed languages, he answered:

> I try not to mix, but my pronunciation is Ukrainian. When I go to Leningrad, then I see right away that I have an accent. But later, when I've been there with them, then already I speak in Russian. Later, in Moscow, when I am getting closer to the Kyiv train station, again I hear [my] native [speech]. Even though they speak Russian, I already understand that they are Ukrainians.

The scholar Vitalii Radchuk (2000b) took the argument even further that Russian is just as impure as Ukrainian, presenting scientific evidence that all languages are surzhyk mixtures, even though they are not recognized as such. Radchuk cited a 1957 study by the Russian scholar O. Trubachov of 10,779 Russian words whose etymologies were provided in M. Fasmer's four-volume etymological dictionary of Russian. Trubachov found that only 0.9 percent of the words were exclusively Russian; of the rest, 58.5 percent were late borrowings, 10.3 percent were onomatopoeic or of unclear origin, 29.5 percent were general Slavic and early borrowings, and only 0.8 percent were shared only by the eastern Slavic languages. This evidence refuted the supposedly unique linguistic closeness of Belarusian, Ukrainian, and Russian (which had been used by pro-Russian scholars to argue for the naturalness of the unification of these nations). By citing Trubachov's study, Radchuk also sought to return linguistic legitimacy to Ukrainian, which was often discredited for its lack of a "pure form"—after all, even the prestigious Russian was a thorough mixture. Radchuk did not consider surzhyk a positive phenomenon, but he tried to minimize its threat to the construction of a prestigious Ukrainian language by scientifically arguing for the normalcy of language mixing, in that all standard languages had "mixed" histories. Radchuk's argument can be seen as an effort to even out the terms of the struggle over the values of Ukrainian and Russian.

Radchuk's effort to make people conscious of the historically mixed nature of languages did not make a big impact, and the ideology of pure language continued to prevail. This ideology of purity was part of the iconization of language that is key in nationalism, and it led people to ignore the linguistic facts that Radchuk pointed out (Irvine and Gal 2000).[8] People's gut feelings (their inculcated habitus) and intentions in social positioning determined whether they judged a language to be pure and socially valuable.

The ideas of one young man in Lviv illustrate another aspect of the conflict between embracing and rejecting surzhyk. He told me that a literary language that is "too pure" loses "its charm" and becomes a "dry language," and that using a word that is more full of life, even if it is Russian-based slang, can be much more expressive. He bemoaned the fact, however, that his parents used Russified words and did not adhere to pure Ukrainian at home. His contradictory views underscored the difficulty of drawing the line between the informal and expressive use of Russified terms versus the Russification of the Ukrainian language.

In an interview I conducted in 1992, in Kyiv, a man told me that he occasionally used surzhyk for its humorous value. Although he was careful to say that

---

8. As discussed in chapter 2, iconization is the process through which linguistic features associated with particular social groups come to represent them, "as if a linguistic feature somehow depicted or displayed a social group's inherent nature or essence" (Irvine and Gal 2000, 37).

he was not making fun of the people who regularly use this language, he believed
that surzhyk in itself can convey jokes that a standard language simply cannot.
He described this joking as a play on the subtleties of expression: a nonstandard
language could be particularly useful in conveying satire and irony about the current state of affairs. This use of surzhyk came to prevail in Ukrainian popular culture during the first decade of independence, although some people found even
humorous uses of surzhyk distasteful and dangerous.

Surzhyk, Creativity, and Cultural Alternatives

Surzhyk was used in literature and performance in a variety of ways, ranging
from serious to humorous, and from neutrally realistic to clearly condemnatory.
On one end of the spectrum of literary functions was serious, nonjudgmental realism, which depicted the nonstandard speech of people of low social status and
little education—usually villagers—without implying anything negative about
their character, only perhaps the tragedy of their circumstances. On the other end
of the spectrum, surzhyk was used as an embodiment of cultural degradation or
even moral depravity, often presented as bitter humor. The connotations of
surzhyk between these extremes were ambiguous.

Some people did not tolerate the use of surzhyk anywhere, but others argued
that freedom of expression was essential for the development of a "complete"
Ukrainian culture, with both its high and low aspects (Masenko 1994). As the author Poderevians'kyi (1999) wrote in defense of the use of surzhyk, "Now is a very
interesting moment in the life of the language: we have the concurrent existence
of literary Ukrainian, the Galician variant of the language, surzhyk. And each
variant has the right to exist, because it is alive."

An example of serious nonjudgmental use of surzhyk is Miastkivs'kyi's
(1989) story set in and near the southern city of Odesa at the time of the 1933
famine engineered by Stalin. The story was narrated in standard Ukrainian, and
surzhyk was used to depict the speech of homeless children who had come to the
city from villages to beg for food. The nonstandard speech served as a reflection
of the lack of education and tragic circumstances of the starving children.

In the "new literature" of Ukraine, writers used surzhyk in more controversial ways, tackling many formerly taboo topics of city life (Masenko 1994). Andrukhovych (1991, 1993) and Zabuzhko (1996) used elements of surzhyk
selectively: their educated, urban characters only occasionally mixed Ukrainian
and Russian, reflecting the coexistence of the two languages in their environment. Their use of surzhyk functioned to impart a gritty realism, bringing us
closer to the protagonists by showing the imperfection of the cultural elite. This
was not a neutral realism in that it carried connotations of roughness and some
degradation.

In the first Ukrainian best-selling novel *Field Research in Ukrainian Sex,* author Oksana Zabuzhko described the intimate struggle against the intrusion of other languages into the protagonist's native Ukrainian, through a semi-auto-biographical account (the protagonist is a writer also named Oksana, and the events described correlate with some of the author's experiences) set in the late Soviet–early post-Soviet period.[9] The story includes experiences during a stay in the United States, comparing the pressures of English with that of Russian, and underscoring the foreignness of Russian to Ukrainian through this comparison. In her account Oksana seemed powerless to resist the intrusion, although the "foreign" words were offset from her "own" language in her mind (Zabuzhko 1998, 28; in the English translation italics highlight codeswitches into other languages from Ukrainian):

> От чим же, до речі, паршива чужа країна—набиваються, натрушуються, як пух у ніздрі, напохватні чужинецькі слівця й звороти, заліплюють пори в мозкові, нахабно тиснуться попідруч, навіть коли ти наодинці з собою,—і незчуваєшся, як починаєш балакати "хеф-напів," тобто повторюється те саме, що вдома (вдома? схаменися, кобіто,—де він, твій дім?), ну, гаразд, у Києві в Україні— з російською: всякає ззовні накрапами, зсихається-цементується, і мусиш— або повсякчас провадити в умі розчисний синхронний переклад, що звучить вимучено й ненатурально,—або ж приноровитися, як усі ми, самим голосом брати чужомовні слова в лапки, класти на них такий собі блазнювато-іронічний притиск як на забуцім-цитати (наприклад [...] «Ти себе що—"побєдітєльніцей" почуваєш?»).

> And this, exactly, is what makes a foreign country so wretched—incidental little foreign words and turns of phrase pack in, get stuck like fuzz in your nostrils, they clog up the pores in your brain, impertinently they squeeze right up under your fingertips, even when you are alone with yourself,—and you do not even realize it when you start speaking *half* [in English] and half, that is, the same thing starts happening as at home (at home? come to your senses, *woman* [Polish-based Galician slang]—where is your home, anyway?), well, okay, in Kyiv, in Ukraine—with Russian: it seeps in from outside drop by drop, sets in—cements itself, and you must either carry on a constant purify-

---

9. Oksana Zabuzhko (b. 1960) is one of the most prominent Ukrainian post-Soviet writers. Her 1996 novel, *Field Research in Ukrainian Sex,* was very popular in Ukraine and was also translated into Polish, Russian, Czech, Hungarian, and English. As the author acknowledged in an interview, the title is deceptive in that the book does not deal all that much with sex. Zabuzhko agreed with the observations of a reviewer that "these 'studies in sex' are nothing but a 'pathogenesis of our solitude,' meaning solitude not just in personal terms, but also in historical, cultural, and even linguistic terms. Quite a perceptive resume of the entire twentieth-century Ukrainian history: a lost, 'forgotten' country, with a historical memory that's been deliberately erased, subjected for so long to all kinds of humiliation" (http://www.zabuzhko.com/en/interviews.html; accessed August 2004).

ing synchronic translation in your mind, which sounds forced and unnatural—or subdue yourself, like all of us, putting those foreign words into quotes with just your voice, putting them under the same mocking-ironic pressure as on a pseudo-citation (for example, "What, do you feel like the '*winner*' [*in Russian*] now?)

In Oksana's rejection of the intrusion of other languages into her native Ukrainian she asserted a commitment to Ukrainian purity, while admitting the difficulties of maintaining such purity. In her novel Zabuzhko used surzhyk and Russian sparingly, to add realism to urban dialogue or to highlight irony. In the passage above, the protagonist's rejection of English, the knowledge of which is generally viewed as a prestigious asset in Ukraine, heightened the cultural exclusivity of her stance. As a writer in Ukraine, Oksana (whether the author or the character) filled a role traditionally regarded as that of a language arbiter, and her admission of vulnerability to linguistic impurity is clearly depicted as an unfortunate weakness.

The writer Bohdan Zholdak became known for pushing the use of surzhyk even further, although a writer colleague of his told me that he is the "biggest purist of them all." Zholdak used surzhyk as an embodiment of the baseness of post-Soviet reality: the surzhyk of his characters corresponded to their intellectual and cultural lowness—its humor was bitter (1992, 1998).[10] Zholdak's (1992) story "Mania chy Tania" was written wholly in surzhyk, told in the voice of a man of limited intellect, embodying the degradation of Soviet life. Here surzhyk was not safely contained in the context of a story told in standard Ukrainian but permeated from beginning to end. What hemmed it in was the protagonist's circumscribed view of the world.

Les' Poderevians'kyi's use of surzhyk is similar in embodying the baseness of Soviet and post-Soviet life but is much more extreme. In his 2001 collection of avant-garde plays, although the narration is mostly in standard Ukrainian, characters speak surzhyk that is full of expletives and of prison and army jargon, depicting an absurd, depraved, surreal world. An introduction to the book labels these writings a grotesque "literary Chernobyl." This introduction attempts to fit Poderevians'kyi's works within the logic of Ukrainian nation building by arguing that the writings underscore the alienness of degenerate Russian-origin expletives and late Soviet spiritual emptiness to true Ukrainian culture (Lapins'kyi 2001). Nevertheless, the warnings "Attention! Non-normative lexicon" and "Careful! Non-normative lexicon" appear on the cover and in the front matter to alert those with delicate linguistic sensibilities (and to attract those who are eager for the carnivalesque release of the non-normative).

Poderevians'kyi's writings and performed readings developed a cult following in the 1990s and 2000s. They presented an extreme in pushing the boundaries

---

10. See Koznarsky 1998 for a literary analysis of language in Zholdak's works.

of linguistic and social propriety that was particularly attractive to youth who rejected rigid norms, whether they were Soviet or national Ukrainian. The academic Maksym Strikha (1990, 141) argued that surzhyk was a necessary manifestation of a counterculture:

> Surzhyk has taken an important place in youth subculture, where it spread in the underground culture of the 70's and finally asserted itself in the first "Červona Ruta Festival" of 1989 (the texts of Braty Had'ukiny, Sestryčka Vika). And it should be said openly that these crippled, and from a purist point of view, hideous lines like "you be my jackhammer" ["ty bud' mojim *otbojnym* molotkom"—Russified term italicized] did a lot more for the awakening of Ukrainian consciousness in the generation of teenagers than the poems of laureates about the melodic nightingale-language [kalyno-solovjina mova]. The reason for this phenomenon is rather simple: the older students of PTU [Profesijno Texnične Učylyšče (Professional-Technical School)] suddenly realized that the Ukrainian language is no worse than Russian at serving their really limited spiritual desires, and the broken surzhyk gave the texts a hint of forbidden riskiness.

The countercultural and rebellious function of surzhyk appeared most often in the songs of popular music groups, such as the rock groups Vopli Vidopliassova (VV), Braty Had'ukiny, Lesyk Bend, Vika, and the hip-hop group Tanok Na Majdani Kongo (TNMK). Nonstandard language had a subversive quality: it challenged authority and constructed an alternative to the government-endorsed standard Ukrainian culture.

Like politicians, musicians also faced censure for the use of surzhyk. In a television interview in May 2000 with the Ukrainian folk-inspired rock group Mandry, the interviewer questioned the group's choice of even singing in Ukrainian at all, given that their language is "checkered" like the shirt they sing about (one of their popular songs is "Kartata Soročka" 'checkered shirt'). The lead singer Foma defended his use of Ukrainian by relating the Ukrainian expertise of his mother and his time spent in the village. Indeed, the challenge to his use of Ukrainian language at first seemed odd to me, given that, in my estimation, most of his songs were predominantly in standard Ukrainian, with only rarely a lexical dialectism or Russianism. However, as I witnessed several times, the inclusion of any surzhyk in a speaker's or performer's repertoire affected judgments of his or her language as a whole. A form of misrecognition was again operating here.[11]

On Mandry's 1999 album titled *Romansero pro Nižnu Korolevu* 'Romance about the Gentle Queen,' one song was clearly in surzhyk, whereas the others were Ukrainian with only a few Russianisms. This markedly surzhyk language

---

11. Misrecognition, as defined by Bourdieu (1990:140–141), is "an alienated cognition that looks at the world through categories the world imposes, and apprehends the social world as a natural world." In this case, a few Russified elements lead to the classification of a whole linguistic repertoire as surzhyk, according to a strict social logic of linguistic purism.

song, "Amore Mio," was the last song on the album, and it is telling that it was the only song whose lyrics were not provided in the CD booklet.[12] The Ukrainian-Russian surzhyk and behaviors depicted identified the protagonist as a lower-class urban man who sings of romantic fantasies on palm beaches and addresses his love with the Italian phrase *amore mio* 'my love'. The contrast between the exalted vision of his romance and the mundane details of his everyday life is humorous. The surzhyk is not clearly depicted as negative: it is associated with belonging to a lower class, but it is also the vehicle for idealized romance. I suspect that the lyrics of this song were not printed since a written embodiment of surzhyk that was not clearly critical would elicit more criticism, for in printed matter there is a greater presumption of legitimacy (Annamalai 1989, 230; Jaffe 1999, 215).

Surzhyk figured prominently in the rap of TNMK, one of the most successful music groups in Ukraine.[13] The group's songs on the 2001 album *N'eformat* were mostly in Ukrainian, with many surzhyk elements and some segments in Russian. In an interview I conducted in 2002 with the rapper and songwriter Sasha Sydorenko a.k.a. Fozzi, he explained that surzhyk attracted him because it was alive. He and his fellow musicians had grown up speaking Russian in the city of Kharkiv, and received very positive audience responses to their early experiments with Ukrainian-surzhyk songs. Ultimately Fozzi continued to compose only in Ukrainian and surzhyk, since he felt that it works much better for rap than Russian does. The success of the group in Ukraine and in Russia was a source of pride among young people in Ukraine, and had added to the appeal of the Ukrainian language. As far as language purity, Fozzi argued that "it would not be completely honest if we were to write like people who used Ukrainian from the beginning, people would sense that this isn't completely honest, so we feel comfortable using surzhyk." Fozzi also challenged purism in saying that "there are actually many Ukrainian languages. There isn't one standard. The correct language isn't completely alive. Each city has its own language. It's got to be alive, with new words coming about."

A brief narrated track between song tracks on the *N'eformat* album tackles the fetishization of "authentic language" directly. This track begins with a "sexy" young female voice speaking standard Ukrainian, as if she were advertising a phone sex hotline. Instead of sex she is selling Ukrainianness, and her words are interspersed with samples of an older woman speaking in a heavy Ukrainian village dialect that is hard to understand. This spoof on phone-sex advertisements

---

12. The use of the Italian phrase *amore mio* in the lyrics, and the listing of the song title in roman letters, added another dimension of complexity to the linguistic mixing in the song.

13. The group's name, Tanok Na Majdani Kongo, translates as "Dance on Congo Square," referring to the New Orleans Congo Square that is considered the birthplace of jazz.

substitutes for sex the supposed pleasure of listening to "authentic" dialect. The text is as follows:

> Today we propose that you dive into the fairytale world of the Ukrainian language. [Passage in heavy dialect.][14] Our linguistettes and linguists[15] are waiting for you twenty-four hours a day. [Passage in heavy dialect.] Only for the underaged. Call telephone number 8 900 800 [fades out, followed by a passage in heavy dialect.] One minute of talk costs [pause] normally[16] [Final passage in heavy dialect].

In the phone-sex spoof narrative and the following song, "ПоRAPалося серце" (*poRAPalos'a serce;* a Ukrainian-English play on words meaning "my heart has gotten rapped/roughed up"), TNMK critiqued the iconization of Ukrainian identity while simultaneously embracing, incorporating, and transforming folk styles and themes.[17] In some of the other passages between songs and in the songs themselves, TNMK took on the divisive Russian versus Ukrainian issue head-on and joked about it. The rivalry was both a joke and a serious matter—final meanings were left unstated and ambiguous. Thus TNMK went against the prevailing trends of purism and of sweeping ethnic tensions under the rug. Even so, Fozzi (who gave the interview in good standard Ukrainian) expressed his desire to improve his language and admitted to consulting with musicians from western Ukraine to check on correct forms. His friend Sasha Polozhyns'kyi, lead singer of the alternative group Tartak, gave Fozzi two lengthy dictionaries of Ukrainian synonyms for his birthday, supposedly so that he would have to call him less to consult about correct Ukrainian forms. But Polozhyns'kyi did not see himself as a language authority. In an interview he expressed concern over language purity

---

14. The content of the dialect passages, some of which are quite difficult to understand on first hearing, is not important to the skit, but it does evoke some rural stereotypes. The "heavy dialect" passages translate as follows: "Be it—no matter what money you've got, you need a friend for a day, I know, I'm not giving anything"; "Listen, *kumočko* [diminutive feminine form of address between parents and godparents], now tho- those are bells ringing, oh, we'll just drink up and go, don't worry"; "Drink it up [unintelligible] and she sa- now listen *kumočko*, now I'm not all burned up. And I [unintelligible] give us and these in one go we'll drink up, and we'll go"; "And goodnight to Safronia. And with that the end."

15. In the original a made-up ("incorrect") feminine form of the word "linguists" (*movoznavky*) is used along with the usual (male and unmarked) form (*movoznavci*). By using a made-up female form along with the neutral/male form, the text further sexualizes the "linguist."

16. The term *normal'no* 'normally' is meant here to translate "as one would expect," "just right," "not too much."

17. The music video for the song "PoR A Palos'a serce" takes the syncretism of the song to another level. While the audio blends rap and hip-hop elements with Ukrainian folk melodies and verses, the video blends typical hip-hop video elements (break-dancing, undulating sexy female dancers, the performers posturing in typical hip-hop clothing) with Ukrainian imagery (folk graphic designs framing the video and a Ukrainian flag appearing as the final backdrop.)

and a desire to improve his Ukrainian, for although he had grown up in a western Ukrainian town, he stated that it was not a purely Ukrainian language environment. One would expect surzhyk to have a place in hip-hop, inasmuch as it is parallel in many ways to African American English, but the logic of legitimacy through correctness nevertheless affected the performers of this countercultural genre.

Verka Serduchka: Post-Soviet Icon of Surzhyk

While much public discourse and academic commentary decried linguistic impurity as an evil, and performers who used it expressed ambivalence about it, the comedian Andrii Danylko made surzhyk the centerpiece of his carnivalesque role cross-dressed as "Verka Serduchka."[18] He rose to stardom in Ukraine and beyond, in Russia, and his signature character, Verka Serduchka, emerged as the quintessential icon of post-soviet surzhyk. Verka is a surzhyk-speaking female character whose official lowly profession is that of a *providnyc'a*—a train car attendant, responsible for collecting tickets and distributing linen and tea. Since most people in Ukraine travel by train and use the train as an individualized parcel service, almost everyone has dealt with such typically provincial *providnyc'i*. Danylko's portrayal of Verka, a train attendant turned pop star, parodied Ukraine's envisioned transformation from a Soviet backwater to the "center of Europe" (Hrytsenko 1999, 18).

Danylko's role as the exaggeratedly crass Verka began as an advertisement for a bank in 1995, continued in theater performances, and in late 1996 culminated with Verka Serduchka's own talk show *CB Шoy* 'SV Show' on the most popular Ukrainian TV channel, "1 + 1" (Hrytsenko 1999, 16).[19] This show aired for several years and went off the air by the summer of 2002. In 2002 Danylko-as-Verka continued to perform at concerts, released a few popular song CDs, and performed in humorous televised films. In the largely improvised *SV Show* program, the Verka character chatted about various mundane topics with guests who were famous cultural figures from Ukraine and other countries of the former USSR. The show supposedly took place in a train compartment, the first-class *spal'nyj*

---

18. The name is pronounced "V'erka Serd'uchka," but it is rendered "Verka Serduchka" when appearing in roman letters on CDs and on the official website. Here I use the spelling used by the performer.

19. See also the show's website: http://www.1plus1.net/programs/sv_show.phtml. The slogan for the "1 + 1" /*odyn pl'us odyn*/ channel, "ти не один/*ty ne odyn*/" 'you are not alone,' also exemplifies surzhyk/syncretism, as pointed out by V. Kulyk (personal communication). The correct standard way to say "you are not alone" in Ukrainian would be ти не сам /*ty ne sam*/. This correct form, however, does not tie into the channel's name. Thus, for the sake of achieving the cute play of words for the slogan, a translation of Russian phrasing (a calque) is used.

vagon 'sleeping wagon,' abbreviated in Ukrainian and Russian to SV, and hence the title *SV Show*.[20] Verka mercilessly satirized pop stars, Ukrainian traditions, politics, and foreign culture. Verka left no sphere of cultural values untouched and often managed to make fun of the stars who were her guests, particularly if they appeared to think too highly of themselves. Danylko's act was refreshing to people who felt stifled by the attention to cultural and linguistic correctness.

With his unprecedented success as Verka, Danylko brought surzhyk to prominence. His Verka Serduchka was not alone on television in her use of surzhyk, and at the turn of the millennium there were various comedy acts that used nonstandard mixed language along with slang, including "Krolyky" 'the little rabbits' and "Dovhonosyky" 'Long-noses' who both appeared on television in skits or shows. But these acts presented surzhyk in its habitual context of informality and "low culture," whereas Verka took surzhyk to the top, claiming stardom and producing hit albums, and rubbing elbows (or cuddling under one blanket on the couch of the staged train compartment) with other pop stars. Verka became the poster girl for surzhyk, figuring on the cover of a handbook titled "Let's Avoid Russianisms in Ukrainian Language! A Brief Dictionary-Anti-surzhyk for Deputies of Parliament and Everyone Who Wants Their Ukrainian Language to Not Resemble the Language of Verka Serduchka" (Hnatkevych 2000).

Verka's surzhyk was not only linguistic: she transgressed and undermined all cultural values, blurring high culture and low culture, male and female, pre- and post-Soviet life. Her costumes combined sequined glitz and holey woolen tights, blending the markers of poverty and wealth. Verka was both pop star and lowly train attendant, blending together fame and the mundane. Reality itself was brought into question: Was Verka an act, or was she real? Often Verka was discussed without mention of the actor who played her, even in serious contexts using the pronoun "she," reinforcing her reality above the (male) actor's. Verka made fun of fame, but she became famous herself. While Verka was deconstructing and undermining categories and values, some thought that the success of this character was constructing legitimacy for surzhyk. Initially Verka's performance was more clearly a parody of a low cultural type, but her wild popularity brought this into question—the spoof of pop stars had become a pop star herself. A Ukrainian radio personality, Anatolij Vekskliarskyj, who used to be a surzhyk-talking disc jockey but gave up this role in favor of standard language use, criticized people's perceptions of Verka:

> In general, people are wrong in their understanding of the image of Verka Serduchka. They consider her "their own," a kindred spirit that is accessible and understandable.

20. V. Kulyk pointed out another level of polysemy: "SV" can also stand for "Serduchka Verka" (last-name-first is common usage in official documents in Ukraine), and thus the *SV Show* is simply the show named after the character.

Cover of book published in 2000 by Yurii Hnatkevych, titled *Let's Avoid Russianisms in Ukrainian Language! A Brief Dictionary—Anti-surzhyk for Deputies of Parliament and Everyone Who Wants Their Ukrainian Language to Not Resemble the Language of Verka Serduchka*. Pictured are the Parliament building and the actor Andrii Danylko in the guise of surzhyk-speaking train car attendant cum pop star Verka Serduchka.

In reality Verka is a disgusting creature, she is malicious. She considers herself the lead train conductor, but her place is that of a janitor.

When I was DJ Tolia [when he used surzhyk] acquaintances who hung out in the "higher spheres" told me: "You need to understand, they won't get it," that they are being made fun of, they consider you one of their own. The same is the case today with Andrii Danylko. His Verka is considered one of their own by those whom he is criticizing. (Hal'kovs'kyi 1998, 2)

In the quote Vekskliarskyj tried to delimit and control the meaning of Verka's performances, defining them as a parody of low culture that is not recognized as demeaning by people of the lower classes. But such assertions did not eliminate the polysemy of Verka Serduchka. Rather than being a clear parody or a strategic effort at bivalency, in Verka's performances intertextuality and ambiguity appeared as ends in and of themselves. Danylko-as-Verka reveled in superimposing cultural oppositions and revealing the absurdity of constructions of prestige and fame, his/her own included. Whether Verka Serduchka was beneficial or harmful for the development of Ukrainian independence was unclear, as unclear as Verka's gender and cultural status.

When I was in Ukraine in May 2000 I took every opportunity to ask people what they thought of Verka Serduchka, and I received a wide range of responses. One taxi driver (who at the end of our long conversation confided in me that he was an undercover officer of the Ministry of Internal Affairs) described Andrii Danylko, the actor who plays Verka, as "the only real actor in Ukraine," talented and hardworking. In contrast, the rector of Kyiv State University referred to Verka as "a two-headed monstrosity from Chernobyl." Many educated Ukrainians shared this negative opinion, although not all expressed themselves so colorfully. After all, Verka made fun of the Ukrainian intellectual elite as well. Others had enjoyed Verka's acts at first but found that they lost appeal after their initial impact.

While Danylko's creativity and skill were undeniable, many people found his satire objectionable for several reasons. It continued a history of demeaning and trivializing Ukrainian language and culture, just as many people felt that the acts of the 1960s performers Tarapun'ka and Štepsel' did (Hrytsenko 1999, 17). By associating Ukrainianness with surzhyk and provincialism, the performances reinforced self-perceptions of inferiority. Some people also expressed the fear that the preponderance of base surzhyk-language humor would lead to the expectation that humor requires degraded language, extinguishing the practice of standard language humor.

The demeaning of Ukrainian language and identity was all the more problematic when it was taken beyond Ukraine. Few Ukrainian cultural products were exported to Russia, and Verka Serduchka was one of them. Ukrainianness may have developed some countercultural chic in Russia, as evident in the success of Ukrainian rock and hip-hop groups VV, Okean El'zy, and TNMK, but this success was at first demographically more limited compared to Verka's popularity. Verka's *SV Show* was the only Ukrainian television program that I knew of that was broadcast in Russia in the late 1990s. Verka's creator Andrii Danylko traveled widely to perform, including to the Russian Far East and the United States. He achieved success in other roles as well, but Verka remained his dominant role. The popularity of the *SV show* in Russia, and the eventual prevalence of Russians as the show's guests, led to a decrease in the Ukrainian component of Verka's surzhyk. Reportedly the show had become more popular in Russia than in Ukraine (Hrytsenko 1999, 16). In the early years of the new millennium Verka's language still bore markers of Ukrainian mixed in, but, as a whole, the language was more Russian, which made it more intelligible to wider (non-Ukrainian) audiences. Many people saw it as a problem in that only demeaning images of Ukraine were exported to Russia. That was the only kind of Ukraine that Russia wanted to see, not a high-cultural, prestigious image. Thus laughter could be a double-edged sword.

Danylko rejected the blame that he was harming and demeaning Ukrainian culture. He argued (in Lihachova 1998, 4):

> From Rukh [the political party] they write petitions: take away Danylko, he is making fun of Ukraine, the Ukrainian people.... But I don't understand, why can't we make fun of ourselves? Fun of that which has been revived, of that which is dead but people pretend is alive? Why does Ukrainian national humor have to be so full of pathos, so falsely elevated?

National self-caricature can be a step in the development of a healthy nation, since it requires a certain self-confidence to laugh at oneself (Lihachova 1998, 1). But was Ukraine's self-confidence strong enough to withstand the parody of the cultural values that were defining it? Danylko's right to criticize was questioned by people who asserted that he cannot speak standard Ukrainian even outside his role, that he can only speak surzhyk. This was brought forth as evidence of his personal and cognitive shortcomings, and was meant to further delegitimize his performances (which always relied heavily on surzhyk). The implication was that if at least he commanded standard Ukrainian, his performances could be regarded as skillful, but that in fact they represented his limitations and lowness.

Judgments of whether Danylko could actually speak standard Ukrainian may have been strategic efforts to discredit him or the result of misrecognition or both. A professor of Ukrainian literature who saw one of Danylko's performances in Kyiv gave a positive assessment of his ability to speak the standard language. I only heard Danylko speak Russian in television interviews, and both were with Russophone hosts, but in one of his early televised skits (in the role of a male villager) he did speak standard Ukrainian well. In this skit he used literary Ukrainian, except for a few Russian diminutive forms of names that he listed near the end. After viewing this skit with me, one viewer who did not like this comedian asserted that the language in the skit was surzhyk and not standard Ukrainian. The few Russified name forms led her to hear all his language as illegitimate. She disapproved of his reputation as a "surzhyk speaker," and so, consciously or not, her judgment served to deny him legitimacy. Jaffe provides a reverse example of this kind of misrecognition in her study of the sociolinguistic situation in Corsica: an interviewee asserted that a comedian whom she liked always spoke Corsican, despite the fact that the comedian's skits relied heavily on language mixing—"so closely was a pure, monolingual norm linked with value in her mind, that she retroactively read out abundant heterogeneity in her recollection of something that she had liked" (Jaffe 1999, 268).

Andrii Danylko's popularity in his role as Verka had much to do with his talent as a comedian and actor but also had to do with the carnivalesque power of his act. Verka's parodies of people who had recently risen to the top of the social hierarchy were particularly appreciated by those who felt left behind by the new system. The social and cultural values imposed by the Soviet regime had been replaced by the dogma of purist nationalism or mimicry of Western styles. Danylko-as-Verka exposed the shallowness of these practices, proposing that people laugh and take cultural authorities less seriously.

Surzhyk as a Symbol of Post-Soviet Chaos

Danylko's Verka Serduchka broke many of the rules of correct cultural and linguistic behavior. Rather than cause a change in the rules, Verka became a focal point for negative attitudes of purists and galvanized the articulation of even stronger opposition toward surzhyk than before, reinforcing its marginalization in many ways. Perhaps in response to the initially wild popularity of Verka and the visibility of her surzhyk, some efforts to restrict the use of surzhyk in public spheres were formulated as part of language legislation proposed in 1997 (but not passed). The proposed clause read: "The only form of use of the state language in all spheres of social life is its normative form. In using the state language deviations from its normative form are inadmissible" (cited in Taranenko 2001, 7). It would be very controversial to pass such a law, as it would bring the purist-surzhyk struggles over authority into the legal sphere, and would outlaw acts such as Verka Serduchka. While such restrictive legislation might reduce public airtime for surzhyk, it would also add importance and the appeal of the forbidden to something many people simply write off as bad taste. Also, judgment of how well one can speak is not a purely objective matter, but, as I have argued here, is shaped by the negotiations of status, politics, and morality, so the implementation of the proposed law could be explosive indeed.

So far there has been no regulation of printed matter other than that of editors at printing presses and the control of the Kyiv Academy of Sciences committee over government-funded dictionaries and grammar books. Authors and singers are free to use whichever language they like, and the legitimacy of the language of writings or performances is judged and debated by its audiences. Verka's use of surzhyk for parody was troubling to purists because of its popularity, but as parody, by definition, it was not an authoritative paradigm. In contrast, many people were critical of what they judged to be the heavily Russified Ukrainian language in serious television programs, which they found to be a much more insidious surzhyk because it purported to be the voice of authority, and it was more subtle (Matsiuk 2000). The anxiety of purists over the poor quality of Ukrainian on television was coupled with anxiety that a relatively small percentage of televised content was in Ukrainian, revealing its tenuous cultural hold.

Some saw the dominance of surzhyk and lack of pure Ukrainian as an appropriate metaphor for the chaos and absurdity in Ukrainian life of the 1990s and 2000s in general. As expressed by two journalists:

> In our day, in the linguistic space of Ukraine surzhyk reigns supreme. But is it only in the linguistic sphere? What about in politics, economics, in our daily life—is it not the same duplicity of absurdity, the half-baked quality of decisions and the lack of definition of goals and plans? Strictly speaking, it [surzhyk] is not only a hit in the repertoire of humorists, but it is also the character of the general situation in the whole country. It is probably from this that stems the love of all the people that has been won by "Krolyky" [a surzhyk-speaking pair of comedians], and Virka [Verka Serduchka], and of course the dear monstrosities, the eternal Dovhonosyky ["Long-noses," another comedy act relying on surzhyk]. [. . .] In answer to the question of *The Day* [Ukrainian newspaper]: "How will such a large quantity of monstrosities affect television?" Špykul'ak [one of the "Long-nose" comedians] replied: "In every barrel of tar there should be at least one spoonful of honey." And as for the possibility of the appearance of a "long-nose" newspaper [which would be a newspaper of surzhyk and low-brow humor], Šaryk [another "Long-nose" comedian] answered with a joke: "They are already published for us. Take a look in the kiosks." (Klochko and Krotkov 1998)

Some feel that the government can solve Ukraine's problems by intervening with support for worthy cultural and linguistic resources, and that these will ultimately triumph over surzhyk. For example, in an article arguing for national support in preserving and popularizing the art of the set designer Yevhen Lysyk from Lviv, a journalist argues that, "the next steps are in the hands of the state, which has to finally understand that Lysyk is the hardest national currency. An artist of Yevhen Mykytovyč Lysyk's caliber is the 'gold reserve' of the nation. Furthermore, this is also the wall that will withstand any surzhyk of mass culture, no matter how well financed" (Kosmolins'ka 2000). This quote portrays "correct" high culture as a bastion that must withstand the onslaught of impurity. The statement exemplifies the tension between different visions of culture and struggle for control over legitimacy and authenticity.

Surzhyk reflects a long history of linguistic domination but also a rejection of disempowering and restrictive standards. The negative value of the term has overridden alternative interpretations, although some performers, writers, and singers have reveled in its carnivalesque and countercultural power. In aspirations for the correctness and legitimacy of newly independent Ukraine and the recently designated Ukrainian state language, people have used the label surzhyk pejoratively as a weapon in negotiations of status. By labeling someone's language as "polluted," "incorrect," or "broken"—in other words, surzhyk—people could bring into question that person's integrity, education, and worth. Relatively subtle deviations from the standard, such as a Russian accent, or one or two Russian words used in otherwise Ukrainian speech, were at times the object of vehement criticism. As confidence in the status of Ukrainian increases, I would expect a relaxation of some of the anxieties over impurity and surzhyk. It might also signal something more revolutionary: the social recognition of mixing as a norm.

6 ## Concealing Tensions and Mediating Pluralisms

Nobody from her borderland believed any single language
could ever convey all one's needs or say the world in its fullness.

— ASKOLD MELNYCZUK, *AMBASSADOR OF THE DEAD*

Legitimacy, Ambiguity, and Nonreciprocal Bilingualism

As years accrued onto Ukraine's independent statehood, belief in the country's legitimacy became more widespread. Many of the newly established institutions of independent Ukraine became habitualized and taken for granted. Fifteen years after the 1989 law declared Ukrainian the sole state language, the status of Ukrainian and of Russian was still the object of public and political contest, but, overall, the status of Ukrainian had decidedly risen. The changes were particularly evident in the newly dominant roles of Ukrainian in public signage, official paperwork, and education (Hrycak in press). Ukrainian was also used more widely than before in everyday public urban life, in television programming, and in popular music. Language use continued to vary markedly between the largely Russophone urban east and Ukrainophone west, but even in the east, Ukrainian was often used in prestigious contexts.

Ukrainian citizens everywhere had a diverse array of experiences from which to construct their identity. Even in the Ukrainianized west, Russian television, music, and literature still had a significant presence, and most Ukrainians had a Soviet/Russian component to their identity, except for the youngest generations. Middle-aged and older men had the experience of serving in a Russian-speaking Soviet army, and even a decade after independence Russian continued to be widely used in the Ukrainian military. People everywhere still cited lines from popular Soviet Russian films. The idiosyncrasies of the Soviet system were a vivid memory, sometimes bitter, sometimes humorous. Only the youth had not experienced life as Soviet citizens, although they had grown up within many of the systems set up in Soviet times. The celebrations of national holidays throughout Ukraine were still shaped by Soviet-era traditions, only partly transformed to align symbolically with independence (Wanner 1999).

In the new millennium Ukrainian traditions had also taken root where they used to be largely excluded. In the east Russophone urbanites had studied Ukrainian and were hearing it increasingly in the media, leading more young people to identify linguistically and ethnically with Ukrainianness. Even staunchly Russophone Ukrainian citizens came to feel their Ukrainianness in encounters with Russians from Moscow or Saint Petersburg because of linguistic and cultural differences. Russophones living in Ukraine had experiences that allowed them to feel a Ukrainian component in their identity, just as many Ukrainophones could feel a Russian component. Whether they chose to emphasize or stifle this component depended on economic, political, and spiritual factors. One young Russian man in Lviv wrote: "Young Russians in Lviv wield Ukrainian well. I had a period when I not only spoke Ukrainian at work, but also started to think in Ukrainian. That is when I understood that it is time to seriously start thinking about the preservation of my Russian identity. In the conditions of Lviv, one can lose it quickly" (Arbatov 2002). This man's experience testified to the new strength of Ukrainian language and culture, since in the Soviet period it was almost always non-Russian identities that were at risk.

The differences between the largely Russophone urban east and Ukrainophone west could be seen as opposed cultural-linguistic poles, which Mykola Riabchuk (1992) dubbed "two Ukraines." The different linguistic situations and cultural histories of the east and west were clear, but it was not apparent where the boundary between the "two Ukraines" lay. In the capital city of Kyiv the statuses of the languages were difficult to define, since they were caught in the tension between the opposing diglossic orders of east and west. Although Ukrainian had become widespread in educational and governmental institutions, Russian still prevailed in Kyivan public life—particularly in business interactions and on the street—except in pockets around universities and academic institutes. In other areas of the city in 2002 it was still somewhat unusual to hear well-dressed young urbanites speaking Ukrainian with one another in casual situations.

The ambiguity of language statuses in Kyiv was paralleled by pervasive ambivalence in the attitudes held by a large portion of Ukraine's population as a whole, according to polling, voting, and survey data. While some people clearly supported one direction, many more were undecided, did not care, or preferred contradictory paradigms (such as nationalism and communism, Russian language and Ukrainian language) to find a way to coexist. Riabchuk (1992) referred to this ambivalent population as a "third Ukraine," neither fitting the paradigm of the culturally more Russian "east" or culturally more Ukrainian "west." This resonates with Kulyk's (2002, 2004a, 2004b) arguments that a "centrist," status quo ideology was gaining momentum, which he saw as ultimately favoring Russian, because it was better established as a language of power.

Material concerns, cynicism, and disillusionment with politics led many people to detach themselves from political views altogether, but in daily life they still had to choose which language(s) to speak. Bilingual practices provided a middle way for the undecided and for those who were disillusioned with the categorically opposed alternatives. The desire to "have it both ways," allowing the co-presence of both Ukrainian and Russian, could be seen as strategic syncretism and active resistance to the imperatives of a traditionally construed nationalism rather than as apathy or ambivalence.

Nonreciprocal bilingualism was particularly effective in defusing the political implications of language choice. In this practice both languages were present in interactions, with each person speaking his or her preferred language and not accommodating to other speakers. This paradigm of interaction became widespread starting in the late 1990s on television and in public life in Kyiv.[1] It was a new twist on Soviet-era bilingual practices in that it represented an ideology of equality of the two languages, as opposed to the Soviet paradigm of a lesser regional language competing with an international language. In theory, the choice of either language was equivalent.

Nonreciprocal bilingual interactions allowed for the mixing of languages in conversation while preserving the imperative of language purity for any given speaker. Correspondingly, in some printed newspapers and journals the languages appeared side by side on the same page, co-present but not mixed, with some articles and advertisements in Ukrainian, others in Russian. While this practice challenged a monolingual model of nation, it upheld the ideology of linguistic separation and purity.

Some individuals had gone against the grain in Soviet times by using only Ukrainian with their Russian-speaking colleagues in their public and professional lives, also creating nonreciprocal bilingual interactions. They were exceptions whose behaviors were seen as politically motivated. Less politicized were families who maintained a bilingual state of affairs in private, with husband and wife speaking different languages to each other, as exemplified in Sophia's interview in chapter 2. In three such cases I learned about in more detail, one partner did accommodate in the early stages of acquaintance, but part of the path to marriage included "being true to oneself." In the two relationships that began before independence, the initial interactions were in Russian, whereas the couple who

---

1. The degree to which nonreciprocal bilingual interactions are present in other areas of Ukraine remains to be researched. Kulyk (2004a) describes these practices as generally typical in Ukraine.

met after independence began their relationship in Ukrainian. As the relationships solidified, the person who had been accommodating reverted to his or her "truly native" language, which did not pose any problems in comprehension as both partners were at least passively if not fully bilingual.

The paradigm of nonreciprocal bilingual interaction without mixing or codeswitching appeared on television early in Ukraine's independence, as Ukrainian-speaking journalists interviewed people who preferred to speak Russian. The journalists portrayed the newly official role of Ukrainian, while the interviewees were generally urbanites who did not feel proficient enough in Ukrainian to use it in a public interview. Televised parliamentary sessions also followed this bilingual paradigm, as many politicians spoke Ukrainian, whereas others, especially those from eastern Ukraine, continued to speak Russian despite the mandate to use Ukrainian in public office.

After independence, as the bilingual interviews became common on television, nonreciprocal bilingual interactions became ever more frequent in public city life, particularly in Kyiv, which had previously been almost completely Russophone. People who had formerly spoken Ukrainian only at home began using it in public, adhering to Ukrainian even though the majority of the people they interacted with answered in Russian. With time this behavior became less remarkable. It was expected that everyone living in Ukraine should know both languages at least passively. By the year 2000 in Kyiv, it generally became culturally correct to treat language in public as transparent, reacting neither positively nor negatively to language choice. Russian visitors to Ukraine told me that the bilingual conversations they heard were perplexing, since they could only understand the Russian half of the interaction. Many residents of Ukraine, on the other hand, had grown to think of the languages as mutually intelligible, since they had exposure to both languages through education, the media, and other contexts.

Accommodation by switching to the language of one's conversational partner was acceptable if it was imperceptible, such as in language choice at the beginning of an interaction, and if a speaker was equally fluent in both languages. But if accommodation was noticeable, it could sometimes cause discomfort, by raising awareness of language choice and implying that the languages were not equal. In this trend the standards of correctness took on another dimension, in that people were expected to "be true to themselves" by speaking "their own" language, and to be comfortable with others doing the same. This paradigm for social interaction is reminiscent of the bilingual marriages, in which accommodation in the early stages was a result of tension and newness in the relationship, whereas nonaccommodation signaled relaxation and acceptance of differences. In everyday life, in Kyiv, Ukrainophones were happy to be more comfortable speaking Ukrainian in public, while Russophones had not changed their own speaking habits but became accustomed to hearing and responding to Ukrainian.

Although the overt struggles over control of symbolic values continued, in some spheres nonreciprocal bilingualism served to submerge the tensions between Ukrainian and Russian speakers by eliminating the need for accommodation. People could simply speak as they preferred. In practice, the coexistence of languages did not assure their equality but rather established a situation that could be balanced or tip in favor of either language. For example, language choice could influence how much attention or respect was accorded a given speaker. However, with either language supposedly being equally acceptable on the surface, the workings of symbolic power were less openly contested. The acceptability of both languages provided an outward resolution of the inexorable oppositions between Ukrainian and Russian that had been constructed by politicians, scholars, and others with clearly articulated ideologies.

People who were committed to the revival of Ukrainian feared that nonreciprocal bilingualism ultimately would favor Russian, since it was the more established and powerful language (e.g. Kulyk 2000; Masenko 2004). They were wary of bilingualism in general, because in Soviet times the policies promoting it were unconcealed means of Russification. Political moves that strengthened Ukraine's ties with Russia worsened fears that Ukrainian, a language of the majority whose status was rising, would revert to a marginalized minority status relative to Russian if Ukraine again came more firmly under Russia's influence.

Some people disagreed with these fears and felt that the official status of Ukrainian would sustain its use. For example, in a 2002 interview, the hip-hop musician Sasha Sydorenko a.k.a. Fozzi of the group TNMK stated, "In my opinion things for Ukrainian are going well, even though people are used to Russian being official and Ukrainian being limited to certain channels. Youth view Ukrainian as normal. We don't need two state languages. The new generations accept Ukrainian as their own. Maybe they don't use it much yet, but for them it doesn't have the negative connotations." In concluding, Fozzi asserted, "Ten years from now you'll remember my words—that things will be even better, I'm sure of it." Fozzi's optimism, creativity, and popularity lent weight to the elevation of Ukrainian language status, as his performances "infect[ed] with [their] own intention certain aspects of language" (Bakhtin 1981, 290). But his practices and intentions were by no means simple, as he used both languages and surzhyk in his interactions and performances.

Many people believed that bilingual practices were to be applauded, because they allowed the greatest degree of freedom to language users after decades of authoritarian regulation. In disagreements over legislation, people often ignored the fact that language use is always influenced and regulated by the judgments of speakers, which ultimately add up to the social valuation of linguistic forms. While legislation did have a significant impact on judgments of language, it also embodied ambiguities and conflicts over language in society.

Language Laws and Practices: Media and Politics

Legislation and institutional practices were important factors shaping public language use, even though the regulations left room for interpretation and were unevenly implemented. Following the 1989 Law on Language, which declared Ukrainian the sole official state language, subsequent laws specified language use in particular fields. For example, the Law on Television and Radio Broadcasting, passed in December 1993 by the Verkhovna Rada (Parliament of Ukraine), specified that 50 percent of broadcasts must be produced in Ukraine, and that television and radio organizations must conduct broadcasts in the state language (Ukrainian) but that broadcasts for particular regions could also be conducted in the language of minorities who reside there compactly (Zakon 1993). The law did not specify what constitutes a "compact" population, and whether ethnicity or primary language was the determinant of a minority population. These ambiguities, and the lack of enforcement measures, facilitated the prevalence of Russian-language broadcasting, allowing television companies to capitalize on the availability and popularity of older Soviet films and newer imports from Russia. Post-soviet Ukrainian productions were also often in Russian, with the goal of reaching a wider market in Russia and Ukraine, under the assumption that everyone knew Russian, including Ukrainophone Ukrainians who were at least passively bilingual. Even though issued broadcast licenses routinely stipulated that 50–75 percent of programming had to be in Ukrainian, broadcasters ignored these requirements without any consequences (Maksymiuk 2004a). A 2004 survey of the eastern and southern regions of Ukraine found that the proportion of Ukrainian in broadcasts varied from 14 percent in Crimea to 46 percent in Mykolaiv (Krushelnycky 2004).

In an effort to increase the presence of Ukrainian on the airwaves, in April 2004 the National Council for Television and Radio Broadcasting (established by the 1993 parliamentary law mentioned above) adopted a resolution stipulating that national companies and interregional companies (covering at least half of Ukraine's twenty-five regions) had to broadcast only in Ukrainian (Maksymiuk 2004a). This resolution, like language laws before it, initially elicited anger and criticism. President Kuchma, contradicting the 1993 parliamentary law and the new resolution of the Council, opined that the resolution only had the force of a recommendation and was not legally binding (Prime 2004). Just five months after it was passed the resolution seemed to have failed under pressure from broadcasters in Ukraine and politicians in Moscow (BBC 2004; Fawkes 2004).

The choice of language on television, Ukrainian or Russian, was cause for dispute, particularly in imported foreign programs that were dubbed, as in the case of the U.S.-produced *Santa Barbara* series in Crimea (discussed in chapter 3). Critics often targeted what they judged to be the poor quality of the language of a translation in their disapproval of that language choice. Correspondingly, skillfully used language could transcend ethnolinguistic barriers. A man from Donetsk (Russian language–dominant eastern city) recounted that in 1998 he and his twenty-year-old urban Russophone friends avidly watched *Alf* (a U.S. production about a furry alien creature living with an American family) in Ukrainian, because the translation was so well done. They even started using some of Alf's humorous Ukrainian phrases with one another. The example he provided was, "Ти що, себе Русланою Писанкою вважаєш?" 'Who do you think you are, Ruslana Pysanka?' Ruslana Pysanka was known as the first Ukrainian erotic film actress and was touted as a sex symbol; she later worked as a TV weather announcer. Cultural references in the American show had thus been ably translated to the Ukrainian context and picked up by Donetsk youth, who could revel in the play on language and the interplay of cultures (the alien American Alf with insider knowledge of Ukrainian culture).

The tug-of-war over language also took place when businesses began broadcasting songs in public spaces. In May 2000 tension over the ethnolinguistic question spiked in Lviv when the Ukrainian songwriter Ihor Bilozir died after being beaten by ethnic Russians who did not like that he was singing Ukrainian songs with his friends in a café. None of the perpetrators was prosecuted, and one of the culprits was the son of a Russian police chief. This incident sparked major protests in the city and revealed that despite the apparent strength and spread of Ukrainian in the west of the country, language was still a contentious issue there (Maksymiuk 2000). Although ethnic Russians comprised a relatively small percentage of the population of Lviv (3.6 percent according to the 2001 census, and previously 7.2 percent in the 1989 census), Soviet policies had brought many of them to occupy positions of institutional power, which many still held after independence (Zastavnyi 2003). The stereotypical perception that Russians, as "colonizers," were disproportionately represented among the institutionally powerful and wealthy colored many Ukrainians' resentments.

The Bilozir tragedy served as the impetus in June 2000 for the passing of controversial laws in Lviv for the "protection of the sound environment," banning songs with "amoral content and low aesthetic level" as a means of limiting the airing of some Russian pop songs (Taranenko 2001, 11). Many Lviv residents felt that the Russian ownership of cafés and other businesses had led to the disproportionate presence of imported Russian music in the public spaces of the city, propagating the legacy of Russian cultural domination. The laws created an uproar about constitutional rights, with authorities from Russia attempting to intervene. The Lviv legislators strove to diminish the controversial ethnic factor by singling out for regulation songs with vulgar content, but the law was clearly directed at limiting Russian pop music. Subsequently prohibitive laws against Russian were replaced by legislation supportive of Ukrainian-language broadcasts and publications (Taranenko 2001, 11). A few years later, in 2004, legislation was again proposed to ban Russian music in Lviv, this time in minibuses, and possibly also in restaurants and bars, again eliciting mixed reactions (Fawkes 2004).

The legislation on language in advertising also had a turbulent history, with international implications. A 1996 Law on Advertising stated that the language of ads should be Ukrainian, except in areas of compact minority populations, corresponding to the current language law of Ukraine (Zakon 1996). Some nationwide television advertisers satisfied this requirement by providing Ukrainian subtitles for ads voiced in Russian. Subtitling was no guarantee of linguistic equality: for example, a 2002 television ad for chocolate voiced in Russian had Ukrainian subtitles as required, but these were so tiny and quickly displayed as to be barely legible. In the case of that ad, the subtitles fulfilled a legal requirement while minimizing its potential communicative function.

A 2003 law was more categorical, asserting that Ukrainian language was to be used in all advertising in all media in Ukraine. Interestingly the law incited outrage from an English-language newspaper catering mostly to expatriates in Ukraine, which did business with advertisers who wanted to reach an English-speaking public. English and Ukrainian share few similarities on the surface, and foreign businessmen who had training in a Slavic language more often had studied Russian rather than Ukrainian. An editorial in the English-language *Kyiv Post* stated that this law "could be one of the worst and most destructive laws passed by the Rada [Ukrainian Parliament] since Ukraine achieved independence," and that "it is not outrageously reductive to state the matter thus: Ukraine has a choice between this law, and Europe" (Anon. Editorial 3, 2003). While the intensity of the statement was in part a result of the newspaper's fears for its survival because the law threatened its advertising revenues, it pointed out the contradictions between institutional support for Ukrainian, and the pressures of the global market and community where English is dominant. The law could be seen as an infringement on the freedom of speech or as an effort to fight the marginalization of Ukrainian language and culture.

Although the law in question was most likely meant to promote Ukrainian over Russian in the bilingual public sphere, the protests of the *Kyiv Post* editors showed that it could be a double-edged sword regarding English and international business relations. No solution could be neutral: even if compromise could be reached hypothetically, by making advertisements bilingual, this would amount to a concession by the English-language paper, because the ads would undoubtly appear more cumbersome and the vehicle of their messages less "smooth," having to share space with an "unneeded" language.

Trademarks were initially an exception to the 1996 law requiring advertising to be in Ukrainian except in areas of compact minority populations. This meant that Russian, English, and other languages had a significant presence in Ukrainian public spaces, although, aside from the brand names, other information in advertisements generally appeared in Ukrainian, at least in Kyiv. A July 2003 act aimed to change this, requiring trademarks to be translated or transliterated into Ukrainian alongside the original form. Complaints from businesses led to the reversal of this act less than a year later in February 2004, again allowing trademarks to appear in their original language without duplication in Ukrainian (Shevchenko et al. 2004).

Tensions over language were also expressed in international politics. Some Ukrainian politicians felt that the language issue was a matter of national security (UNIAN 2004). This opinion was reinforced by statements such as Russian president Putin's June 2000 suggestion that "if Moldova raised Russian to a second state language, Moscow would cease supporting the separatist Transdniester" region of this country (Kuzio 2000). Russia's elimination in 1995 of all taxes on Russian publications gave them a financial advantage over those published in Ukraine, so that, in 2001, five out of the thirteen newspapers with the largest print runs in Ukraine were from Russia (Kuzio 2001). For the Moscow government, use of Russian in former Soviet states assured its continued influence over these countries.

The Russian government disapproved of Ukraine's legislative efforts to promote Ukrainian. For example, a December 1999 ruling of the Ukrainian constitutional court that all state officials should know and use Ukrainian, in keeping with the constitutional definition of Ukrainian as the sole state language, resulted in heated exchanges with Russia. Although the Russian government found Ukraine's policies objectionable, it nevertheless implemented similar policies to legally promote Russian in Russia. In January 2000 President Putin formed a Council on the Russian Language whose first actions included an order to the Ministry of Education to fine Russian officials who had a poor command of Russian (Kuzio 2000). Despite the seemingly stronger position of Russian as an established language of power, concerted effort was still required to maintain centralized control of a standard.

Language legislation in Ukraine constituted a significant influence on public language use. The impact of laws was complex: the laws themselves were like conversational moves, variously interpreted and manipulated in the struggle over language values. Individuals, businesses, broadcasters, and neighboring governments all strove to bend or challenge Ukrainian laws to their own benefit, their own ideology. Discourses of nation, justice, freedom, and human rights clashed in the tensions over language regulation.

Public Signage and Advertising: English in the Mix

The role of English deserves more attention, having played a unique role in the development of the language situation in Ukraine. Since independence, English had become more and more widespread, visible, and desirable in Ukraine. Many people saw the presence of English as less threatening to the Ukrainian language and nation than the use of Russian. In many Ukrainian schools Russian ceased to be taught, while the demand for English language teachers was very high. In part this was a response to opening opportunities with the West. The growing use of English as an additional language facilitated the resurgence of Ukrainian over Russian: English, a language of prestige, wider communication, "hipness," and access to science and technology, more than fulfilled some of the primary reasons for learning Russian.

Soon after independence, an increasing number of official buildings declared their identity in bilingual plaques that were Ukrainian-English, replacing Ukrainian-Russian plaques. In downtown Kyiv the new signboards of businesses were often Ukrainian-English, owing in part to their foreign clientele and in part to the growing fashion for English. Some of the earliest examples, in 1991, were "Українські Ласощі/Ukrainian Sweets," "Кентукі Бейрут Курка/Kentucky Beirut Chicken," and "Пункт Обміну Іноземних Валют/Foreign Exchange." Western commodities that people craved came with packaging covered with English words or with other languages using roman letters, marking them as Western. In the first years after independence, the packaging itself was valued, cherished, and displayed in many Ukrainian homes as a marker of prestigious Western exoticism.

During my visit in the year 2000, the conflicting new statuses of languages struck me immediately when I got off the plane in the remodeled Kyiv-Boryspil Airport. While the sign above the entryway to the terminal declared "приліт/arrivals" (in Ukrainian and English), the advertising billboards inside were mostly in English and Russian. The visa in my passport was in Ukrainian and English, but the additional visa paperwork I received at the airport was printed in Russian. The customs agent wanted to speak English with me, probably because of my U.S. passport, even though I had addressed him in Ukrainian and had heard him speak Russian to his colleague.

Younger people were especially attracted to English since it afforded direct access to the once forbidden West—to science and technology, music and business. In the early to mid-1990s in Ukraine I saw more young people wearing caps and T-shirts with American flags than I had seen in the United States (although this trend ebbed by the late 1990s). However, other (usually older) people were annoyed by incomprehensible English words in storefronts and elsewhere—at least Russian was legible and understandable to them. The situation in Ukraine contrasted with Lithuania, where English was considered the major threat once Russian had been effectively displaced (Newman 1993). Much as in France, a special Lithuanian commission crusaded against the use of foreign (not just English) words such as "hotel," "night bar," and "ravioli," to the annoyance of business owners who wanted to use the newer, fashionable Western words. In Ukraine several people I spoke with voiced their misgivings about the wholesale influx of English words into Ukrainian usage, and it had become a concern for linguists (Radchuk 1999, 2000a). Even so, the attractiveness and prestige of English continued to fuel borrowing in many spheres, from political and economic terms to street slang.

Russian as well as Ukrainian speakers were attracted to English. For Ukrainophones, English was an international language without the local history of Russian signifying colonial oppression. Meanwhile, given the choice between Ukrainian and English as a second language, Russians tended to prefer English despite its difficulty. While Ukrainian still bore some of the stigma of a peasant language, English epitomized worldliness. As an international language, English was viewed as offering wider opportunities than Ukrainian. In a matched-guise language attitude test I conducted in 1995, the English guise was heavily favored over the Ukrainian guise of an English-Ukrainian bilingual reader by both ethnic Russian and Ukrainian respondents (Bilaniuk 1998a).

For Russian speakers, learning Ukrainian was complicated by the fact that Russian-accented Ukrainian speech (difficult to avoid for adults who have spoken Russian their whole lives) bore the stigma of impurity—of being low-status surzhyk—whereas a Slavic accent in English did not have such connotations in Ukraine. Several Russians who did not know Ukrainian even told me that it is easier for them to try to learn English than Ukrainian, even though Russian is closely related to Ukrainian. A couple of Ukrainophone interviewees told me that they preferred using English (instead of Russian) in situations where a Russophone did not seem to understand Ukrainian, since this put them on more equal footing, with both speakers using a foreign language. Although the presence of English was still limited, it was growing and affecting the dynamics of Ukrainian-Russian language status.

Ukrainian-English and Russian-English mixing was much more prevalent in pop culture and advertising than Ukrainian-Russian language mixing. While mixing the two Slavic languages had negative connotations or was marked as alternative or comic, intertextual mixing with English had become fashionable in many spheres (Azhniuk 2001, 52; Hrabovych 1998, 21). I found many examples, particularly in pop music and technology, of playing on cross-linguistic ambiguities by mixing English with Ukrainian or Russian. A creative example of such mixing comes from an album of the popular Ukrainian rock group Vopli Vidopliassova, or VV. Their Ukrainian album title *Krajina Mrij* technically translates as "country of dreams/hopes." But the English translation of the album title listed on the CD spine is "Cry in a Dream"—a play on the Ukrainian word *krajina* 'country,' which sounds like the English words "cry in a." Another example is a chocolate candy bar labeled in Ukrainian "Солодкий дотик" (*Solodkyj dotyk*) and in English "Sweet Touch," the original motivation for the name being a play on the name of the confection's manufacturer, "Світоч"/svitoč/.

Wrapper from chocolate bar named "Solodkyj Dotyk" 'Sweet Touch' by confectionery firm "Svitoč."

Creative intertextual mixing with English was especially frequent in advertising. A billboard promoting the Ukrainian television music channel posted the question, "TVій формат?" 'Your format?' in which the roman letter *v* stands for the corresponding Cyrillic letter for that sound, "в". The result is that the first two letters are "*tv*"—evoking the hipness of English in naming the medium. A similar play on words through the mixing of alphabets appeared on another billboard advertising a laptop brand called "Versija" 'Version'. By highlighting in red the letters *PC* in the Cyrillic "ВЕРСИЯ" (the letters "PC" make the sounds [rs] in Cyrillic), the ad evoked the English acronym "PC" (for personal computer), creating positive associations with English and Western technology. The billboard also showed a degree of Ukrainian-Russian bivalency. Of the two words that stood out in large format (the second in capitals), "Твоя ВЕРСИЯ," the first word (meaning "your") is written identically in Russian and Ukrainian. The second word would be read *Versija* in Russian, meaning "version." The letter "и," which represents the Russian high front vowel [i], is identical to the Ukrainian letter for the mid front vowel [y], so the brand name is still technically readable in Ukrainian as *Versyja* although this is not a standard word form. The word "version" in Ukrainian would be written "ВЕРСІЯ." A trademark symbol after the brand name on the billboard acted as a legitimator for the departure of the name from Ukrainian orthographic standards. While the brand name was really Russian, the small-print information on the board was in Ukrainian.

The frequency in advertising of play on the ambiguities and bivalencies of Ukrainian and English, or Russian and English, contrasted with the rarity of such word play between Ukrainian and Russian. This might be surprising given an audience that used both languages, but Ukrainian-Russian mixing often evoked connotations of low prestige, which were brought even more into everyone's consciousness by the phenomenon of Verka Serduchka, and other performances and writings that used surzhyk to depict social baseness. That does not mean that advertisers did not attempt to capitalize on ambiguities between Russian and Ukrainian. A few people I interviewed who worked in advertising firms said that they did try to find ways to appeal to both Russian and Ukrainian speakers by minimizing differences, often minimizing the use of words altogether. The strategy of minimalism—using as few words as possible and relying mostly on images— also allowed advertisers to avoid ethnic markedness. When possible, ad designers chose word forms that were least marked as being Ukrainian or Russian.

While the strategies of linguistic minimalism, Ukrainian-Russian bivalency, and play on English were evident, nevertheless the overwhelming majority of text in posted ads in Kyiv in 2002 was unambiguously Ukrainian, as the law required. Posted ads in Kyiv were one field in which the official role of Ukrainian had been rather effectively instituted, asserting the official public presence of this language in the city.

Language Politics on Television

Language use on television was less clear-cut than in posted advertising. The expense of production for broadcasting originally limited the quantity and quality of Ukrainian-language shows, but marketing strategies and the inclinations of producers maintained a high degree of Russian language content even later, despite legal requirements, as discussed above. Laws requiring Ukrainian-language broadcasting may have been the impetus for the increase in bilingual shows, because a bilingual format could satisfy both ethnolinguistic sides. The lack of translation of Russian speakers on otherwise Ukrainian shows served to normalize the presence and understandability of Russian in Ukraine (Kulyk 2004b,8).

In the first decade of independence, except for the nonreciprocal bilingual interviews and parliamentary sessions, Ukrainian and Russian languages generally coexisted on television only in separate shows, their boundaries kept clear. In the late 1990s Verka Serduchka's surzhyk-speaking character and a few other comedy shows disrupted this trend by bringing the maligned Ukrainian-Russian mixed language into a prominent position on the airwaves. Other programs took the middle road between purism and mixing, using limited code switching and occasional Russianisms in Ukrainian speech that amounted to a less blatant surzhyk than that of Verka Serduchka. In this manner they strove for bivalency and ambiguity, actively avoiding committing to a single lingua-political choice while also side-stepping the stigmatized surzhyk (Heller 1988a,11; Woolard 1998b).

An example of an approach that took the middle road in order to appeal to a broad public in Ukraine was a game show called *Field of Wonders*[2] that aired in Kyiv in May 2000. This show was among the first in what would become a popular genre of Western-modeled game shows a few years later. It appeared to be designed in order not to alienate any linguistic groups but still to be nominally "in Ukrainian," in response to the increasing government demand for Ukrainian television content. This was accomplished by having a show host who spoke Ukrainian but whose pronunciation and use of lexical Russianisms indicated that Russian was his better language. Some contestants were at ease speaking Ukrainian, and others appeared less comfortable. One young man from southeastern Ukraine said little, using Russian or responding by simply repeating some of the Ukrainian words just spoken by the host (e.g., host: "We'll continue?" contestant: "We'll continue"). When this man won a car at the end of the show, he was much more expressive, in Russian. While the show was largely conducted by the host in Russian-accented Ukrainian, the musical interlude act performed by a coy young female pop singer was in Russian. The show as a whole seemed awkward, the host's exuberance contrasting with the contestants' reserve and skepticism regarding the bizarre new practices they were asked to engage in, the garish Western-styled game props clashing with the drab post-Soviet look of the contestants. In more ways than one, this Ukrainian TV game show was syncretic, suffused with awkward intertextuality, actively embraced only by the host and, in the end, by the game winner.

Two years later, in 2002, as noted above, game shows had become a popular television genre, with the airing of versions of recent Western shows such as *The Weakest Link*, as well as renditions of older concepts such as *The Newlywed Show* (in which newlyweds were tested in their knowledge of each other) or *Love at First Sight* (in which unmarried contestants vied to be matched with dates). Other game shows presented a uniquely Ukrainian twist, using Ukrainian sets or themes. There were also at least two different lottery shows, which included a televised game component in addition to the drawing of winning numbers for

---

2. The show was called *Pole Chudes* 'Field of Wonders' and aired on Friday evenings on the channel "UT-3-Inter." The games included spinning a large wheel and setting forth an uneven bouncing ball that knocked over standing pins on a table. A contestant won if his or her pin remained standing.

lottery tickets purchased nationwide. The multitude of game shows in 2002 was striking given their complete absence several years earlier.

Along with game shows, talk shows had also become a popular genre after independence. In 2002 the numerous talk shows included one-on-one formats, discussion groups convened by a regular single host, and shows hosted by male-female couples. Sometimes the talk shows had call-in components or live studio audiences. Both the game shows and talk shows, with contestants, callers, participants, and studio audiences gathered from all over Ukraine, were a potential national community-building force, bringing together people from different regions and of varying professions into the same context, and airing their personal experiences and viewpoints. Some of the one-on-one or group discussion shows were exclusively in Ukrainian (usually on topics of education or Ukrainian culture), and others that included more participants and aimed to attract wider audiences were either bilingual or in Russian.

On programs that had Ukrainian-speaking hosts, like *Sejf,* and *Intellekt-Show LG Evryka,* contestants could speak either Ukrainian or Russian. The degree of codeswitching by contestants varied with age. On the trivia quiz show *Sejf,* where both host and contestants were middle-aged, there was no code switching, and Russophone contestants adhered to Russian while the host spoke Ukrainian. The youth-oriented *LG Evryka* had two Ukrainophone hosts who appeared to be in their early twenties, and Russophone contestants often introduced themselves and conversed with the hosts in Ukrainian but reverted to Russian for tasks in which they had to speak under pressure. Contestants on *LG Evryka* also sometimes threw in a few English words in their introductions, such as "Good luck." The hosts did not switch but adhered to Ukrainian, which was presumably their designated role.

A trivia show called *D'ikan'ka* or *Dykan'ka* (depending on whether one used Russian or Ukrainian pronunciation) presented a different Ukrainian-Russian hybridity. Although the show was conducted completely in Russian, its theatrical set was designed to evoke a folkloric Ukrainian village, and at times contestants had to choose their prizes hidden in antique-looking traditional pots and carved wooden trunks. The printed name of the show, "диканька," was bivalent in that it read normally in both Ukrainian and Russian, although with slightly different pronunciations, since the second letter "и" represents the phoneme [i] in Russian and [y] in Ukrainian. The title image of the program was animated, showing the second letter in the title swinging down, as if on a broken hinge, leaving the letter "i" in its place, a letter that represents the phoneme [i] in Ukrainian but is absent from the Russian alphabet. The supposedly Ukrainian spelling resulted in the Russian pronunciation of the village name, and thus the title image made a (cynical?) nod at the need for being bilingual.

In the early 2000s several television shows began using the format of nonre-

Title images from *Dykan'ka* game show, aired in 2002, showing transformation from bivalent spelling to markedly Ukrainian spelling of the Russian pronunciation of the show's name.

ciprocal bilingualism between cohosts.[3] In the summer of 2002 there were five regular television shows that had male-female cohost couples who spoke differ-ent languages to each other and to their guests, not switching to accommodate—each host sticking to his or her assigned language, one always speaking Ukrai-nian, the other always speaking Russian. Guests or contestants on these shows sometimes did codeswitch to accommodate the hosts who remained in their des-ignated guise, but the majority adhered to one language of their choice, avoiding codeswitching just like the hosts. Switching by the hosts was either very mini-mal, done within a specific framework, or explicitly managed with megalinguis-tic commentary. The five shows were *L'ubov z peršoho pohl'adu* 'Love at First Sight,' a weekly newlyweds' game; *Loto-Zabava* 'Loto-play,' a weekly lottery game show; *Pidjom* 'Wake-up,' a daily morning talk show; and *Xorošou* (a play on the Russian word *xərašo*, meaning "good," and the English term "show"), a daily afternoon talk show on the Ukrainian music channel. In the first three programs the female hosts spoke Ukrainian and the male hosts spoke Russian. In the latter two it was the other way around. While both languages were always present, surzhyk was absent, except on one of the lottery shows, where a team of male comedians ap-pearing clownish in oversized shoes and colorful suits occasionally did mix lan-guages and use a few nonstandard forms. This exception proved the rule: only clowns would mix languages and use surzhyk. Among "normal, respectable" peo-ple, linguistic boundaries were meant to be coterminous with personal bound-aries, although they were not necessarily meant to correspond with clear-cut ethnic identities.

The M1 music channel talk show *Xorošou* was the newest of the bilingual co-hosted shows and first aired in the summer of 2002. The hosts of *Xorošou* embod-ied ethnolinguistic ambiguity in the lack of ethnic correspondence between their names and languages. The female host had a typically Ukrainian surname—end-ing in *-enko*—but she spoke exclusively Russian; the male host had a typically Russian name—ending in *-ov*—but he spoke mostly Ukrainian. In an article that previewed their show, language choice was not mentioned and the surnames of the hosts were not given, avoiding ethnolinguistic markedness. The nonrecipro-cal bilingualism on the show was not balanced or peaceful; rather, there was a constant conversational struggle going on between the young man and woman. The struggle was not overt but took the form of the speakers vying to be the one speaking and providing information (often talking over each other). Sometimes they appeared to be trying to influence language choice when interacting with callers by trying to get their hellos in first. This was one of the least scripted of the bilingual shows.

Unlike the other shows in which all contestants were from Ukraine and

---

3. In 2002 there were also radio shows in Kyiv with this bilingual dual-host format.

therefore were presumed to understand Ukrainian, *Xorošou* occasionally hosted musicians from Russia. In these cases the Ukrainian-speaking male host did codeswitch into Russian to accommodate, but he did not do so for Russian speakers who were from Ukraine. He would sometimes make mistakes about when he was supposed to be accommodating, either reverting to Ukrainian with monolingual Russians or catching himself accommodating to Russophone Ukrainian citizens and self-correcting back to Ukrainian. His linguistic accommodation was contextualized as an exception by the extensive metalinguistic commentary that often accompanied his codeswitches. The commentary helped maintain the boundaries between languages and offset the switch so that it would not be seen as language mixing. The male host would remark that he had to prepare himself mentally for the switch, and, in one case I documented, he narrated his switching process while his cohost talked over him, presenting the next topic. He said, "O.K., now I will readjust to Ukrainian language, so you go ahead and converse a bit for now. [He tilted his head down.] Ukrainian language, Ukrainian language, that's it, I've switched [and he lifted his head up and started participating in the conversation]." Lack of symmetry was evident in the fact that the Russian-speaking female host never switched to Ukrainian to accommodate. While there was some code switching by the male host, *Xorošou* nevertheless reinforced categorical ethnic and linguistic distinctions by limiting the accommodation to foreigners and marking the switches through metalinguistic commentary.

The television shows with bilingual interactions functioned to make language less of an issue, but they were not devoid of imbalance and struggles over language values. For example, on the *LG Evryka* game show the Ukrainophone hosts sometimes commented on the importance of cultivating Ukrainian, although there were no negative sanctions for competing in Russian. On the *Medovyj Mis'ac'* show, the Russophone host switched to Ukrainian when it was his turn to read official game questions, serving to construct Ukrainian as an official institutional language. More often, however, conversational practices appeared to favor Russian. On both *L'ubov z peršoho pohl'adu* and *Loto-Zabava,* cumulatively the male Russophone hosts spoke more than the Ukrainophone female hosts. While the hosts of *L'ubov z peršoho pohl'adu* did not codeswitch on the show, out-takes aired at the end of a program revealed that the Ukrainian host switched to Russian when she made insider's comments to her colleagues that would not normally be aired. This provided viewers with the evidence that Russian was the more accepted language of communication on the set. On *Xorošou,* the Ukrainophone host was not as fluent in Ukrainian as his cohost was in Russian, resulting in unequal representation of the languages. Nevertheless, these inequalities and struggles were hidden beneath a normalizing layer, since nonreciprocal bilingualism was instituted as normal, and language choice was usually not made an issue.

The superficial equality and equivalence of Ukrainian and Russian that was presented on television was reinforced in printed television guides. Nowhere was there any indication of the language of any given show or film in the available TV guides.[4] In Kyiv all the available printed guides were in Russian, and all the show titles were translated to Russian. In articles discussing two of the bilingual programs there was also no mention at all of language. This failure to mention the language hid the issue of which language might be dominant. Television shows that did not involve live discussion were usually in one language, and I frequently heard the complaint from pro-Ukrainian individuals that Russian-language shows dominated the airwaves (something that varied with time; see Kulyk 2004b).

Those more cynical of the media viewed the new nonreciprocal bilingualism on television as the result of producers doing the minimum to include Ukrainian content while continuing to give Russian priority. The intentions of producers likely varied in their efforts to find a balance between legal and financial concerns, the available talent, and their own artistic and cultural inclinations. Television in Ukraine, as elsewhere, was clearly a powerful medium in the politics of language and identity.[5] It propagated ideas and information, and contributed to the construction of language ideologies in the way languages were represented in programming.

Language Ideology and Social Change

Social and legislative changes that were instituted during the first fifteen years of Ukraine's independence brought issues of language and identity to the fore. As in the rest of Europe, language was integral in the imagining of a national community, but the unity and homogeneity of language are never faits accomplis but are themselves imagined—that is, they are ideological constructs (Anderson 1991; Silverstein 2000). Ideologies of unitary standard language, rather than homogeneous practices, are the forces that help maintain particular social unities and hierarchies (Lippi-Green 1997). Language is always suffused with struggle, and the

---

4. In my examination of media in the field, I never found any mention of the language of television programs in listings or articles discussing shows. See also Kulyk 2004, 6.

5. The significance of television was underscored by the findings of yearly nationwide surveys representative of the adult population of Ukraine, conducted by the Institute of Sociology of the Ukrainian Academy of Sciences. The surveys found that of all the possible leisure-time activities, respondents engaged in watching television by far the most frequently. From 1994 to 2000 the percentage of people who had watched television at least once in the week prior to the survey had increased from 79 percent to 87 percent. The next most popular activity was reading newspapers, which had increased from 54 percent to 70 percent during the same period. I am grateful to Oxana Shevel for sharing this database with me.

status of people in power is maintained by repeated interactions that reassert a given social hierarchy. As Voloshinov argued, "the ruling class tries to impart a supraclass, eternal character to the ideological sign, to drive inward the struggle between social value judgments which occurs in it, to make the sign uniaccentual" (Voloshinov 1973, 23). In times of social instability, as in post-Soviet Ukraine, the struggle over symbolic values becomes more vivid, and interactions and the value judgments that steer them become more openly conflicting and contested.

In Ukraine in 1991 the nation abruptly became a legal fact, while the means of imagining it, including the ideology of a national language, were fragmented and poorly institutionalized, in tension with the ideologies propagated in the Soviet system. The construction of post-Soviet Ukrainian identities was full of conflicting forces, pulling one way into an idealized traditionalism, another way for maintenance of a Soviet paradigm and the Russian-dominated status quo, and still another into globalization and postmodern hybridity. Ukrainian citizens did not all want the same thing, and while, for some, the drastic social changes galvanized their sense of self, many were not sure what their identity should be. The institutional forces that might cull variability and uncertainty did much to bolster the status of Ukrainian, but they themselves were variable and contested. As discussed above, the stipulations of laws went back and forth and these were variously interpreted and implemented. Different political factions, media productions, performers and performances exerted their sway on ideologies and practices of language, "attracting its words and forms into their orbit by means of their own characteristic intentions and accents" (Bakhtin 1981, 290). Legislation, institutionalization, and interpersonal relations all played a role in the struggles over the values of linguistic forms in Ukraine.

The close genetic relationship of Ukrainian and Russian underscored how even small differences in linguistic variants could accrue great symbolic weight. Debates over the appropriate roles of languages centered on the simply labeled "Ukrainian" and "Russian," but it was in the interstices and intersections of these categories where the fundamental fault lines in the social fabric lay. The stigmatization of the mixed Ukrainian-Russian surzhyk language could be invoked to discredit its speakers, but surzhyk also had carnivalesque power, and was used by comedians, musicians, and in everyday interactions to evoke laughter and to challenge established categories and authorities.

A different level of mixing, in the form of nonreciprocal bilingualism, worked to resolve some of the tensions between Ukrainian and Russian, by allowing both Ukrainian and Russian to coexist in conversation while maintaining the purity of individual speakers. Nonreciprocal bilingualism entailed another kind of correctness—the idea that each speaker should be "true" to a particular ethnolinguistic identity. On one level this practice resolved ethnolinguistic tensions, making the choice of either language available. However, this essentialization of individual ethnolinguistic identities created an obstacle for those who envisioned the Ukrainianization of Ukrainian citizens as the necessary path of cultural and linguistic correction.

In contesting the different ideologies of correctness, people tried to influence the (re)shaping of social hierarchies in Ukraine. In this book I argued that a key means of doing this was by striving to influence how the links between linguistic forms and social positions were reforged, through judgments of value and efforts to "correct" cultural and linguistic practices. The social turbulence in Ukraine after the disintegration of the Soviet Union disrupted the existing linguistic marketplace and made more vivid these struggles that take place in every linguistic regime. Social stability and the institutionalization of standards obscure the processes of contestation and correction beneath ideologies of what is "normal," "acceptable," or "common sense" (part of habitus), but this normality is never static. The definition of languages is always intertwined with political, economic, and social interests, continually re-created in everyone's words.

Epilogue

The Languages of Ukraine's
Orange Revolution

In the fall of 2004 the people of Ukraine carried out a revolution. Making news around the world, hundreds of thousands of people took to the streets in Kyiv and other cities throughout Ukraine to protest the widespread fraud that gave the run-off presidential election win to Viktor Yanukovych. Yanukovych, prime minister at the time, was favored by the regime of the incumbent president Kuchma, and publicly backed by Russia's president Putin and by the Kremlin. His opponent, Viktor Yushchenko, promised to eradicate the widespread political and economic corruption in Ukraine, to promote democracy, and to integrate Ukraine more closely with Europe.

During my research stays in Ukraine I found that many people were pessimistic about the possibility of eliminating the corruption in the political and economic systems in their country. Protests had occurred occasionally. For example, in 2000 demonstrators called for President Kuchma's ouster when audio tapes allegedly implicated him in the murder of the journalist and government critic Heorhii Gongadze. But these protests failed to have much impact, seemingly reinforcing the public's general sense of disempowerment. Furthermore, sociological research showed that a large portion of Ukraine's population was politically noncommittal (Kulyk 2004a, 2004b; Riabchuk 1992, 2002).

In the fall of 2004 things changed. The manipulation of the November 21 election was too blatant. Internet news sites, and two television stations that had held out against government control, were key in disseminating the news of the large discrepancies between the official results and the exit polls, as well as reports of disappearing inks, ballot stuffing, people bussed to vote multiple times, and other transgressions in the electoral process. One of the first dissenters in the state-run media was the sign-language interpreter Natalya Dymitruk, who, instead of conveying news of Yanukovych's supposed victory, told hearing-impaired viewers not to believe the rigged results, that, in fact, Yushchenko was the true winner, and apologized for having conveyed previous untrue statements

Protesters in the Orange Revolution, on November 25, 2004, the fifth day of protests. Photograph by Yuriy Verbovskyy.

(Vasovic 2004). Many other journalists and reporters in the state-run media also refused to report the government-dictated untruths and joined the demonstrations. Yushchenko's once handsome face, disfigured by the attempt on his life by dioxin poisoning in September 2004, was a poignant symbol of what was at stake: the choice was between a more open and fair government versus the existing trend of Soviet-Style control of information, including efforts to eliminate problematic dissenters such as Gongadze and Yushchenko.

During the days of the protests a friend from Kyiv wrote to me that, in contrast to the usual cynical mood regarding politics, for the first time she saw faces beaming with hope and optimism, and she felt herself swept up in the atmosphere of generosity and good-will among the people in the streets of the city. A Western observer described the mood during the protests as utopian, a mood embodied in the fact that the city's crime rate went down despite the hundreds of thousands of visitors to the city (Way 2005). Vivid on the black and white wintry landscape, the orange color of Yushchenko's campaign was visible everywhere in ribbons, flags, and anything orange that people could find to wear or display. Many popular musicians had joined the protests, helping to create a festive and defiant atmosphere despite frigid temperatures. A rap song, "Razom nas bahato, nas ne podolaty" 'together we are many, we will not be defeated' resounded among the protesters, and became recognized as the "Hymn of the Orange Revolution." Enacting the disruption of traditional value systems characteristic of liminal revolutionary times, otherwise conservative middle-aged people confessed to having learned to like rap during the demonstrations (Wagstyl and Warner 2004).

As the world watched, the massive protests and political negotiations ultimately prevailed against the fraudulent election and a new, more carefully monitored election was held on December 26. Yushchenko won this election by a comfortable 8 percent margin, and was inaugurated president on January 23, 2005. This win was a triumph of the democratic process and a major challenge to authoritarian regimes of the post-Soviet region. It was also a turning point in debates over cultural and political correction.

As in the previous elections in independent Ukraine, language was a divisive issue. The status and spheres of use of Ukrainian had clearly increased since independence, inevitably encroaching on what had previously been exclusively Russian spheres, and disrupting the dominant status of Russian. Yanukovych hoped to capitalize on any misgivings Russophones might have by promising to make Russian a second official language, just as the incumbent president Kuchma had once promised. Kuchma had not carried through with his campaign promise: it was easier to leave aside the controversial issue that would entail constitutional amendments, allowing language dynamics to work themselves out at lower levels. But for Yanukovych, the language issue was again a way to appeal to Russophones and to attempt to alienate them from Yushchenko, by depicting the opposition leader as hostile to Russian.

Writers supporting Yushchenko challenged Yanukovych's legitimacy and fitness for leadership on the basis of his poor language skills (just as Yushchenko had been challenged in 2002 [Semenova 2002]). One writer argued that "it is difficult for him [Yanukovych] even to speak—not only Ukrainian, but even his native Russian" (Andrukhovych 2004). Yanukovych's lack of command of Ukrainian was exemplified in his spelling mistakes in filling out the documents to register as a presidential candidate. The inadequacy of his Russian was pointed out in his use of nonstandard lexicon, referred to as *blatniak* 'prison jargon.' His use of *blatniak* was furthermore taken to reflect his corrupt character, reinforcing the fact that he had a criminal record of robbery and assault (Andrukhovych 2004; BBC News 2004). In criticizing Yanukovych's linguistic shortcomings, a group of Ukrainian writers went even further, arguing that the Russian language used in Ukraine as a whole was a "language of [low-quality] pop and prison jargon." This fueled a heated debate over the relative values of Ukrainian and Russian (BBC Russian.com Forum 2004). These skirmishes in the politics of linguistic correction contributed to the portrayal of the Yanukovych-Yushchenko opposition as a Russian-Ukrainian, East-West divide.

The simplistic presentation of an East-West split as explanatory of the division between supporters of Yanukovych versus those favoring Yushchenko was politically misleading: it reduced the opposition between the candidates to a regional-cultural difference, diverting attention away from the legitimate political issues. Yanukovych represented a corrupt autocracy (continuing the status quo of Kuchma's regime) whereas Yushchenko represented a promise of democratic reform. But support for Yushchenko was not unanimous: 44 percent of all voters in the December 26, 2004, election, mostly in the east and south of the country, voted for Yanukovych. Part of the explanation lay in the restricted and manipulated flow of information to eastern regions. Where there were "so many nice things" (as one Crimean woman put it) said about Yanukovych on state-controlled television and newspapers, there were rumors in both Donetsk and Crimea that Yushchenko was doing America's bidding and would close down Ukrainian mines in order to store American toxic waste (Mulvey 2004; Trofimov 2004). Soviet-era fears of American malicious intentions were apparently still alive.

Another segment of support for Yanukovych was more opportunistic. In a system where favors and connections play a significant role in administrative appointments at every level, some people feared they might lose their jobs and their influence if Yushchenko should win and subsequently crack down on corruption (Melnyk 2004). Pensioners and workers in southeastern Ukraine were given raises shortly before the election, and while some saw this as a blatant effort at bribery, others believed that this was evidence that their local candidate, Yanukovych, was looking out for their interests and that they should vote for him to retain these benefits (Meek 2004).

In addition to the opportunism, misinformation, and wild rumors, support for Yanukovych in the southeast of the country also stemmed from an ideological preference for Slavic unity, especially with powerful neighboring Russia. Many people, especially in eastern Ukraine, had familial ties in Russia. After decades of open borders between the Soviet republics, Yanukovych's promise of instating dual Ukrainian-Russian citizenship was appealing to those who had found that crossing new post-Soviet international borders had become onerous.

Yanukovych, even with his criminal record, represented a comforting familiarity to many Ukrainians. For entrepreneurs, doing business with Westerners often meant prioritizing efficiency and impartiality, and doing away with the Soviet/Slavic social rituals through which mutual understandings were established and business dealings were personalized. Openness to the West and Western products had coincided with drastic economic instability for many people. Yushchenko's platform of striving for greater integration with Europe was seen by some as leading to the further erosion of a familiar way of life.

In late November 2004, when politicians in the southeastern Ukrainian regions recognized that Yushchenko's presidential bid might be successful and thus threaten their access to power, they attempted to capitalize on regional differences by proposing a move toward regional autonomy. A meeting of about four thousand local councilors from southeastern Ukrainian regions in Donetsk oblast was also attended by the Moscow mayor Yurii Luzhkov, who referred to the pro-Yushchenko Orange Revolution as "the Sabbath of witches who have been fattened up with oranges" (Maksymiuk 2004b). Many Ukrainians saw Russia's support of separatism (through Luzhkov) as an effort to divide and conquer, aided by regional politicians who wanted to hold on to their influence. In the end, the threat of separatism fizzled, lacking both grass-roots support and economic viability (Blinova and Glinkin 2004; Schwabe 2004).

Families and friendships were bitterly divided by their support of different candidates in the last election, but few people wanted to see Ukraine break apart (Riabchuk 2004). Earlier analysts had faulted Ukrainians for being politically noncommittal, but it may be that the penchant for "having it both ways" worked to bring together Ukrainophones and Russophones—as well as those who do not fit neatly into either category—to join under the orange banners to fight for their civil rights. The Orange Revolution brought people together across regional and cultural divisions.

Yushchenko himself is from a northeastern Ukrainian city, Sumy, 40 kilometers from the Russian border. His most visible campaign supporter, Yulia Tymoshenko, appointed as Yushchenko's prime minister, grew up speaking Russian in the southeastern city of Dnipropetrovsk and reportedly did not speak Ukrainian until after independence. Her case is similar to that of Borys Tarasyuk, who was appointed Yushchenko's foreign minister (whose linguistic life history is presented in chapter 2). While Yushchenko was against legislation granting Russian language official status alongside Ukrainian, he made a point of occasionally speaking publicly in Russian during his campaign to emphasize his acceptance of this language as part of Ukrainian life.

There were significant public shows of support for Yushchenko in some eastern as well as western cities, and centrally located Kyiv, the site of the most massive public support for Yushchenko, is difficult to characterize with simple linguistic or cultural labels. In Kyiv the protesters of the Orange Revolution spoke and carried signs in both languages, and language did not appear to be a divisive issue among them. But ethnolinguistic tensions in the city had not disappeared entirely. A friend of mine in Kyiv, who generally preferred to speak Ukrainian, wrote in December 2004 that, with people speaking Russian, she switched to Russian so as not to risk arousing anger against Ukrainians or against "the orange ones" (Yushchenko supporters). She felt that it was still a safer bet to use Russian publicly in Kyiv, as she had during the Soviet period, so she tended to begin interactions in Russian with people she did not know, reserving Ukrainian for

Viktor Yushchenko appearing before the protesters in Kyiv on December 4, 2004. "These hands are clean," he said. "I have never stolen anything in my life. I have not been convicted and I lead an honest life." Pictured from left to right (and the posts they came to occupy once Yushchenko became president in January 2005) are Mykola Tomenko (vice prime minister of humanitarian policy), Oleksandr Zinchenko (state secretary), Yushchenko, a bodyguard, Anatolij Kinakh (first vice prime minister), Yulia Tymoshenko (prime minister), and Yurij Karmazin (member of parliament, head of the Parliamentary Committee for Fighting Organized Crime). Photograph by Yuriy Verbovskyy.

friends or people she heard using Ukrainian. The acceptability of nonreciprocal bilingual interactions had apparently not defused all the political implications of language choice. Paradoxically my friend could be characterized as a Ukrainophone who contributed to Russian dominance in public spaces of the city.

Yushchenko's win would likely make it more comfortable for people who would prefer to speak Ukrainian in public in Kyiv and elsewhere to do so. Yushchenko's vision of Europeanization and democratization entails linguistic and cultural correction of another sort: the accrual of linguistic capital through widespread multilingualism. Yushchenko idealistically insisted that neither language would be promoted at the expense of the other, but that both, and others as well, needed to be mastered, to return Ukraine and Ukrainians to an empowered and prestigious cultural position. As reported by an observer of a speech to protesters in Kyiv on December 3, 2004:

Of late, Yushchenko has made a habit of talking about the grandeur of Ukraine's history, and how "European" it is. Tonight, he repeated in Russian, a little story that he had told in Ukrainian several days ago, about the Patriarch of Constantinople traveling through Ukraine in the 1640s and being very surprised that Khmelnytsky was able to speak seven languages, including fluent Latin, and that in every village "even the women and children knew how to read." He also pointed out that 600 years before that, when princess Anna (the daughter of King Yaroslav the Wise of Kyivan Rus) was getting married to the French king, she signed her name on the marriage document in full, while the French king was only able to write an "X." All of this was said in the context of arguing the European-ness of the Ukrainian nation, and it was said in Russian in an effort to counter the propaganda of the regime which for months has tried to convince eastern Ukrainians that Yushchenko is a nationalist, and that he will ban Russian once he becomes President. Yushchenko's argument was that because Ukraine is part of Europe, every Ukrainian should speak Ukrainian, Russian, English, French and German, and only then will the population of "his nation" be able to catch up on the time lost since the 1640s. (Wynnyckyj 2004)

Yushchenko's multilingual vision is not within reach for most Ukrainians, but he expressed a pluralistic ideal that was likely the best bet for forging a democratic future in Ukraine. Any simple solution in favor of only Ukrainian or Russian was bound to fan ethnolinguistic tensions. Ukrainian-Russian bilingualism was controversial, because it was seen as a continuation of Soviet policies that ultimately worked in favor of Russian. Yushchenko insisted that everyone should know not only both languages but others as well, and argued that (triple or quadruple) multilingualism was a normal European condition that Ukrainians needed to seek to achieve a better life (Yushchenko 2005). But, in the end, the idea that all Ukrainians should know Ukrainian, along with other internationally powerful languages, was already a huge step favoring Ukrainian, a language that tsarist and Soviet ideologies had repressed and designated for nonexistence or extinction.

APPENDIX **A Comparison of Ukrainian and Russian**

There is no simple way to characterize the degree of mutual intelligibility of Ukrainian and Russian. People who grew up with both languages may think that they are completely mutually intelligible, whereas those familiar with only one may understand very little of the other. People do not necessarily speak the standard language but mix the two languages and use regional variants, which makes the judgment of understanding more complicated.

In my own experience (learning Russian as an adult after having learned Ukrainian as a child), the greatest barrier to understanding was the different vocabulary. The grammatical structures of Ukrainian and Russian are mostly very similar, but some differences do exist. Much can depend on the context, the topic, the speed and clarity of speech. It helps to be familiar with the phonological differences and regular sound correspondences between the two languages. In some cases written language may be easier to understand than speech, because some words that appear identical in writing may be pronounced differently because of different letter values and phonological rules. Three letters that are written identically have different sound values in the two languages: и, е, and г. While Ukrainian spelling is largely phonetic (read exactly the way it is written), Russian pronunciation diverges from orthography according to a set of rules, including the following: unstressed "o" is pronounced [a] or [ə], "e" in a stressed syllable sometimes becomes [jo], and voiced consonants (b, d, g, v, z, ž) become devoiced (p, t, k, f, c, š) at the end of words or before other unvoiced consonants. The focus here is on understanding spoken interactions, so only transcriptions are provided. The phoneme transcribed as "y" is pronounced [ɪ] in Ukrainian and [i] in Russian, but I do not show this distinction here. The stress on a syllable is indicated when this is the only difference between pronunciations in the two languages.

The list of common terms and phrases that follows is meant to give readers who are unfamiliar with one or both of the languages a sense of the similarities and differences one would encounter in everyday life. The list is not random and is not meant to be the basis for a quantitative assessment of similarity. The listed terms are standard, and regional variants may present either more similarity or divergence. In some cases more than one widely used variant is listed for a given term.

English	Ukrainian	Russian
greetings	vitan'n'a	pr'iv'etstv'ijə
hi	pryvit	pr'iv'et
good morning	dobroho ranku	dobrəjə utrə
good day	dobryj den'	dobryj d'en'
good evening	dobryj večir	dobryj v'eč'ir
thank you	djakuju, spasybi	spas'ibə
do you know? (plural/formal)	čy vy znajete?	n'i znajit'i l'i vy?
where are you going? (fam.)	kudy ty ideš?	kuda ty id'oš?
here	tut	z'd'es' (colloq.: tut)
there	tam	tam
where	de	gd'e
everywhere	vs'udy	v'iz'd'e
nowhere	n'ide	n'igd'e, n'egd'i
somewhere	des'	gd'e-tə
where from?	zvidky?	atkuda?
this (m., f., n.)	cej, c'a, ce	etət, etə, etə
that (m., f., n.)	toj, ta, to	tot, ta, to
what for?	naviščo?	zač'em?
why?	čomu?	pəč'imu?
I (fem.) lost (something)	ja zhubyla	ja uran'ilə
I (masc.) found (something)	ja znajšov	ja našol
you ask	ty pytaješ	ty sprašyvajiš
you answer	ty vidpovidaješ	ty atv'ičajiš
he searched	vin šukav	on iskal
she saw	vona bačyla	ana v'id'elə
we will talk	my hovorytymemo, my budemo hovoryty	my bud'im gəvar'it'
you will write	vy pysatymete, vy budete pysaty	vy bud'it'i p'isat'
they cannot sing	vony ne možut' spivaty	un'i n'l mogut p'et'
building	budynok	zdanijə
house/home	d'im	dom
floor	pidloha	pol

English	Ukrainian	Russian
ceiling	stel'a	pətalok
wall	st'ina	s't'ina
door	dveri	dv'er'
table	st'il	stol
chair	kr'islo	stul
bed	l'ižko	kravat'
pencil	ol'ivec'	kərandaš
paper	papir	bumagə
book	knyha	kn'igə
next stop	nastupna zupynka	s'l'edujuš'š'əjə astanofkə
street	vulyc'a	ul'ica
car	mašyna	mašyna
train	pojizd, pot'ah	pojist
airplane	l'itak	səmal'ot
clothing	od'ah	ad' eždə
shirt	soročka	rubaškə
pants	štany	br'uk'i, štany
skirt	spidnyc'a	jupkə
tie	kravatka	galstuk
scarf	šalyk	šarf
hat	šapka, kapel'ux	šl'apə
footwear	vzut't'a	obuf'
shoes	čerevyky	bat'ink'i
boots	čoboty	səpagi
body	t'ilo	t'elə
head	holova	gəlava
forehead	čolo	lop
eye	oko	glas
nose	n'is	nos
lips	usta, huby	guby
mouth	rot	rot
elbow	l'ikot'	lokət'
arm/hand	ruka	ruka
leg/foot	noha	naga
knee	kol'ino	kal'enə
finger/toe	palec'	pal'ic
muscle	mjaz	myšcə

English	Ukrainian	Russian
food	*jida*	*jida*
breakfast	*sn'idanok*	*zaftrək*
lunch	*obid*	*ab'et*
dinner	*večer'a*	*užyn*
butter	*maslo*	*maslə*
oil	*olija*	*maslə*
bread	*xl'ib*	*xl'ep*
salt	*s'il'*	*sol'*
milk	*moloko*	*məlako*
sugar	*cukor*	*saxər*
flour	*muka*	*muka*
egg	*jajce*	*jijco*
juice	*s'ik (sok)*	*sok*
beer	*pyvo*	*p'ivə*
vodka	*hor'ilka*	*votkə*
apple	*jabluko*	*jabləkə*
onion	*cybul'a*	*luk*
garlic	*čysnyk*	*č'isnok*
tasty	*smačno*	*fkusnə*
thirst	*spraha*	*žaždə*
hunger	*holod*	*golət*
people	*l'udy*	*l'ud'i*
person	*l'udyna*	*č'ilav'ek*
boy	*xlopec'*	*mal'č'ik*
girl	*d'ivčyna*	*d'evuškə*
man	*čolovik*	*muš'š'inə*
husband	*čolovik*	*muž*
woman	*žinka*	*žen'š'š'inə*
wife	*žinka*	*žyna*
family	*s'imja*	*s'im'ja*
father	*bat'ko*	*at'ec*
dad	*tato*	*papə*
mother	*maty*	*mat'*
mom	*mama*	*mamə*
child	*dytyna*	*r'ib'onək*
brother	*brat*	*brat*
sister	*sestra*	*s'istra*
time	*čas*	*vr'em'ə*
hour	*hodyna*	*č'as*

English	Ukrainian	Russian
minute	*xvylyna*	*minutə*
day	*den'*	*d'en'*
week	*tyžden'*	*n'id'el'ə*
month	*mis'ac'*	*m'es'ic*
year	*r'ik*	*got*
Monday	*poned'ilok*	*pən'id'el'n'ik*
Tuesday	*vivtorok*	*ftorn'ik*
Wednesday	*sereda*	*sr'ida*
Thursday	*četver*	*č'itv'erk*
Friday	*pjatnyc'a*	*p'atn'icə*
Saturday	*subota*	*subotə*
Sunday	*ned'il'a*	*vəskr'is'en'jə*
January	*s'ičen'*	*jinvar'*
February	*l'utyj*	*f'ivral'*
March	*berezen'*	*mart*
April	*kviten'*	*apr'el'*
May	*traven'*	*maj*
June	*červen'*	*ijun'*
July	*lypen'*	*ijul'*
August	*serpen'*	*avgust*
September	*veresen'*	*s'int'abr'*
October	*žovten'*	*akt'abr'*
November	*lystopad*	*najabr'*
December	*hruden'*	*d'ikabr'*
when	*koly*	*kagda*
now	*teper*	*t'ip'er'*
now-immediately	*zrazu*	*s'ičas*
later	*pizn'iše*	*pož'ž'i*
still a long time	*šče dovho*	*jiš'š'o dolgə*
in an hour	*za hodynu*	*č'ir'is č'as*
once (some time ago)	*kolys'*	*adnaždy*
What time is it?	*kotra hodyna?*	*skol'kə čisof?*
	(lit., which hour)	(lit., how many hours)
concepts	*pon'at't'a*	*pan'at'ijə*
(I) understand	*rozumiju*	*pən'imaju*

English	Ukrainian	Russian
love (general)	*l'ubov*	*l'ubof'*
love (romantic)	*koxan'n'a*	*l'ubof'*
hate	*nenavis't'*	*n'enəv'is't'*
I like	*men'i podobajet's'a*	*mn'e nrav'iccə*
I advise	*ja radžu*	*ja savjetuju*
language	*mova*	*jizyk*
announcement	*ohološen'n'a*	*abjavl'en'ijə*
independence	*nezaležn'is't'*	*n'izav'is'iməs't'*
government	*ur'ad*	*gəsudarstvə*
small (masculine)	*malén'kyj*	*mál'in'k'ij*
small (feminine)	*malén'ka*	*mál'in'kəjə*
small (neuter)	*malén'ke*	*mál'in'kəjə*
big	*velykyj*	*ba'lšoj*
huge	*velyčeznyj*	*agromnyj*
very	*duže*	*oč'in'*
main	*holovnyj*	*glavnyj*
half	*piv*	*pol*
whole	*c'ilyj*	*celyj*
many	*bahato*	*mnogə*
difference	*riznýc'a*	*ráz'n'icə*
similarity	*pod'ibn'is't', sxožis't'*	*padob'ije, sxoctvə*
let it be	*nexaj bude*	*pus't' bud'it*

References

Abdulaziz, Mohamed H., and Ken Osinde. 1997. "Sheng and Engsh: Development of Mixed Codes among the Urban Youth in Kenya." *International Journal of the Sociology of Language* 125:43–63.

Alvarez-Cáccamo, Celso. 1998. "From "Switching Code" to "Code-Switching": Towards a Reconceptualization of Communicative Codes." In *Code-switching in Conversation: Language, Interaction, and Identity,* ed. Peter Auer, 29–48. New York: Routledge.

Anderson, Benedict. 1991. *Imagined Communities.* New York: Verso.

Andrukhovych, Yurij. 1992. "Rekreatsiji." *Suchasnist'* 369, no. 1 (January): 27–85.

———. 1993. "Moscoviada." *Suchasnist'* 381, no. 1(January): 40–84; no. 2(February): 10–53.

———. 2004. *The Color of Freedom and Oranges.* Translated by Michael M. Naydan. Electronically distributed letter, November 22, 2004.

Annamalai, E. 1989. "The Linguistic and Social Dimensions of Pluralism." In *The Politics of Language Purism,* ed. Björn H. Jernudd and Michael J. Shapiro, 225–231. New York: Mouton de Gruyter.

Anonymous Editorial, 1. 1995. "Chomu ne vykonuiet'sia 'Zakon pro movy v Ukraïni?'" *Shliakh Peremohy,* no. 8 (2132), March 4, 6.

Anonymous Editorial, 2. 1995. "Chernomyrdin zashchytil 'Santa-Barbaru' grudiu." *Komsomol'skaia Pravda,* no.169 (21179), September 16, 4.

Anonymous Editorial, 3. 2003. "A Disaster of a Law: Editorial." *Kyiv Post,* September 25. Posted in the Ukraine List (UKL #212), electronic news list compiled by Dominique Arel.

Arbatov, Kyrylo. 2002. "Davaite spil'no zakhyshchaty kul'turu: ukraïns'ku—v Krymu, rosiis'ku—u L'vovi." *Kryms'ka svitlytsia,* March 15, 6.

Arel, Dominique. 1993. "Language and the Politics of Ethnicity: The Case of Ukraine." Ph.D. diss., University of Illinois at Urbana-Champaign. Ann Arbor: University Microfilms International.

———. 2002. "Interpreting "Nationality" and "Language" in the 2001 Ukrainian Census." *Post-Soviet Affairs* 18 (3): 213–249.

Argentier, Joan A. 2001. "Code-Switching and Dialogism: Verbal Practices among Catalan Jews in the Middle Ages." *Language in Society* 30:377–402.

Auer, Peter. 1999. "From Codeswitching via Language Mixing to Fused Lects: Towards a Dynamic Typology of Bilingual Speech. *International Journal of Bilingualism* 3 (4): 309–332.

Auer, Peter, ed. 1998. *Code-switching in Conversation: Language, Interaction, and Identity.* New York: Routledge.

Azhniuk, Bohdan. 2001. "Movni zminy na tli dekolonizatsiï ta hlobalizatsiï." *Movoznavstvo* 3:48–54.

Bakhtin, Mikhail M. 1981 [1934–35]. "Discourse in the Novel." In *The Dialogic Imagination,* ed. Michael Holquist, trans. Caryl Emerson and Michael Holquist, 259–422. Austin: University of Texas Press.

Balla, Mykola Ivanovych. 1996. *English-Ukrainian Dictionary in Two Volumes.* Kyiv: Osvita.

Barker, Adele Marie, ed. 1999. *Consuming Russia: Popular Culture, Sex, and Society since Gorbachev.* Durham, N.C.: Duke University Press.

Barthes, Roland. 1989. "The War of Languages; The Division of Languages." In *The Rustle of Language,* trans. Richard Howard, 106–124. Berkeley: University of California Press.

BBC News. 2004. "Anger at Ukraine's Ban on Russian." *BBC News Online,* April 15, 2004. Available at http://news.bbc.co.uk/go/pr/fr/-/2/hi/europe/3630631.stm (accessed September 2004).

BBC Russian.com Forum. 2004. "Russkii na Ukraine: 'iazyk popsy i blatniaka'?" Discussion forum. Available online at http://news.bbc.co.uk/hi/russian/talking_point/ newsid_3945000/3945397.stm (accessed October 28, 2004).

Bex, Tony, and Richard Watts, eds. 1999. *Standard English: The Widening Debate.* New York: Routledge.

Bezhbovska, Liliana. 1995. Will the Sun Stop Shining if the National Academy of Government Start Talking in Ukrainian? *Chas-Time,* no. 28 (April 14, 1995): 14.

Bider, Herman. 1997. "Ukraïns'ka mova v Habsburgz'kii monarkhiï (1772–1918)." *Movoznavstvo* 1:24–29.

Bilaniuk, Laada. 1993. "Diglossia in Flux: Language and Ethnicity in Ukraine. *Texas Linguistic Forum* 33: 79–88.

——. 1997a. "Matching Guises and Mapping Language Ideologies in Ukraine." *Texas Linguistic Forum* 37:298–310.

——. 1997b. "Speaking of Surzhyk: Ideologies and Mixed Languages." *Harvard Ukrainian Studies* 21 (1/2): 93–117.

——. 1998a. "The Politics of Language and Identity in Ukraine." Ph.D. diss., University of Michigan.

——. 1998b. "Purity and Power: The Geography of Language Ideology in Ukraine." *Michigan Discussions in Anthropology* 13:165–189.

——. 2003. "Gender, Language Attitudes, and Language Status in Ukraine." *Language in Society* 32:47–78.

———. 2004. "A Typology of *Surzhyk:* Mixed Ukrainian-Russian Language." *International Journal of Bilingualism* 8 (4): 409–425.

Blinova, Ekaterina, and Maksim Glinkin. 2004. "Too Many Ukrainians: A Titular Nationality Dominates in the Eastern Regions of Ukraine That Allegedly Supported Yanukovych." *Nezavisimaia Gazeta* (Moscow), December 4. Translated by Lisa Koriouchkina for the Ukraine List (UKL #300), electronic news list compiled by Dominique Arel.

Blommaert, Jan, ed. 1999. *Language Ideological Debates.* New York: Mouton de Gruyter.

Blommaert, Jan, and Jef Verschueren. 1992. "The Role of Language in European Nationalist Ideologies." *Pragmatics* 2 (3): 355–375.

Bonfiglio, Thomas Paul. 2002. *Race and the Rise of Standard American.* New York: Mouton de Gruyter.

Bourdieu, Pierre. 1977a. *Outline of a Theory of Practice.* Cambridge: Cambridge University Press.

———. 1977b. "The Economics of Linguistic Exchanges." *Social Science Information* 16 (6): 645–668.

———. 1984. *Distinction: A Social Critique of the Judgement of Taste.* Cambridge, Mass.: Harvard University Press.

———. 1990. *The Logic of Practice.* Stanford: Stanford University Press.

———. 1991. *Language and Symbolic Power.* Edited by J. B. Thompson. Translated by G. Raymond and M. Adamson. Cambridge, Mass.: Harvard University Press.

Bugarski, Ranko. 1992. "Language in Yugoslavia: Situation, Policy, Planning." In *Language Planning in Yugoslavia,* ed. Ranko Bugarski and Celia Hawkesworth, 9–26. Columbus, Ohio: Slavica.

Buriachok, A. A., et al. 1999. *Slovnyk Synonimiv Ukraïns'koï Movy.* Vol. 1. Kyiv: Naukova Dumka.

Busel, Viacheslav Tymofiiovych. 2001. *Velykyi Tlumachnyi Slovnyk Suchasnoï Ukraïns'koï Movy.* Kyiv: Perun.

Cameron, Deborah. 1995. *Verbal Hygiene.* New York: Routledge.

Chaban, Mykola. 1994. "Jak z' hortalasia ukraïnizatsiia na prydniproví." *Borysfen,* no. 10 (40). (Dnipropetrovsk monthly journal).

Cheboksarov, N. N. 1970. "Problems of the Typology of Ethnic Units in the Works of Soviet Scholars." *Soviet Anthropology and Archaeology* 9 (2): 127–153.

Chihirinskaia, Ol'ga. 1995. "Ot pervogo litsa: Khrammatyka e vyskus'tvo chytaty y pysaty . . ." *VLD Press Torhovyi Dom,* no. 25 (96), June 23, 1.

Chizhikova, L. N. 1968. Ob etnicheskikh protsessakh v vostochnykh raionakh Ukraïny." *Sovietskaia Etnografiia* 1:18–31.

Chykalenko, Je. 1955. *Spohady (1861–1907).* New York: Ukrainian Academy of Arts and Sciences in the United States.

Clark, Katerina, and Michael Holquist. 1984. *Mikhail Bakhtin.* Cambridge, Mass.: Harvard University Press.

Comrie, Bernard. 1987. "Russian." In *Languages and Their Status*, ed. Timothy Shopen, 91–151. Philadelphia: University of Pennsylvania Press.

Conquest, Robert. 1986. *The Harvest of Sorrow: Soviet Collectivization and the Terror-Famine*. New York: Oxford University Press.

Council of Europe. 1992. *European Charter for Regional or Minority Languages*. Strasbourg, 5.XI.1992. Available at http://conventions.coe.int/Treaty/en/Treaties/Html/148.htm (accessed July 20, 2004).

Dashkevych, Ja. R. 1990. "Ukraïnizatsia: Prychyny i naslidky." *Slovo i chas* 8:55–64.

Davis, Hayley. 1999. "Typography, Lexicography, and the Development of the Idea of 'Standard English.'" In *Standard English: The Widening Debate*, ed. Tony Bex and Richard Watts, 69–88. New York: Routledge.

Derkach, B. A. 1972. "H. S. Skovoroda—pys'mennyk." *Hryhorii Skovoroda: Literaturni Tvory*. Kyiv: Naukova Dumka.

Desheriev, Ju. D., and I. F. Protchenko. 1972. "Soiuz ravnopravnykh narodov i russkii iazyk." *Russkaia Rech'* 5.

Dingley, James. 1990. "Ukrainian and Belorussian—a Testing Ground." In *Language Planning in the Soviet Union*, ed. Michael Kirkwood, 174–188. New York: St. Martin's.

Dmytryshyn, Basil. 1970. Introduction to *The Suppression of the Ukrainian Activities in 1876*, by Fedir Savchenko. Harvard Series in Ukrainian Studies, vol. 14, xv–xxix. Munich: Wilhelm Fink Verlag.

Douglas, Mary. 1966. *Purity and Danger: An Analysis of the Concepts of Pollution and Taboo*. New York: Ark Paperbacks.

Drinov, D., and P. Sabaldyr. 1934. *Proty natsionalizmu v matematychnii terminolohiï. Matematychnyi Terminolohichnyi Biuleten'*. Kyiv: Vseukraïns'ka Akademiia Nauk.

Dunham, Vera. 1990. *In Stalin's Time: Middleclass Values in Soviet Fiction*. Enlarged and updated edition. Durham, N.C.: Duke University Press.

Dunn, Stephen P. 1975. "New Departures in Soviet Theory and Practice of Ethnicity." *Dialectical Anthropology* 1:61–70.

Dziuba, Ivan. 1990. *Bo to ne prosto mova, zvuky . . .* Kyiv: Radians'kyi Pys'mennyk.

Emerson, Caryl. 1984. Editor's preface to *Problems of Dostoevsky's Poetics*. Edited and translated by Caryl Emerson, xxix–xliii. Minneapolis: University of Minnesota Press.

Errington, Joseph. 1998. *Shifting Languages: Interaction and Identity in Javanese Indonesia*. Studies in the Social and Cultural Foundations of Language 19. Cambridge: Cambridge University Press.

Fasold, Ralph. 1984. *The Sociolinguistics of Society*. New York: Basil Blackwell.

Fawkes, Helen. 2004. "Ukraine Drive to Keep Russian off Buses." *BBC News Online*, June 18, 2004. Available at http://news.bbc.co.uk/go/pr/fr/-/2/hi/europe/3783353.stm (accessed September 2004).

Fedyk, Ol'ha. 1991. "Fenomen Linhvohipnozu." *Dzvin* (11):138–142.

Ferguson, Charles. 1959. Diglossia. *Word* 15:325–340.

Fishman, Joshua A. 1975. "The Spread of English as a New Perspective of the Study of 'Language Maintenance and Language Shift'; Knowing, Using and Liking English as an Additional Language." In *The Spread of English*, ed. Joshua A. Fishman, Robert L. Cooper, and Andrew W. Conrad, 108–133, 302–310. Rowley, Mass.: Newbury House.

Flaitz, Jeffra. 1988. *The Ideology of English: French Perceptions of English as a World Language.* New York: Mouton de Gruyter.

Flier, Michael. 2000. "Surzhyk: The Rules of Engagement." *Harvard Ukrainian Studies* 22:113–136.

———. 2002. "Surzhyk at the Top: The Linguistic Dimension of Kuchmagate." Paper presented at the Convention of the Association of the Study of Nationalities, Columbia University, April 11.

Foer, Jonathan Safran. 2002. *Everything Is Illuminated.* New York: HarperCollins Perennial.

Franceschini, Rita. 1998. Code-switching and the Notion of Code in Linguistics: Proposals for a Dual Focus Model." In *Code-switching in Conversation: Language, Interaction, and Identity*, ed. Peter Auer, 51–72. New York: Routledge.

Friedrich, Paul. 1989. "Language, Ideology, and Political Economy." *American Anthropologist* 91:295–312.

Frolov, Sergey. 1995. "Iak Dzhina pidmanula Meisona." *Komsomol'skaia Pravda*, no. 167 (2177), September 14, 1.

Gal, Susan. 1995. "Lost in a Slavic Sea: Linguistic Theories and Expert Knowledge in 19th Century Hungary." *Pragmatics* 5:155–166.

———. 2001. "Linguistic Theories and National Images in Nineteenth-century Hungary." In *Languages and Publics: The Making of Authority*, ed. Susan Gal and Kathryn A. Woolard. Manchester, England: St. Jerome.

Gal, Susan, and Judith T. Irvine. 1995. "The Boundaries of Languages and Disciplines: How Ideologies Construct Difference." *Social Research* 62 (4): 967;1001.

Gal, Susan, and Kathryn A. Woolard. 1995. "Constructing Languages and Publics: Authority and Representation." *Pragmatics* 5 (2): 129–138.

Gardner-Chloros, Penelope. 1995. "Code-switching in Community, Regional, and National Repertoires: The Myth of the Discreteness of Linguistic Systems." In *One Speaker, Two Languages: Cross-disciplinary Perspectives on Code-switching*, ed. Lesley Milroy and Pieter Muysken, 68–89. Cambridge: Cambridge University Press.

Giles, H., R. Y. Bourhis, and D. M. Taylor. 1977. "Towards a Theory of Language in Ethnic Group Relations." In *Language, Ethnicity, and Intergroup Relations*, ed. H. Giles, 307–348. New York: Academic Press.

Goodman, Elliot R. 1968 [1960]. "World State and World Language." In *Readings in the Sociology of Language*, ed. Joshua A. Fishman, 715–736. The Hague: Mouton. Reprinted from *The Soviet Design for a World State.* (New York: Columbia University Press, 1960), 264–284.

Goujon, Alexandra. 2000. "Ethno-politologie, ethnicité et état dans l'Ukraine post-sovietique." In *Post-socialisme, Post-colonialisme, et Posteriorité de l'Idéologie*, ed. Tristan Landry and Clemens Sobel, 83–95. Paris: Centre d'Études Africaines et École de Hautes Études en Sciences Sociales.

Grant, Bruce. 1995. *In the Soviet House of Culture: A Century of Perestroikas.* Princeton, N.J.: Princeton University Press.

Grosjean, F. 1982. *Life with Two Languages: An Introduction to Bilingualism.* Cambridge, Mass.: Harvard University Press.

Haeri, Niloofar. 1997. "The Reproduction of Symbolic Capital: Language, State, and Class in Egypt." *Current Anthropology* 38 (5): 795–816.

Hal'kovs'kyi, Oleksandr. 1998. "Anatolii Vekskliarskyi. Vid DJ do 'Talking Head.'" *Den'*, no. 68. Available at http://www.day.kiev.ua/1998/68/time-out/to4.htm.

Handler, Richard. 1988. *Nationalism and the Politics of Culture in Quebec.* Madison: University of Wisconsin Press.

Hanitkevych, Yaroslav. 1995. *Slovnyk Rusyzmiv u Movi Medykiv.* Lviv: Lviv State Medical Institute.

Haugen, Einar. 1972. *The Ecology of Language.* Selected and introduced by Anwar S. Dil. Stanford: Stanford University Press.

Heller, Monica. 1988a. Introduction to *Codeswitching: Anthropological and Sociolinguistic Perspectives,* ed. Monica Heller, 1–24. New York: Mouton de Gruyter.

———, ed. 1988b. *Codeswitching: Anthropological and Sociolinguistic Perspectives.* New York: Mouton de Gruyter.

Hill, Jane H., and Kenneth C. Hill. 1980. "Mixed Grammar, Purist Grammar, and Language Attitudes in Modern Nahuatl." *Language in Society* 9:321–348.

———. 1984. *Speaking Mexicano.* Tucson: University of Arizona Press.

Himka, John-Paul. 1999. Book review of *Die Russophilen in Galizien,* by Anna Veronica Wendland. *Harvard Ukrainian Studies* 23 (3/4): 195–199.

Hirsch, Francine. 1997. "The Soviet Union as a Work-in-Progress: Ethnographers and the Category Nationality in the 1926, 1937, and 1939 Censuses." *Slavic Review* 56, no. 2 (summer): 251–278.

Hnatkevych, Yurii. 2000. *Unykaimo rusyzmiv v ukraïnskii movi! Korotkyi slovnyk-antysurzhyk dlia deputativ Verkhovnoï Rady ta vsikh, khto khoche shchob ioho ukraïns' ka mova ne bula skhozhoiu na movu Vierky Serdiuchky.* Kyiv: Prosvita.

Hobsbawm, Eric. 1983. "Inventing Traditions. Mass-Producing Traditions: Europe, 1870–1914." In *The Invention of Tradition,* ed. Eric Hobsbawm and Terence Ranger. New York: Cambridge University Press.

Hoffmann, David L. 1994. *Peasant Metropolis: Social Identities in Moscow, 1929–1941.* Ithaca, N.Y.: Cornell University Press.

———. 2003. *Stalinist Values: The Cultural Norms of Soviet Modernity, 1917–1941.* Ithaca, N.Y.: Cornell University Press.

Holian, Ya. 1991. Introduction to *Pro Ridnu Movu i Ukraïns'ku Shkolu* by M. Hrushevs'kyi. Kyiv: Veselka.

Holmes, Steven A. 1996. "Black Voice of the Streets Is Defended and Criticized: Oakland, Calif. School Board's Resolution on Black English." *New York Times, late ed.,* December 30, A9.

Hrabovych, Hryhorii. 1998. "Kokhannia z vid'mamy." *Krytyka* 2:19–24.

Hrinchenko, Borys. 1909. *Slovar' Ukraïns'koï Movy.* Kyiv: Redaktsiia Zhurnala Kievskaia Staryna. Reprinted in 1959, Kyiv: Vydavnytstvo Akademiï Nauk Ukraïns'koi RSR.

Hrycak, Alexandra. In press. "Schooling, Language, and the Policy-making Power of State Bureaucrats in Ukraine." In *Rebounding Identities: The Politics of Identity in Russia and Ukraine,* ed. Dominique Arel and Blair Ruble. Baltimore, M.D.; Johns Hopkins University Press.

Hrytsenko, Oleksandr. 1999. Ukrainian Contents. *Krytyka* 10 (24): 16–19.

Humphrey, Caroline. 2002. *The Unmaking of Soviet Life: Everyday Economies after Socialism.* Ithaca, N.Y.: Cornell University Press.

Irvine, Judith T. 1985. "Status and Style in Language." *Annual Review of Anthropology* 14:557–581.

———. 1989. "When Talk Isn't Cheap: Language and Political Economy." *American Ethnologist* 16:48–67.

Irvine, Judith T., and Susan Gal. 2000. "Language Ideology and Linguistic Differentiation." In *Regimes of Language,* ed. Paul V. Kroskrity, 85–138. Santa Fe: School of American Research Press.

Ivanov, V. V., and N. G. Mikhailovskaia. 1982. "Russkii iazyk kak sredstvo mezhnatsional'nogo obshcheniia: aktual'nye aspekty i problemy." *Voprosy Iazykoznaniia* 6:3–13.

Ivanyshyn, V., and Ya. Radevych-Vynnytskyi. 1990. *Mova i Natsiia.* Drohobych: Lvivs'ka Oblasna Orhanizatsiia Tovarystva Liubyteliv Knyhy.

Jacobs, Timothy. 2004. "Talk Latvian in Latvia? Russian Speakers Balk." *Seattle Times,* April 5, 2004, A13.

Jaffe, Alexandra. 1999. *Ideologies in Action: Language Politics on Corsica.* New York: Mouton de Gruyter.

Jahn, Jens-Eberhard. 1999. "New Croatian Language Planning and Its Consequences for Language Attitudes and Linguistic Behavior—the Istrian Case." *Language and Communication* 19:329–354.

Jernudd, Björn H., and Michael J. Shapiro. 1989. *The Politics of Language Purism.* New York: Mouton de Gruyter.

Kalynovych, M., and D. Drinov. 1935. "Likviduvaty natsionalistychne shkidnytstvo v radianskii fizychnii terminolohiï." In *Fizychnyi Terminolohichnyi Biuleten',* 3–19. Kyiv: Vseukraïns'ka Akademiia Nauk.

Kaplan, Fred. 1994. "Moscow Homecoming Greeted by 5,000, Solzhenitsyn Ends Trip with Renewed Attack." *Boston Globe,* July 22, 1994, 2.

Karavans'kyi, Sviatoslav. 1994. *Secrety Ukraïns'koï Movy.* Kyiv: Kobza.

———. 2000. "Do pytannia pro neperekladnist'." *Ukraïns'ka Mova ta Literatura* 2 (162): 8.

Karpenko, Vitalii. 1990. "Mova tsia velychna i prosta . . ." Introduction to *Bo to ne prosto mova, zvuky . . .* by Ivan Dziuba. Kyiv: Radians'kyi Pys'mennyk.

Klochko, Diana, and Ihor Krotkov. 1998. "I eto ishcho ne vsie." *Den'*, no. 183 (September 25). Available at http://www.day.kiev.ua/1998/183/tele/te6.htm.

Kocherga, Olha, and Volodymyr Kulyk. 1994. "Ukraïns'ki terminolohichni slovnyky dovoiennoho periodu v bibliotekakh Kyieva ta L'vova." *Visnyk Akademiï Nauk Ukraïny* 2:55–61.

———. 2002. "To chy bude novyi ukraïns'kyi pravopys?" *Ukraïna Moloda* 62, no. 1868 (April 3): 1.

Kosmolins'ka, Natalka. 2000. "'ART-TERRA' dlia Domu Lysyka u Lvovi." *Postup*, no. 162 (606), September 30. Available at http://postup.brama.com/000930/162_9_3.html.

Koznarsky, Taras. 1998. "Notatky na berehakh makabresok." *Krytyka* 5 (7): 24–29.

Kravtsiv, Bohdan, and Volodymyr Kubijovyc. 1993. "Shevchenko Scientific Society." In *Encyclopedia of Ukraine*, ed. Danylo Husar Struk, 4:657–660. Toronto: Toronto University Press.

Kroskrity, Paul. 2000. *Regimes of Language.* Santa Fe: School of American Research Press.

Kroskrity, Paul, Bambi Schieffelin, and Kathryn Woolard, eds. 1992. *Pragmatics* 2(3). Special issue on language ideologies.

Krouglov, Alex. 2002. "Language Politics in Ukraine." Paper presented at the Convention of the Association of the Study of Nationalities, Columbia University, April 13.

Krushelnycky, Askold. 2004. "Ukraine: Kyiv Imposes Controversial Ban on Russian-language Broadcasts." Radio Free Europe/Radio Liberty, April 16, 2004. Available at http://www.rferl.org/featuresarticleprint/2004/04/cda8b69c-7f6d-42c0-8417-cfc66fa1545d.html.

Kuchma, Leonid. 2001. Published quote from television appearance. *Poliotyka i Kul'tura* 41(124):24.

———. 2003. *Ukraina—Ne Rossiia.* Moscow: Vremia.

Kulish, Mykola. 1955. *Tvory.* New York: Ukrainian Academy of Arts and Sciences in the United States.

Kulyk, Volodymyr. 2001. "Pravopysne bozhevillia." *Krytyka* 5 (43): 6–13.

———. 2002. "Constructing Common Sense: Discourses on Ethnolinguistic Problems and Transformation of Identity in Post-Soviet Ukraine." Paper presented at the Convention of the Association of the Study of Nationalities, Columbia University, April 13.

———. 2004a. "Mova pro movu: normalizatsiia ambivalentnosty, 1. Kraini ta tsentr." *Krytyka* 5 (79): 19–24.

———. 2004b. "Mova pro movu: normalizatsiia ambivalentnosty, 2. Normal'ni novyny." *Krytyka* 6 (80): 4–11.

Kuzio, Taras. 2000. "Language and Nationalism in the Post-soviet Space." RFE/RL Newsline, vol 4, no. 110, part II, August 3, 2000. Available at http://www.ualberta.ca/~cius/stasiuk/st-articles/an-lang-nat.htm (accessed September 2004).

———. 2001. "Status of Russian Language again Threatens Ukrainian-Russian Relations." RFE/RL Newsline, vol. 5, no. 6, part II, January 10, 2001. Available at http://www.ualberta.ca/~cius/stasiuk/st-articles/an-rus-lang.htm (accessed September 2004).

Labov, William. 1972a [1969]. "The Logic of Nonstandard English." In *Language and Social Context*, ed. P. P. Giglioli, 179–215. London: Penguin Books.

———. 1972b [1970]. "The Study of Language in Its Social Context." In *Language and Social Context*, ed. P. P. Giglioli, 283–307. London: Penguin Books.

Laitin, David D. 1998. *Identity in Formation: The Russian-speaking Populations in the Near Abroad.* Ithaca, N.Y.: Cornell University Press.

Lapins'kyi, Ihor. 2001. "Sho ne iasno?" Introduction to *Heroi Nashoho Chasu* by L. Poderevians'kyi. Lviv: Kal'varia.

Lemon, Alaina. 2000. *Betweeen Two Fires: Gypsy Perfromances and Romani Memory from Pushkin to Postsocialism.* Durham, N.C: Duke University Press.

Leonovich, Sofia. 2001. "Mova nasha—mova Rosii?" *Hrani* 29 (41). Available at http://www.grani.kiev.ua/2001/text/41/Leonovich18L_ukr.htm.

Levbarh, Ovsii. 1998. "Nad usiieiu Afiniieiu bezkhmarne nebo." *Den'*, no. 163. Available at http:///www.day.kiev.ua/1998/163/tele/te2.htm.

Lewin, Moshe. 1985. *The Making of the Soviet System: Essays in the Social History of Interwar Russia.* New York: Pantheon Books.

Lewis, E. Glyn. 1972. *Multilingualism in the Soviet Union: Aspects of Language Policy and Its Implementation.* The Hague: Mouton.

Liber, George. 1991. "*Korenizatsiia:* Restructuring Soviet Nationality Policy in the 1920s." *Ethnic and Racial Studies* 14 (1): 15–23.

———. 1992. *Soviet Nationality Policy, Urban Growth, and Identity Change in the Ukrainian SSR, 1923–1934.* Cambridge: Cambridge University Press.

Lihachova, Natalia. 1998. "Andrii Danylko: 'Ja ne rozumiiu, chomu my ne mozhymo smiiatysia nad samym soboiu?'" *Den'*, no. 28. Available at http://www.day.kiev.ua/1998/28/osoba/os1.htm.

Limon, Jose E. 1998. "*Carne, Carnales,* and the Carnivalesque: Bakhtinian *Batos,* Disorder, and Narrative Discourses." In *The Matrix of Language: Contemporary Linguistic Anthropology,* ed. D. Brenneis and R.K.S. Macaulay, 182–203. Boulder, Colo.: Westview.

Linde, Charlotte. 1993. *Life Stories: The Creation of Coherence.* New York: Oxford University Press.

Lippi-Green, Rosina. 1997. *English with an Accent: Language, Ideology, and Discrimination in the United States.* New York: Routledge.

Lomtev, T. P. 1949. "I. V. Stalin o razvitii natsional'nykh iazykov v epokhu sotsializma." *Voprosy filosofii,* no. 2, 136–137.

Mace, James E., and Leonid Heretz, eds. 1990. *Investigation of the Ukrainian Famine, 1932–1933: Oral History Project of the Commission on the Ukraine Famine.* Washington, D.C.: U.S. Government Printing Office.

Makitra, Roman. 2000. "Letter to the editor." *Postup* 199 (563). Available at http://postup.brama.com/000715/119_8_1.html.

Makley, Char. 1998. "The Power of the Drunk: Humor and Resistance in China's Tibet." *Michigan Discussions in Anthropology* 13:39–79.

Maksymiuk, Jan. 2000. "Composer's Death in Lviv Incites Anti-Russian Sentiment." RFE/RL Poland, Belarus, and Ukraine Report, vol. 2, no. 21, June 6, 2000. Available at http://www.rferl.org/pbureport/2000/06/21-060600.html.

——. 2004a. "The End of Russian-Language Broadcasting in Ukraine?" RFE/RL Analytical Reports, vol. 4, no. 8, April 22, 2004. Available at http://www.rferl.org/featuresarticleprint/2004/04/a25ea3c5-6d63-4054-807d-fd2553c4bd6b.html.

——. 2004b. "Will Ukraine Split in Wake of Divisive Ballot?" RFE/RL Newsline, vol. 8, no. 223, part 2, November 30.

Mannheim, Bruce. 1991. *The Language of the Inka since the Spanish Invasion.* Austin: University of Texas Press.

Markus, Vasyl. 1984. "Famine." In *Encyclopedia of Ukraine*, ed. Volodymyr Kubijovyc, 1:853–855. Toronto: University of Toronto Press.

Markus, Vasyl, and Roman Senkus. 1993. "Language Policy." In *Encyclopedia of Ukraine*, ed. Danylo Husar Struk, 3:46–48. Toronto: University of Toronto Press.

Martin, Terry. 2001. *The Affirmative Action Empire: Nations and Nationalism in the Soviet Union, 1923–1939.* Ithaca, N.Y.: Cornell University Press.

Masenko, Larisa. 1994. "Z pokhmuroi zony zaboron . . . deshcho pro movu 'novoï khvyli.'" *Slovo* 4 (84): 6.

——. 2004. *Mova i suspil'stvo: postkoloniial'nyi vymir.* Kyiv: Kyievo-Mohylians'ka Akademiia.

Matsiuk, Roman. 2000. "Surzhyk dlia inteligentsiï." *Postup* 95 (539): 15; 96 (540): 15; 99 (543): 15. Available at http://postup.brama.com/000602/95_15_2.html.

Matvienko, Antonina. 1994. *Ridne Slovo.* Kyiv: Prosvita.

Meek, James, 2004. "Divided They Stand." *The Guardian* (UK), December 10, posted in the Ukraine List (UKL #309), electronic news list compiled by Dominique Arel.

Meeuwis, Michael, and Jan Blommaert. 1998. "A Monolectal View of Code-Switching: Layered Code-switching among Zairans in Belgium." In *Code-switching in Conversation: Language, Interaction, and Identity*, ed. Peter Auer, 76–98. New York: Routledge.

Melnyczuk, Askold. 2001. *Ambassador of the Dead.* Washington, D.C.: Counterpoint.

Melnyk, Oleksandr. 2004. "Why Does the East and South Vote Yanukovych?" Electronic letter, November 13, posted in the Ukraine List (UKL #263), electronic news list compiled by Dominique Arel.

Miastkivs'kyi, Andrii. 1989. "Odesa-mama." *Kyïv*: 11–25.

Milroy, Lesley. 1999. "Standard English and Language Ideology in Britain and the United States." In *Standard English: The Widening Debate*, ed. Tony Bex and Richard Watts, 173–206. New York: Routledge.

Milroy, Lesley, and Pieter Muysken. 1995. "Introduction: Code-switching and Bilingualism Research." In *One Speaker, Two Languages: Cross-disciplinary Perspectives on Code-switching*, ed. Lesley Milroy and Pieter Muysken, 1–14. Cambridge: Cambridge University Press.

——, eds. 1995. *One Speaker, Two Languages: Cross-disciplinary Perspectives on Code-switching.* Cambridge: Cambridge University Press.

Mokrenko, Anatolii. 2001. "Surzhyk." *Ukraïns'ka Hazeta*, no. 20 (212), November 22.

Morozov, Kostiantyn P. 2000. *Above and Beyond: From Soviet General to Ukrainian State Builder.* Cambridge, Mass.: Harvard University Press.

Motyl, Alexander, and Bohdan Krawchenko. 1997. "Ukraine: From Empire to Statehood." In *New States, New Politics: Building the Post-Soviet Nations*, ed. Ian Bremmer and Ray Taras, 235–275. Cambridge: Cambridge University Press.

Mulvey, Stephen. 2004. "Ukraine's Loyal Industrial heart." *BBC News* (Donetsk), December 3, posted in the Ukraine List (UKL #299), electronic news list compiled by Dominique Arel.

Mustiatsa, P., ed. 1935. *Vykorinyty natsionalizm u vyrobnychii terminolohiï. Vyrobnychyi Terminolohichnyi Biuleten'.* Kyiv: Vseukraïnska Akademiia Nauk.

Muzychenko, Yaroslava. 2002. "U-movne isnuvannia." *Ukraïna Moloda*, February 20, 10.

Natalka. 2002. Letter to the editor. *Moloko* 1(10):64.

Newman, Barry. 1993. "Lithuanian Linguists Resist Attacks on Native Tongue: After Surviving the Red Army, Language Is under Assault by Fast Food and Ravioli." *Wall Street Journal*, midwest edition, April 12, 1993, vol. 74, no. 125, A1, A5.

Nicholson, Alex. 2003. "Leonid Kuchma Releases Book Ukraine Is Not Russia. *St. Petersburg Times*, September 5. Posted in the Ukraine List (UKL #211), electronic news list compiled by Dominique Arel.

Okara, Andrii M. 2001. "Na zakhyst rosiis'koï movy." *Kurier Kryvbasu*, no. 134: 3–10.

Ostrianyn, D. Kh., P. M. Popov, and I. A. Tabachnykov. 1961. "Vydatnyi ukraïns'kyi filosof i pys'mennyk." *Hryhorii Skovoroda: Tvory v Dvokh Tomakh*, 1:XI–XL. Kyiv: Vydavnytstvo Akademiï Nauk.

Ozhegov. S. I. 1986. *Slovar' Russkogo Iazyka.* Moscow: Russkyi Iazyk.

Pachlovska, Oxana. 1998. *Civiltà Letteraria Ucraina.* Rome: Carocci editore.

Pan'ko, T. I. 1991. "Mova i Kul'tura Natsiï, ed. T. I. Pan'ko, 3–7. Lviv: Lviv State University.

Parakrama, Arjuna. 1995. *De-Hegemonizing Language Standards: Learning from (Post)Colonial Englishes about "English."* New York: St. Martin's.

Parkin, David. 1994. "Language, Government, and Play on Purity and Impurity: Arabic, Swahili and the Vernaculars in Kenya." In *African Languages, Development and the State*, ed. Richard Fardon and Graham Furniss, 227–245. New York: Routledge.

Perlez, Jane. 1994. "Fear of Russia Is a Way of Life for Ukraine." *New York Times*, January 16, 3.

Poderevians'kyi, Les'. 1999. "Statement in 'Oksamytova Ukraïnizatsiia.'" *Den'*, no. 203 (November 2): 7.

———. 2001. *Heroi Nashoho Chasu.* Lviv: Kal'varia.

Podvesko, M. L. 1962. *Ukrainian-English Dictionary.* Offset reprint of *Ukrains'ko-anhliis'kyi slovnyk.* Kyiv: Radians'ka shkola, 1957.

Polevs'ka, Liudmyla. 1995. "Replika: *Volodymyr Maiakovs'kyi*: 'Tovarishch moskal', na Ukraïnu shutok ne skal'.'" *Vysokyi Zamok* (Lviv newspaper), no. 128 (562), September 21, 1.

Ponomariv, Oleksandr. 2001. "Pravopys: suddi khto?" *Ukraïna Moloda,* February 1, 5.

———. 2004. "Ternystyi shkliakh ukraïns'koho pravopysu." *Svoboda,* no. 42 (October 15): 16–17.

Prima News Agency. 2004. "Ukrainian President Opposes Monopoly of Official State Language on TV." PRIMA News Agency, April 26, 2004. Available at http://www.prima-news.ru/eng/news/news/2004/4/29/28350.html (accessed September 2004).

Prosvita Ukrainian Language Society. 1991. *Materialy pro Rozvytok Mov v Ukraïnskii RSR.* Kyiv: KKDNK.

Pujolar, Joan. 2001. *Gender, Heteroglossia, and Power: A Sociolinguistic Study of Youth Culture.* New York: Mouton de Gruyter.

Pullum, Geoffrey K. 1997. "Language That Dare Not Speak Its Name." *Nature,* March 27, 386:321–322.

Pylyns'kyi, M. M. 1976. *Movna Norma i Styl'.* Kyiv: Naukova Dumka.

Radchuk, Vitalii. 1999. "Zabobon neperekladnosti." *Ukraïns' ka Mova ta Literatura* 40 (152): 3–4.

———. 2000a. "Implementatsiia chy vprovadzhennia?" *Shliakh Peremohy* 32 (2415): 10.

———. 2000b. "Surzhyk iak nedopereklad." *Ukraïns'ka Mova ta Literatura* 11 (171): 11–12.

———. 2002. "Mova v Ukraïni: stan, funktsiï, perspektyvy." *Dyvoslovo* 2 (540): 2–5.

Rakhmanin, Sergey. 2002. "Korolevstvo razbitykh zerkal." *Zerkalo Nedeli,* no. 51 (375), December 29, 2001–January 11, 2002. Available at http://www.zerkalo-nedeli.com/print.php?id=33374.

Reid, Anna. 1997. *Borderland: A Journey through the History of Ukraine.* Boulder, Colo.: Westview.

Riabchuk, Mykola. 1992. "Two Ukraines?" *East European Reporter* 5 (4).

———. 2002. "Ambivalence to Ambiguity: Why Ukrainians Remain Undecided? Paper presented at the conference "L'Ukraine et le monde exterieur dix ans après l'independence" at the Centre d'Etudes et de Recherches Internationales, Paris, April 5.

———. 2004. "The Ukrainian Fault-Line: Citizens versus Subjects." *Berliner Zeitung* 3 (December), posted in the Ukraine List (UKL #297), electronic news list compiled by Dominique Arel.

Rich, Vera. 1992. "Ukraine in Terminology Move: To Standardize Ukrainian Scientific and Technical Terminology." *Times Higher Education Supplement* 1039 (October 2): 11.

Ries, Nancy. 1997. *Russian Talk: Culture and Conversation during Perestroika.* Ithaca, N.Y.: Cornell University Press.

Romaine, Suzanne. 1989. *Bilingualism.* New York: Basil Blackwell.

Rowenchuk, Katherine Marie. 1992. "The Standardization of Modern Ukrainian (1909–1929)." Ph.D. diss., University of Michigan. Ann Arbor: University Microfilms International.

Samoylovich, Oleg. 1995. Electronic-mail message, subj.: Russkyi shovinizm, on DN.TALKS conference, FIDONET, June 17.

Savchenko, Fedir. 1970 [1930]. *The Suppression of the Ukrainian Activities in 1876.* Harvard Series in Ukrainian Studies, vol. 14. Munich: Wilhelm Fink Verlag.

Schieffelin, Bambi B., Kathryn A. Woolard, and Paul V. Kroskrity, eds. 1998. *Language Ideologies: Practice and Theory.* New York: Oxford University Press.

Schiffman, Harold E. 1996. *Linguistic Culture and Language Policy.* New York: Routledge.

Schwabe, Alexander. 2004. "The Leeches of Ukraine." *Spiegel Online International* (Germany), December 3, posted in the Ukraine List (UKL #300), electronic news list compiled by Dominique Arel.

Semenova, Marina. 2002. "Yushchenko razgovarival s krymskoi molodëzhu na raznykh iazykakh." *Ukraine.ru.* Available at http://www.ukraine.ru/reporting/114239.html.

Serbens'ka, Oleksandra. 1994. Preface to *Anty-Surzhyk,* ed. O. Serben'ka. Lviv: Vydavnytstvo Svit.

——, ed. 1994. *Anty-Surzhyk.* Lviv: Vydavnytstvo Svit.

Shchurat, Stepan Vasylievych. 1956. *Rannia Tvorchist' Ivana Franka.* Kyiv: Vydavnytstvo Akademiï Nauk Ukraïns'koi RSR.

Shevchenko, Taras. 1964. *Lysty, Notatky, Fol'klorni Zapysy.* Vol. 6 of *Povne Zibrannia Tvoriv u Shesty Tomakh.* Kyiv: Vydavnytstvo Akademiï Nauk Ukraïns'koi RSR.

Shevchenko, Didkovskiy and Partners. 2004. "New Game Rules for Advertising in Ukraine." *World Services Group.* Available at http://www.worldservicesgroup.com.

Shevelov, George Y. 1980. "Ukrainian." In *The Slavic Literary Languages,* ed. A. M. Schenker and E. Stankiewicz, 143–160. New Haven: Yale Concilium on International and Area Studies.

——. 1986. "The Language Question in the Ukraine in the Twentieth Century (1900– 1941)," part 1. *Harvard Ukrainian Studies* 10, nos. (1–2): 71–170.

——. 1987. "The Language Question in the Ukraine in the Twentieth Century (1900– 1941)," part 2. *Harvard Ukrainian Studies* 11 (1): 118–224.

——. 1989. *"The Ukrainian Language in the First Half of the Twentieth Century (1900–1941): Its State and Status.* Cambridge, Mass.: Harvard University Press.

——. 1993. "Standard Ukrainian." In *Encyclopedia of Ukraine,* ed. Danylo Husar Struk, 5:7–9. Toronto: University of Toronto Press.

Shumylov, Oleksandr. 2000. "Mova, surzhyk, 'iazyk': iednist' ta borot'ba protylezhnostei na mezhi tysiacholitt'." *Suchasnist',* no. 10, 110–124.

Shynkaruk, V., and I. Ivanio. 1973. "Hryhorii Skovoroda." In *Hryhorii Skovoroda: Povne Zibrannia v Dvokh Tomakh,* 1:11–57. Kyiv: Vydavnytstvo Naukova Dumka.

Silverstein, Michael. 2000. "Whorfianism and Nationality." *Regimes of Language.* Santa Fe: School of American Research Press.

——. 2003. "The Whens and Wheres—as Well as Hows—of Ethnolinguistic Recognition." *Public Culture* 15 (3): 531–557.

Slezkine, Yuri. 1994. "The USSR as a Communal Apartment; or, How a Socialist State Promoted Ethnic Particularism. *Slavic Review* 53 (2): 414–452.

Slovnyk Ukraïns'koi Movy. 1978. Kyiv: Naukova Dumka.

Smirnova, Daria. 1998. Jak dubliuiut' nashi uliubleni serialy. *Den'*, no. 139. Available at http:///www.day.kiev.ua/1998/163/tele/te2.htm.

Smith, Graham, Vivien Law, Andrew Wilson, Annette Bohr, and Edward Allworth. 1998. *Nation-building in the Post-Soviet Borderlands: The Politics of National Identities.* Cambridge: Cambridge University Press.

Smith, Michael G. 1998. *Language and Power in the Creation of the USSR, 1917–1953.* New York: Mouton de Gruyter.

Smith, Sidonie, and Julia Watson. 2001. *Reading Autobiography: A Guide for Interpreting Life Narratives.* Minneapolis: University of Minnesota Press.

Solzhenitsyn, Aleksandr Isaevich. 1990. *Kak nam obustroit Rossiiu? Posilnye soobrazheniia.* Paris: YMCA Press.

———. 1991. *Rebuilding Russia: Reflections and Tentative Proposals.* Translated and annotated by Alexis Klimoff. New York: Farrar, Straus and Giroux.

Ssorin-Chaikov, Nikolai V. 2003. *The Social Life of the State in Subarctic Siberia.* Stanford: Stanford University Press.

Staryts'kyi, Mykhailo. 1945 [1883]. *Za Dvoma Zaitsiamy.* Kyiv: Mystetstvo.

Stavyts'ka, Lesia. 2001. "Krovozmisne dytia dvomovnosti." *Krytyka* 10 (48): 20–24.

Stepanenko, Je. H., ed., and editorial board. 1995. *Hovorit' pravyl'no ukraïnskoiu movoiu. Sich-eslavs'kyi Yarmarok,* no. 4 (4): 4 (Dnipropetrovsk newspaper).

Strikha, Maksym. 1990. "Mova i nauka: harmoniia chy konflikt?" *Nauka i Kul'tura,* 158–162.

———. 1997. "Surzhyk." *Berezil',* no. 3–4: 135–142.

Stroud, Christopher. 2004. "Rinkeby Swedish and Semilingualism in Language Ideological Debates: A Bourdieuian Perspective." *Journal of Sociolinguistics* 8 (2): 196–214.

Subtelny, Orest. 1988. *Ukraine: A History.* Toronto: University of Toronto Press.

Szporluk, Roman. 1975. "Russians in Ukraine and Problems of Ukrainian Identity in the USSR." In *Ukraine in the Seventies,* ed. Peter J. Potichnyj, 195–217. Oakville, Ontario: Mosaic.

Taniuk, Les'. 2003. "Zaborony Ukraïns'koï movy." Report no. 06-7/10-151 to the Verkhovna Rada (Parliament) of Ukraine, in hearings "The Functioning of Ukrainian Language in Ukraine," March 11, 2003.

Taranenko, Oleksandr O. 2001. "Ukraïns'ka mova i suchasna movna sytuatsiia na Ukraïni." *Movoznavstvo* 4:3–19.

Tedlock, Dennis, and Bruce Mannheim, eds. 1995. *The Dialogic Emergence of Culture.* Chicago: University of Illinois Press.

Thomas, George. 1991. *Linguistic Purism.* New York: Longman.

Thompson, John B. 1991. Editor's introduction to *Language and Symbolic Power,* ed. J. B. Thompson. Cambridge, Mass.: Harvard University Press.

Todorov, Tzvetan. 1984. *Mikhail Bakhtin: The Dialogical Principle.* Translated by Wlad Godzich. Minneapolis: University of Minnesota Press.

Trofimov, Yaroslav. 2004. "Yushchenko's Formidable Challenge." *Wall Street Journal*, December 20, posted in the Ukraine List (UKL #317), electronic news list compiled by Dominique Arel.

Trosset, Carol S. 1986. "The Social Identity of Welsh Learners." *Language in Society* 15:165–192.

Trubachov, O. 1957. "Printsipy postroeniia etimologicheskikh slovarei slavianskikh iazykov." *Voprosy Iazykoznaniia* 5:67.

Trudgill, Peter. 1974. *The Social Differentiation of English in Norwich.* London: Cambridge University Press.

Tynianov, Yuri. 1981 [1924]. *The Problem of Verse Language.* Edited and translated by M. Sosa and B. Harvey. Ann Arbor: Ardis.

UNIAN. 2004. "National Council for Television and Radio Broadcasting Surprised with Kuchma's Statement on 'Unconstitutionality' of Air Ukrainization." UNIAN news, April 23, 2004.

Ukraïns'ka Radians'ka Entsyklopedia (URE). 1962. "Moskofily." In *Ukrainian Soviet Encyclopedia*, 9:391. Kyiv: Akademiia Nauk Ukraïns'koi RSR.

———. 1964. "Iazychie." In *Ukrainian Soviet Encyclopedia*, 16:460. Kyiv: Akademiia Nauk Ukraïns'koi RSR.

Vasovic, Aleksandar. 2004. "State Controlled Media Turning More Critical." *Seattle Times*, December 1, A13.

Verdery, Katherine. 1996. *What Was Socialism, and What Comes Next?* Princeton, N.J.: Princeton University Press.

Verkhovodov, Petro. 2000. "Standartna chy sovkova ukraïns'ka nasha mova?" *Suchasnist'*, no. 10: 159–160.

Voloshinov, V. N. 1973 [1929]. *Marxism and the Philosophy of Language.* Translated by Ladislav Matejka and I. R. Titunik. Cambridge, Mass.: Harvard University Press.

Vynnychenko, Volodymyr. 1980. *Diary*, vol. 1 (1911–1920). Edited by Hryhory Kostiuk. New York: Canadian Institute of Ukrainian Studies, Ukrainian Academy of Arts and Sciences in the United States.

Wagstyl, Stefan, and Tom Warner. 2004. "Dancing in the Streets as 'a Nation Is Born.'" *Financial Times*, December 4, posted in the Ukraine List (UKL #299), electronic news list compiled by Dominique Arel.

Wanner, Catherine. 1998. *Burden of Dreams: History and Identity in Post-Soviet Ukraine.* University Park: Pennsylvania State University Press.

———. 1999. "Crafting Identity, Marking Time: An Anthropological Perspective on Historical Commemoration and Nation-Building in Ukraine. *Harvard Ukrainian Studies* 23 (3/4): 105–131.

Way, Lucan. 2005. "Failed Authoritarianism in Ukraine: Why Kuchma Fell." Lecture presented at the University of Washington, February 24, 2004.

Wendland, Anna Veronica. 2001. *Dis Russophilen in Galizien: Ukrainische Konservative Zwischen Österreich and Rußland, 1848–1915.* Studien zur Geschichte der Österreichisch-ungarischen Monarchie, 27. Vienna: Verlag der Österreichischen Akademie der Wissenschaften.

Wexler, Paul N. 1974. *Purism and Language: A Study in Modern Ukrainian and Belorussian Nationalism (1840–1967)*. Bloomington: Indiana University Press.

Williams, Brackette F. 1989. "A Class Act: Anthropology and the Race to Nation across Ethnic Terrain." *Annual Review of Anthropology* 18:401–444.

Winford, Donald. 2003. *An Introduction to Contact Linguistics*. Oxford: Basil Blackwell.

Woolard, Kathryn A. 1985. "Language Variation and Cultural Hegemony: Toward an Integration of Sociolinguistic and Social Theory." *American Ethnologist* 12:738–748.

———. 1988. "Codeswitching and Comedy in Catalonia." In *Codeswitching: Anthropological and Sociolinguistic Perspectives*, ed. Monica Heller, 53–76. New York: Mouton de Gruyter.

———. 1989. *Double Talk: Bilingualism and the Politics of Ethnicity in Catalonia*. Stanford: Stanford University Press.

———. 1992. "Language Ideology: Issues and Approaches." *Pragmatics* 2 (3): 235–249.

———. 1998a. "Introduction: Language Ideology as a Field of Inquiry." In *Language Ideologies: Practice and Theory*, ed. Bambi B. Schieffelin, Kathryn A. Woolard, and Paul V. Kroskrity, 3–47. New York: Oxford University Press.

———. 1998b. "Simultaneity and Bivalency as Strategies in Bilingualism." *Journal of Linguistic Anthropology* 8 (1): 3–29.

Woolard, Kathryn A., and Bambi B. Schieffelin. 1994. "Language Ideology." *Annual Review of Anthropology* 23:55–82.

Woolhiser, Curt. 2001. "Language Ideology and Language Conflict in Post-Soviet Belarus." In *Language, Ethnicity, and the State*. Vol. 2: *Minority Languages in Eastern Europe Post-1989*, ed. Camille C. O'Reilly, 91–122. New York: Palgrave.

Wynnyckyj, Mychailo. 2004. "Yushchenko Redeemed." Electronic letter, December 2, posted in the Ukraine List (UKL #297), electronic news list compiled by Dominique Arel.

Yushchenko, Viktor. 2005. "Rozhromnyj vystup Yushchenka v Donets'ku." *Ukraïns'ka Pravda*, February 13. Available online at http://www2.pravda.com.ua/archive/2005/february/13/2.shtml.

Zabuzhko, Oksana. 1998. *Pol'ovi doslidzhennia z ukraïnskoho seksu*. Kyiv: Fakt.

Zakon. 1993. "Zakon Ukrainy pro Telebachennia i Radiomovlennia." Vidomosti Verkhovnoï Rady, no. 3760-12. With amendments through February 2004. Available at http://www/nau.kiev.ua.

Zakon. 1996. "Zakon Ukraïny pro Reklamu." Vidomosti Verkhovnoï Rady, no. 271/96. With amendments through February 2004. Available at http://www/nau.kiev.ua.

Zastavnyi, Fedir Dmytrovych. 2003. "Vseukraïnskyi perepys naselennia 2001 r.: Rezultaty, analiz, otsinka." Lviv: Vydavnychyi tsentr L'vivs'koho Natsional'noho Universytetu im. Ivana Franka.

Zholdak, Bohdan. 1992. "Mania chy Tania" (part of "Seksotesy"). In *Chumat's'kyi Shliakh* 1:58–61.

———. 1998. "My maiemo te, choho ne matymemo." *Krytyka* 5 (7): 30–31.

Index

Note: Page numbers with an *f* indicate figures; those with a *t* indicate tables; those with an *n* indicate footnotes.

Academy of Sciences
  Ukrainian, 151, 171, 191n5
  USSR, 4
accents. *See* dialect(s)
advertising
  English in, 180–85, 184f
  language laws and, 180–82
  surzhyk in, 145–46, 163–65
Aeneid (Kotliarevs'kyi), 76, 107
African American English, 106n5, 146, 165
After Two Hares (Staryts'kyi), 110–12, 111f, 114
akanie, 16, 55–56, 112, 137, 203
Alf (TV show), 179
Anderson, Benedict, 25
Andrukhovych, Yurij, 159, 197
anti-surzhyk manuals, 121f, 146, 156, 167f
archaeological terms, 92t
architectural surzhyk, 104, 105f
Auer, Peter, 122–23, 126t
Austro-Hungarian Empire, 73–78
Azhniuk, Bohdan, 133

Baiul, Oksana, 14n1
Bakhtin, Mikhail, 29–31, 177, 192
"Banderas," 59, 63
Barthes, Roland, 143
Belarus
  East Slavic unity and, 8, 21, 25–26, 158
  UN and, 64n23, 66
Belarusian, 34, 158

Lithuanian and, 72
Sovietization and, 25
trasianka and, 17, 104, 122
Ukrainian and, 3, 73, 86, 118–19, 158
Bible, Kralits'ka, 76
bilingualism
  codeswitching and, 105, 120n23, 133, 176
  English and, 23, 85, 181–83, 201
  family issues with, 41, 42, 46–48, 60–64
  Kuchma on, 147
  language mixing and, 120–22, 128–34, 176
  nationalism and, 174–75
  nonreciprocal, 22, 34, 175–77, 185–92
  Russification and, 9, 10f, 34, 115, 117, 177
  television shows with, 22, 176–77, 185–91
  urban, 126t, 131–34
  Yushchenko on, 200–201
  See also diglossia
Bilozir, Ihor, 179
blatniak ("prison jargon"), 161, 197
Bondarev, Yurij, 61
"bookish" language, 106–7, 113–14. *See also* literary language
Bourdieu, Pierre
  on agency, 28–30
  on education, 26
  on habitus, 27–28, 31, 32
  on language, 26–27, 41
  on misrecognition, 162n11